Riding the Tiger

By the same author

Developmental States in East Asia (editor)
*The Chinese State in the Era of Economic Reform:
The Road to Crisis* (editor)

Riding the Tiger

The Politics of Economic Reform in Post-Mao China

Gordon White
Professorial Fellow
Institute of Development Studies
at the University of Sussex

MACMILLAN

First published 1993 by
THE MACMILLAN PRESS LTD
Houndmills, Basingstoke, Hampshire RG21 2XS
and London
Companies and representatives
throughout the world

ISBN 0-333-45480-4 hardcover
ISBN 0-333-45481-2 paperback

A catalogue record for this book is available
from the British Library.

Copy-edited and typeset by Povey–Edmondson
Okehampton and Rochdale, England

Printed in Hong Kong

Reprinted 1994

骑 虎 难 下

qi hu nan xia

'If you're riding a tiger, it's hard to get off.'

(Chinese saying)

Contents

List of Tables

List of Figures

Abbreviations

FBIS	Foreign Broadcast Information Service, *China: Daily Report.*
GMRB	*Guangming Ribao* (Glorious Daily), Beijing.
NCNA	New China News Agency (*Xinhua*), Beijing.
RMRB	*Renmin Ribao* (People's Daily), Beijing.
SSB	State Statistical Bureau, *Statistical Yearbook*, Beijing.
SWB	British Broadcasting Corporation, *Summary of World Broadcasts: Far East.*
ZGSHTJZL	*Zhongguo Shehui Tongji Ziliao 1990* (Statistical Materials on Chinese Society) Beijing, Chinese Statistics Publishing House, 1990.

Acknowledgements

The author would like to thank the following for their valuable advice and assistance in completing this work: Bob Benewick, Marc Blecher, Robert and Shu Cassen, Jack and Maisie Gray, Barbara Harriss-White, Jude Howell, Julie McWilliam, Peter Nolan, Akio Takahara and Adrian Wood.

I would also like to express my gratitude to numerous Chinese colleagues and friends with whom I have discussed the content of this work, with particular thanks to Shang Xiaoyuan, Yang Mu and Duan Shunchen.

A special debt of gratitude is due to my publisher, Steven Kennedy, who has been patient and supportive throughout.

GORDON WHITE

Introduction

When the Chinese Communist Party came to power in 1949, China was a desperately poor country devastated by decades of civil war and foreign invasion. In the short term, the need was to bring peace, stability and order to the country; over the longer term, like their imperial and Nationalist predecessors, Communist leaders sought to design and implement a strategy of economic development which could transform China into a prosperous and powerful country able to hold up its head proudly in the world of nations. They sought these goals through a strategy of socialist development which would, it was hoped, achieve rapid socio-economic modernisation while avoiding the human costs of early capitalist development, and dependence on the advanced capitalist nations.

In the context of the time, the only model which seemed capable of delivering these objectives was that of the Soviet Union, hammered out under the leadership of Stalin in the dire decades of the 1930s and 1940s. Though the Chinese revolutionary leadership had had their differences with the Soviet Union before 1949 and though the experience of the Chinese revolution differed markedly from that of the Bolshevik Revolution in 1917, they adopted the basic institutional features of the 'Soviet model' in both politics and economics in the early 1950s. This reflected not only a shared ideological heritage of revolutionary Marxism–Leninism, but also the perception that the Soviet Union had achieved, in a relatively short period of time, the kind of rapid economic transformation that China was so eager to achieve. Moreover, the Chinese leadership were pushed towards the Soviet Union by the international environment of the time, the Cold War between the socialist camp and the West and, more powerfully, by the 'hot war' in Korea from 1950 to 1953 which brought Chinese forces into direct combat with those of the Western powers.

During the early and mid-1950s, a massive process of institutional transfer took place as a vast latticework of Soviet-derived political and economic institutions was laid down across China: the Party was extended into every sphere through an apparatus of Party committees and branches which acted as a kind of political nervous system throughout the body of society; a complex edifice of agencies for economic planning and management was established to control the whole economy and move it forward in a decisive dash for industrialisation through a series of five-year plans, the first of which ran from 1953 to 1957; different sectors of the population were incorporated into 'mass organisations' under the Party's command; and productive units were converted into state enterprises and collective farms through the 'socialist transformation' of industry and commerce and agricultural collectivisation.

Though the heyday of the 'Soviet model' was economically successful and is nowadays looked back on nostalgically by older elements of the Party leadership, it brought many problems in its wake: some of these stemmed simply from the imposition of a foreign institutional system in an alien context; some from the inherent deficiencies of that model in terms of its high degree of concentration of political power in the hands of the central organs of the Chinese Communist Party (CCP) and of economic power in the hands of the central planners and administrative agencies; some from the incompatibility between Soviet practices and the institutional and ideological heritage of the Chinese revolution, particularly as interpreted by its supreme leader, Mao Zedong (Mao Tsetung).[1] The result was a search sponsored by Mao and his supporters within the CCP leadership, for a distinctively Chinese form of socialist development which reflected this pre-revolutionary experience, and attempted to grapple with the inherent problems of the Soviet model and attune the institutions of Chinese state socialism towards Chinese socio-economic realities. This 'Maoist' paradigm of development, which began with the convulsive Great Leap Forward of 1958–9, dominated Chinese politics and economics for nearly two decades, culminating in the decade of Cultural Revolution from 1966–76.

In retrospect, 'Maoism' can be seen as a deeply flawed, and ultimately unsuccessful, attempt to construct a distinctively 'revolutionary' and Chinese form of state socialism which, though portrayed as a radical alternative to the Soviet system, failed to break in any decisive way with the latter's fundamental ideological tenets and institutional features. At the time, however, particularly in the latter part of the Cultural Revolution decade in the early–mid-1970s, Maoist developmental experience was the object of admiration both in the West and in the Third World as a possible 'third way' to prosperity and modernity between two equally distasteful paths – Western capitalism and Eastern European socialism. For many socialists, the Maoist experiment seemed to represent a serious attempt to break the classic Soviet mould of communist-led state socialism and establish a new pattern of development led by a new form of state committed to the core socialist values of equality, mass participation and collective solidarity. For theorists and practitioners of Third World development, Maoist innovations struck responsive chords – for example, mobilising mass labour for infrastructural projects; attempting to reduce the privileges and change the workstyles of those death-watch beetles of state socialism, the bureaucratic elite; taking steps to make the educational system more accessible to the mass of the population and more relevant to their needs; organising migration from urban to rural areas rather than the reverse; and encouraging intermediate technology, grassroots initiative and local 'self-reliance'. The 'Chinese model' was widely cited as suitable for emulation, either as a whole or in part, by developmental states in Third World countries (for example, Aziz 1978).

However, after the death of Mao Zedong (Mao Tse-tung) and the arrest of the radical Maoist 'Gang of Four' in late 1976, the policies of the Maoist era were subjected to the most thorough-going and vitreolic criticism in China. In effect, the Chinese themselves repudiated the 'Chinese model'. During the late 1970s, a new model of 'socialist' development, based on market-oriented principles and institutions, emerged under a reorganised CCP leadership headed by Deng Xiaoping (Teng Hsiao-p'ing). This brought changes in ideology and policy so far-reaching that they seemed to vindicate the Manichean notion of the 'struggle between the two lines' depicted by Maoist ideologues during the Cultural Revolution. During this era of economic reform, which still continues into the 1990s, China has experienced a process of rapid change unprecedented in its post-revolutionary history.

Many if not most accounts of the rise and impact of post-Mao market reforms have concentrated on their *economic* aspects: analysing the deficiencies of the previous system of centralised, directive economic planning; describing attempts to reform it by introducing market mechanisms and redefining the ways in which the state regulates the economy; and assessing the economic impact of these changes. By contrast, this book aims to concentrate on the *political* aspects of economic reform: it seeks to trace the political origins of the reform programme in China's previous post-revolutionary experience; to track the political processes which define the nature of reform policies and condition their impact; and to assess the impact of economic changes during the reform era on political ideas and institutions and on relations between state and society.

The Comparative Context of Post-Mao Reforms

Though this is a case-study of Chinese experience, it is written with an eye to comparative experience, of which three aspects are of particular significance.

The Developmental State

The Chinese economic reforms are but one example of a wider phenomenon prevalent in the developing world during the 1980s, the crisis of the developmental state. Since the idea of the 'developmental state' plays an important role in my analysis, some preliminary clarification is in order since the term has passed into common usage attended by a good deal of ambiguity (for an earlier attempt to clarify the concept, see White 1984). One can distinguish a broad and a narrow sense of the term. In the broad sense, the 'developmental state' refers to a historically specific type of state which has evolved, particularly but not exclusively in the post-war era of de-colonisation, with the very notion of 'development' itself. 'Development' has come to mean a process whereby socio-economic change, rather than evolving through some 'spontaneous' dynamic, can be organised and promoted consciously by some organising and directing agent; and that agent *par excellence* is the state. The 'developmental state', therefore, is a state which

sets out to promote national development by means of institutionalised patterns of policy intervention guided by some kind of
'plan' or strategic conception, and plays a central role in that
process. The notion of centrality is important because, although
other kinds of state, notably the traditional liberal *laissez-faire*
state or even the Keynesian managerial state, set out to establish
the preconditions for economic progress, in both cases the overwhelmingly important agent of socio-economic change was outside
the state in the form of a capitalist economy and a civil society.
Unsurprisingly, the 'developing world' has been populated by
developmental states, at least in appearance: some of these have
not measured up to the label, either because the edifice of state
involvement has been more on paper than in practice, or because
'developmentalist' rhetoric has cloaked what might be called
'kleptocratic' regimes, such as Mobutu's Zaire or the Duvaliers'
Haiti which have no interests beyond the self-enrichment of a
narrow political elite.

Although developmental states in this broad sense take a wide
variety of forms, in the context of East Asia they have fallen into
two broad categories: 'state socialist' and 'state capitalist'. In the
latter category, which includes South Korea, Taiwan and Japan, the
state plays a central role as a guiding force for national economic
development, possessing a conception of the national economic
interest and acting to implement that conception by means of
pervasive intervention in economy and society. However, though
these cases may, in the early stages particularly, include direct state
involvement in the economy through the establishment of a
substantial public sector, they must be called 'state capitalist'
insofar as the main economic actors are private, operating in a
more or less competitive capitalist economy. As such, they should
be distinguished from traditional Soviet-style 'state socialist'
regimes in East Asia, such as China, North Korea or Vietnam, in
which the communist Party/state, directly or indirectly, is the
dominant economic actor, virtually to the exclusion of all others.
Although state socialist systems contain enterprises such as
factories and farms, and although these have some degree of
nominal independence, they are all to various degrees directly
controlled by, and dependent on, the Party/state.

Clearly China can be understood as a 'state socialist' developmental state in the above sense. For the purposes of this study,

however, it is useful to identify a narrower, more precise sense of the term 'developmental state', as the state in its developmental capacity: those specific institutions, ideas and policy interventions which embody the socio-economic aims and actions of a given state. We can thus distinguish the state as a developmental entity from the state as a political entity, characterised by a particular set of reigning political ideas, institutions and sources of political legitimacy. This separation between the developmental and political aspects of a state allows us to make a distinction between its developmental (primarily economic) capacity and its political viability. It also allows us to examine the interaction between these dimensions of the state in the real world. As we shall see in this study, the post-Mao era of market reforms has been seeking a new type of socialist developmental state in this second, more precise, sense. This involves a redefinition of the state's role in the economy in ways which bring it closer in many ways to the 'state capitalist' model to the extent that it disengages the state from direct economic involvement and increases the autonomy of productive enterprises, while retaining an integument of socialist political ideas and institutions. This project of 'market socialism' thus involves significant change in the developmental aspect of the state, but not in its political aspect. The contradiction between these two dimensions of change is at the root of the politics of economic reform in contemporary China.

The relationship between the political and developmental aspects of the state are complex and ambiguous. They may undermine each other in various ways. Taking developmental capacity first, failure to achieve proclaimed economic goals may undermine the credibility of the current regime, as witnessed by the popular discontent in the Soviet Union and Eastern Europe over the inability of their economies to compete with those of western countries, particularly in the production of consumer goods. On the other side, economic success may strengthen the credibility of the current political regime, as witnessed by the longevity of authoritarian systems in South Korea and Taiwan. However, developmental success also brings about changes in social structure and attitudes which in the longer term undermine the political *status quo*; this has been a feature of the political evolution of South Korea and Taiwan in the 1980s. Paradoxically, therefore, economic success may lead to political failure.

The Politics of Economic Liberalisation

Over the past decade or more, the theory and practice of the developmental state (in both broad and narrow senses) has come in for much criticism. Whether prompted by internal developmental failure or by external pressures by agencies such as the IMF or World Bank, the governments of many developing countries have sought to redefine the relationship between state and economy by 'rolling back' the state through privatisation and deregulation and increasing the role of markets and private enterprise. This historical shift has been set in train by increasing dissatisfaction with the economic performance of developmental states, particularly those which emerged in the Third World in the aftermath of decolonisation in the 1960s and 1970s. This reaction against the state has been remarkably consistent across the political spectrum, from Thatcherites on one side to communists on the other. Its central thesis is that political leaders who try to sponsor economic progress through heavy reliance on direct and pervasive state involvement have a tendency to become developmental liabilities. This is partly because they transmit the vagaries of politics and the rigidities of bureaucracy to the economy and partly because, like dogs in the manger, they stifle the initiative of other economic actors, be they peasant farmers, industrial capitalists, private traders, co-operative managers or foreign business people.

This critique of the state was not confined to the developing world: it found strong expression in the industrialised capitalist countries of the First World and in the more developed state socialist countries of the then Second World in Eastern Europe in the form of the search for 'market socialism'. Wherever the context, however, and whatever the political complexion of the leadership sponsoring reform, the goals have been similar: to change the balance between state and market in the economy to favour the latter, and to reconstitute the developmental state in a form which retains essential economic functions, but acts to complement rather than inhibit the operation of markets. These are the aims of China's economic reforms in the post-Mao era and they are prompted by profound dissatisfaction with the previous model of Soviet-style state-directed development.

The desire to achieve these goals has taken the form of programmes of economic liberalisation. Comparative studies of the politics of economic liberalisation have demonstrated that reforms designed to change the balance between state and market and redefine the developmental state pose potentially serious challenges to their political sponsors; indeed they can stir up a political hornets' nest (Nelson 1989 and 1990). For example, since economic liberalisation often involves cuts in public expenditure, it causes resentment among former recipients of welfare payments and subsidies. Moreover, different interests in society may suffer or benefit in various degrees from moves towards privatisation and deregulation of the economy. For example, a reduction in the size of the state apparatus threatens civil servants and other public employees with unemployment; a reduction in subsidies to inefficient industries, public or private, threatens both industrialists and industrial workers alike. Since a reduction of the economic responsibilities of state agencies may threaten the power and privileges of state officials, moreover, their resistance can also be expected. Thus, economic liberalisation may well bring social discontent and political conflict. Reforming leaders are likely to face a battery of conflicting pressures which test their political nerve and influence the success or failure of their reform efforts. Since the Chinese economic reforms have attempted to engineer a particularly radical shift in the balance between state and market, we can expect these political stresses and strains to be particularly acute.

Market Socialism

The Chinese reforms are a clear case of the phenomenon of 'market socialism' which began much earlier in the more developed state socialist countries of Eastern Europe. China belongs to a family of nations which adopted (or, in the case of most of Eastern Europe, were forced to adopt) a system of directive, centralised economic planning derived from the Soviet experience of the Stalin period. This system subordinated the economy to state planning and administrative agencies and created systematic inefficiency and waste. The latter became more glaring as these economies became more complex and their need to enter into relations with the international capitalist economy became more pressing. Though the ideas of 'market socialism' had been around much earlier, it was not until the 1960s that they became the basis for practical reform programmes in Eastern Europe, notably the introduction of the New Economic Mechanism in Hungary beginning in 1968. The central ideas behind 'market socialism' were essentially a 'socialist' version of the broader case for economic liberalisation: that centralised, direct and comprehensive state control over the economy was both impractical and undesirable; that the economic involvement of the socialist state should be less pervasive and should operate less through direct controls over enterprises and more through indirect regulation by means of macro-economic levers such as tax or interest-rate policies (this is sometimes called the transition from 'directive' to 'parametric' or 'indicative' economic planning); that markets should be revived and developed to provide the flexibility, dynamism and micro-economic efficiency which were so sadly lacking in the traditional model of central planning (Brus 1972; Nove 1983). While the 'market socialism' paradigm shares these central ideas with the more general rationale for economic liberalisation current in non-socialist contexts (hence the similarities in outlook between communist economic reformers and Thatcherism or Reaganomics), there are certain differences which have important political implications. First, the traditional model of state-socialist economic planning is one where virtually the whole economy is under more or less direct state control. The transition to markets is therefore a much more far-reaching reform than in 'mixed' economies where the role of the state had been more limited; the former is not just a shift in the balance between state and market but a fundamental transformation in the nature of the economic system. Second, this is not merely a question of economics. The notion of 'transition to socialism', as traditionally defined in the Soviet Union, was bound up with the replacement of markets (seen as irrational and unstable operating principles of capitalist economies) by 'scientific' planning. But market socialism, with its optimistic evaluation of the economic benefits of markets and its pessimistic view of the state's capacity for 'scientific' action, implied a radical revision of the very nature of 'socialism' and the 'transition to socialism'. In consequence, though the ideas and policy proposals of market socialists were restricted to the economic sphere, they had profound political and ideological consequences.

When discussing the politics of economic liberalisation above, we viewed 'politics' primarily as a process of conflict and co-operation over the control and exercise of power in furtherance of the interests of different actors in society. In the case of market socialism, politics also takes on the character of a contest between alternative ideologies and social systems, at the extremes between 'capitalism' and 'socialism'. As long as the opposition between East and West was alive, this was not merely a clash between opposing ideological slogans, but between politico-economic systems based on fundamentally opposed principles. In the political sphere the clash was between, on the one side, liberal-democratic polities based on open competition between political organisations and social interests and, on the other side, totalist polities dominated by a single party and ruled by a single ideological orthodoxy with little scope for the autonomous organisation and interplay of social interests. In the economic sphere, the clash was between, on the one side, mixed economies based on a capitalist mode of production and, on the other side, centrally planned economies based on public or social ownership. To its proponents, 'market socialism' could transcend this great divide: it would retain a basically socialist economic system (through a continuation of state planning, albeit in a different form, and a continuing predominance of some kind of 'public' or 'social' ownership), but would incorporate the rational and beneficial elements of capitalist market systems in ways which would improve economic performance, increase social welfare and (implicitly) improve the political appeal of 'socialism'.

In the event, the 'market socialist' project failed in its heartland, Eastern Europe, with the dramatic events of 1989–91. Why was traditional, Soviet-style state socialism unable to reform itself economically? Was it because of inherent contradictions within the basic idea of 'market socialism'; or because the political obstacles stemming from the ideological conservatism and vested interests of the old system were too great, both domestically and internationally as a result of the stifling influence of a Brezhnevist Soviet Union; or because the political and economic stresses of introducing such a radical programme of reform were too over-whelming; or because 'market socialism' was never sufficiently tried out in practice (except in Hungary)? As of the early 1990s, China is one of only two countries (the other is Vietnam) in which the theory and practice of 'market socialism' remains current. As such, it is virtually the last test-case for the viability of the idea and the ability of a traditional state-socialist system to reform itself.

General Theses and Focus

The case material in this book should be situated within these three areas of comparative experience. This, and a detailed analysis of the Chinese case, have generated certain basic theses about the dynamics of economic reform in China. The first is that the project of market-oriented economic reform, while clearly a response to glaring deficiencies in the previous economic system, was given particularly powerful impetus as a response to problems caused by China's previous *political* experience. In essence, the economic reforms were an attempt to re-establish the hegemonic authority of the Communist Party on a different basis: by abandoning the Maoist notion of development as a political struggle and attempting to accelerate economic development and increase the material welfare of the population more rapidly. Success in the latter, it was hoped, would provide a new form of legitimacy for the regime, based on its ability to deliver rapid improvements in welfare. This argument will be developed in Chapter 1.

Second, the book argues the importance of political factors in shaping the content, dynamics and effects of economic reform. It is true that the task of introducing such a profound process of systemic change is technically complex and that there are manifold economic problems to handle in the transition. But it is also crucial to see economic reform as a political process which poses massive problems of political management for the CCP leadership. Indeed, the post-Mao era is characterised by a pervasive tension between the economic and political rationality of reform. This is particularly evident, for example, in what I call the 'hard policy constraint' wherein reform leaders are unwilling to grasp policy nettles which are economically essential but politically difficult. In Chapter 2, we shall analyse the political dynamics of the reform process from 1979 onwards and attempt to identify the ways in which various political factors have conditioned the conduct and impact of the reforms. Chapters 3 and 4 focus this investigation more precisely by looking at the political processes involved in two major areas of policy reform, agriculture and industry. In these two chapters we shall seek to throw light on the complex patterns of political alignment, power and interest which can constrain or realise the intentions of policy-makers.

The third argument also concerns the relationship between the politics and economics of reform. The 'market socialist' project, of which China's is a prime example, contains within it a basic contradiction between economic transformation and political immobility. To the extent that the reforms do in fact achieve their economic aims, however, they set in train basic social and political changes which undermine the legitimacy and effectiveness of the previous state-socialist polity. Thus economic reforms not only fail to restore the legitimacy of Marxist–Leninist socialism; they accelerate its political breakdown. This is partly because of the political stresses involved in any such major attempt at economic liberalisation; partly because of the basic illogic of the market socialist project itself which sets out to bring about radical economic reform without significant political reform; and partly because of the new political ideas, interests and forces created by the reforms which create a social basis for the supersession of the *ancien régime*. These issues are dealt with in Chapters 5 through 7 where I examine the political impact of the reforms on the reigning ideology (Chapter 5), on the hegemonic political institution, the Chinese Communist Party (Chapter 6), and on the relationship between state and society (Chapter 7).

Fourth, reviewing the reform process as a whole, it is argued that, in undertaking a radical programme of market-oriented economic reform, the Chinese regime has faced a historical 'Catch 22'. Failure to reform would have meant increasingly serious economic stagnation, social tension and political decline. Yet successful economic reform creates the basis not only for a new type of economic system, but also for a new social and ultimately political system potentially contrary to the old one (what the Maoists would have called 'bourgeois restoration'). Resolving this dilemma rests on the ability of the reforming leadership to create not merely a new conception of a 'socialist commodity economy', but also of a new form of 'socialist' political system which could serve as alternatives to capitalist economics and liberal-democratic politics. Nowhere in the state socialist world has this been forthcoming and China has been no exception. It is hard to resist the conclusion, therefore, that, in the event, Marxist–Leninist socialism has been incapable of reforming itself and that 'market socialism' , rather than saving its bacon, cooks its goose. Indeed, 'market socialism' would appear to be a chimera, not a new form of socialism but a transition towards capitalism in economics and liberalism in politics (the latter is more uncertain since capitalism can coexist with a wide range of political systems). This may be completed by the route of more or less violent crisis and collapse (along Eastern European lines), or by some form of 'peaceful transition' managed by a reforming Communist leadership. I shall examine the prospects for these alternatives in the concluding Chapter 8.

Although the scope of this book is broad, it does not attempt to be all-encompassing. I shall concentrate largely on *domestic* political processes: the politics of the 'open policy' towards foreign trade and capital require an extended treatment of their own (for example, Howell 1989). Even so, the international dimension cannot be ignored and I shall introduce it into the analysis where relevant. On the domestic scene, I shall deal lightly with themes which have received a good deal of coverage elsewhere, such as the detailed dynamics of leadership conflict or the nuances of ideological debate within the upper reaches of the Chinese Communist Party. There are also important political issues which do not receive the attention they deserve, notably the question of the role of the armed forces which are a crucial determinant of China's political future. In the case of this and other lacunae, I plead limitations of space, time and knowledge. Where relevant, I shall provide references to assist readers who wish to follow up these issues in more detail.

On the question of methodology, a focus on the *politics* of economic reform is no easy matter, since Chinese political and policy processes are frustratingly opaque. Moreover, the Chinese authorities attempt to present a simplified, one-dimensional view of Chinese political realities, seeking to disguise conflict and draw a veil of secrecy over the pulling and hauling which goes on behind the scenes. In analysing the politics of economic reform, therefore, the scholar must borrow the skills of the detective and investigative journalist, drawing together a wide variety of sources and reading as often between as along the lines. It is an exercise in analytical demystification.

A Framework for Analysing the Politics of Economic Reform

Conventional analyses of the politics of economic reform in China have a tendency to focus on the role and impact of the ruling

Communist elite. CCP leaders do in fact act as state managers as do their counterparts in other societies. While their behaviour reflects their own particular beliefs and interests, they also have a capacity to take account of the whole, to deal with questions of national strategy and the overall viability of the polity and economy. To this extent, one can expect their calculations to be influenced by a different, more systemic political logic than that of most other institutions or groups in society which have narrower preoccupations. The very conception and launching of the economic reform project in the late 1970s depended on the ability of certain CCP leaders to perceive systemic problems and come up with systemic solutions, many of which threatened the position of sectional groups and interests.

Political leadership is also crucial in managing the reform process. For example, in the difficult transition from the death of Mao in 1976 to the inauguration of the reform programme in late 1978, a great deal depended on the ability of reformist leaders, led by Deng Xiaoping, to make the most of the political resources at hand in outmanoeuvring and undermining their Maoist opponents. Particularly important was the personal status and political skill of Deng Xiaoping himself, as a paramount figure who was able to win over or neutralise powerful forces which might otherwise have resisted reform (the most important was the People's Liberation Army). While I shall leave analysis of the details of leadership manoeuvres to others (for example, Harding 1987: ch. 3), the importance of committed and skilful political leadership should be emphasised here because it is a crucial factor during the actual conduct of the reforms during the 1980s. To assist the reader, Tables I.1 and I.2 provide some background information on the names and positions of top Party and state leaders and the composition of the crucial leadership nucleus, the Standing Committee of the CCP Central Committee's Politburo, between 1976 and 1991.

Political leadership was important not only because reformist leaders were to encounter opposition from their more conservative colleagues in the higher reaches of the Party, but also because institutions and groups in Chinese society possess political resources which enable them to exert pressures (implicit or explicit, passive or active) which CCP leaders ignore at their cost. The game of Chinese élite politics is not played in an empty stadium; the calculations of

Table I.1   *Top Party and State Leaders, 1976–91*

Party Chairman/General Secretary
Oct 1976–Sept 1982	Hua Guofeng
Sept 1982–Jan 1987	Hu Yaobang
Jan–Oct 1987 (acting)	Zhao Ziyang
Oct 1987–June 1989	Zhao Ziyang

President of the People's Republic of China
June 1983–Mar/April 1988	Li Xiannian
	(V.P. – Ulanhu)
Mar/April 1988	Yang Shangkun
(7th NPC)	(V.P. – Wang Zhen)

State Premier
1976–1980	Hua Guofeng
Sept 1980–88	Zhao Ziyang
1988	Li Peng

Table I.2   *Chinese Communist Party Central Committee: Politburo Standing Committees*

11th Party Congress August 1977	Hua Guofeng Ye Jianying Deng Xiaoping Li Xiannian Wang Dongxing	12th Party Congress September 1982	Hu Yaobang Ye Jianying Chen Yun Deng Xiaoping Li Xiannian Zhao Ziyang
3rd Plenum December 1978	Hua Guofeng Ye Jianying Deng Xiaoping Li Xiannian Wang Dongxing Chen Yun	Party Conference September 1985	Hu Yaobang Chen Yun Deng Xiaoping Li Xiannian Zhao Ziyang
5th Plenum of Central Committee February 1980	Hua Guofeng Ye Jianying Deng Xiaoping Li Xiannian Chen Yun Hu Yaobang Zhao Ziyang	13th Party Congress October/November 1987	Zhao Ziyang Li Peng Qiao Shi Yao Yilin Hu Qili
6th Plenum of Central Committee June 1981	Hu Yaobang Ye Jianying Zhao Ziyang Li Xiannian Chen Yun Hua Guofeng Deng Xiaoping	After the Tiananmen Incident of June 1989, the Standing Committee was changed at the CCPCC Fourth Plenum	Yao Yilin Qiao Shi Jiang Zemin Li Peng Li Ruihan Song Ping

CCP leaders are not made in a political vacuum. The nature of this wider spectrum of political forces can influence significantly the relative power of different individuals or groups within the CCP leadership. Indeed, at times leaders may reach out to encourage an open expression of public feeling to demonstrate their own support and put their political opponents under pressure. Mao Zedong did this in the early years of the Cultural Revolution when he mobilised the 'red guards' and 'revolutionary rebels' against his opponents in the Party leadership; Deng Xiaoping did something similar (though in a much more controlled way) when he encouraged the 'Democracy Wall' movement in Beijing in late 1978 to undercut his more conservative opponents before the crucial Third Plenum of the CCP Central Committee held in December that year.

This broad spectrum of political forces also affects the nature of the reform policy process: by influencing which policy issues actually come to the attention of policy-makers, in what precise shape they emerge from the policy-making process and what happens to them during the process of implementation. The specific nature of this constellation of political forces may change over time. For instance, as the reform process gets under way and reform policies begin to bite, the political advantage deriving from the revulsion against the Cultural Revolution may gradually evaporate; overall approval of the reform project by any particular group may give way to opposition to some of its specific aspects; old interests may realign and new interests may emerge; formerly homogeneous interests may differentiate or fragment. At the root of this view of the politics of economic reform lies *a conception of power, and thus of politics, as pervading the entire political, social and economic systems.* The policy process is embedded in a complex multi-level political process which cannot be captured by conventional methods of 'Pekingology'. Our notion of 'politics' needs to be broadened to comprehend this totality.

We shall be seeking to elucidate some of this complex process more precisely in our detailed examination of the politics of policy reform in agriculture and industry in Chapters 3 and 4. At this stage, however, it is useful to present a simple schema to clarify the overall political process within which the politics of economic policy reform takes place. I find it useful to think of Chinese politics in terms of a dart-board. In the centre (the 'bull's eye') is the political nucleus, the Centre, which comprises the CCP Central Committee and the supreme governmental organ, the State Council, with their affiliated agencies (Figure I.1 provides a simplified map of this central institutional network). Radiating out from the centre to the rim, like the wires on a dart-board (or the spokes on a wheel) are the major institutions of the Party (and its ancillary mass organisations) and state (notably the ministries and their subordinate departments). These are structured into different levels which are like the concentric wire circles on a dart-board (Figure I.2 provides a map of the main politico-administrative layers from central to basic level). The remainder of the board, which underlays and surrounds these three elements, constitutes society, with its complex and changing pattern of interests and attitudes. If one were to look closely at the grain of the board's surface, one would see it criss-crossed by fine networks of personal relationships, *guanxi*, which provide so much of the texture of Chinese social and political life. One could also add an external dimension (if one wanted to stretch the analogy, the extreme periphery of the board beyond the largest wire circle) which is the international political, economic and cultural arena.

In the domestic arena there are *three major types of political actor*: powerful leaders at the centre, institutions which scythe their way down through society and economy, and social classes, strata or groups of various kinds. One can make a simplifying initial assumption that each of these actors has more or less different interests and perspectives which determine their reaction to policy issues which may affect them. They also differ in the extent to which they can mobilise resources to exert political influence, the ways in which they attempt to do so, and the particular arenas in which they may be able to exercise that influence. At this stage of our knowledge of the Chinese political process though we have learned a lot from painstaking work by Western scholars (for example, see Lampton 1987c, and Lieberthal and Oksenberg 1988), the precise content and interplay of interests and perspectives in most specific political arenas remains in large part to be determined by empirical analysis. In future, when a sufficiently rich empirical base has been built up, it may be possible to undertake more formal kinds of political analysis based, for example, on game theory or 'rational choice' methods.

One can make this framework more complex by hypothesising that 'fields' or 'arenas' of politics vary systematically according to specific policy-areas, specific sectors of society or economy, and

Figure I.1   *The Party/State Centre (Simplified)*

Party	Government
Central Committee	State Council
Politburo (executive body)	Executive Cabinet
Standing Committee	Premier, Vice-Premiers, State Councillors, Secretary-General
Secretariat (administrative body)	Commissions, Ministries State Council Offices[2] State Council Institutions[3]
Organisations and institutions directly under the Central Committee[1]	Organisations directly under the State Council[4]

Notes
1. They include important policy organs such as the Central Propaganda Department, Central Secretariat Research Office and Central Party School.
2. Social units with co-ordinating functions in certain policy areas. For example, the State Council Office for Special Economic Zones.
3. These include influential think-tanks such as the Development Research Institute and the Chinese Academy of Social Sciences.
4. Mainly bureaux specialising in certain areas, such as the State Statistical Bureau.

Source: Compiled by Akio Takahara.

different layers of the formal political system. We can then go on to specify a complex array of 'macro-political', 'meso-political' and 'micro-political' arenas to guide our analysis. Whilst mindful that the latter step would be necessary to develop a sophisticated picture of the Chinese political process, it is far too ambitious for this study which will deal mainly with the macro level in the sense of looking at political issues and processes which pervade the national arena of politics with its centre in Beijing. However, as will become apparent later, the 'meso' level of local government is particularly important

Figure I.2 *The Structure of China's Governmental System*

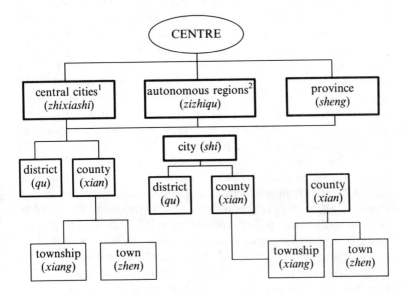

Notes:
1. There are three large cities which are directly administered by the centre (Beijing, Shanghai and Tianjin) and thus equivalent to the province.
2. These are the equivalent of the province in the national minority areas. These are similar differences in labelling at lower levels but these have been omitted for the sake of simplicity.

in the implementation of the reforms, and will receive attention as a major player in the game of national politics and policy. In our detailed studies of agricultural and industrial policy, moreover, we shall investigate the interaction between the macro-political level and the micro-political arenas of village and enterprise.

These multi-layered processes operate within a certain set of *rules of the political game* which rest on the fact that the Chinese political system, on the eve of economic reform and still today, was of the Leninist (i.e. Stalinist) type. This is highly centralised (though less so than was its Soviet counterpart), hierarchically organised and dominated by a ruling Communist party. Thus, to state the obvious, the political rules which regulate the relationship between political and administrative institutions within the Party/state system and between this and the society/economy are very different from liberal-democratic political systems where the political process is rooted in legalised competition between parties and where the policy process is more open and pluralistic. Though the Chinese polity contains strong elements of hierarchy, control and uniformity, however, that does not mean that politics operates in a monolithic way. This system wriggles with politics; it embodies a highly complex, dynamic and multi-layered interaction between various types of actor with competing political aims. Since these actors and interests are for the most part not allowed to organise or voice their claims openly, a great deal of this process is conducted behind the scenes in a kind of 'shadow pluralism' which can be called 'institutionalised' to the extent that it operates according to certain formal or informal rules and regularities. It bears comparison with the 'centralised pluralism' which Alec Nove identified in the Soviet economic policy process (Nove 1977: ch. 3). The process through which this interaction takes place has been described by David Lampton in terms of 'bargaining' (Lampton 1987a), a competitive activity which operates within the constraints posed by a hierarchically organised political and bureaucratic system.

In the analysis which follows, we are interested in the ways in which this political process has affected the nature and course of the post-Mao economic reforms. We shall also be inquiring whether the character of the political process changes under the impact of the economic reforms. We can hypothesise at this stage that the economic reforms will affect the political process in three ways. First, by diversifying the economy, it will increase the number of social and institutional interests in society and thereby make the political process more complex and difficult to manage; second, the decentralisation and dispersion of economic power deriving from the reforms will reduce the power and authority of existing Leninist political institutions and provide potential political resources to this wider array of interests, such that the political system will become more pluralistic and less hierarchical; third, as a consequence of both the above, there will be an increasing tension between the emerging new political process and the old political institutions and rules of the game which will lead to demands to change the latter. This last point leads yet again to the issue of the relationship between economic and political reform which we discuss in our concluding chapter.

1

The Failure of the Maoist Developmental State and the Rise of the Economic Reformers

The chasm between Maoism and the market is wide indeed, yet within a few years of Mao's death, the CCP leadership was trying to leap across it. How can we explain this astounding historical *volte face*? Let us organise our inquiry in terms of three sets of questions.

First, what was distinctive about the Maoist approach to development and why was it repudiated by a majority of the Chinese Party and people? In particular, what was the Maoist conception of the developmental state, in both broad and narrow senses defined earlier, and why did this prove problematic? Second, what were the political interests and pressures in Chinese society in the Maoist period which provided the impetus for the Chinese version of 'market socialism' and what were the political aims of its sponsors in the CCP leadership? Third, what are the main theoretical and policy elements of the programme of economic reforms which have sought to move China in the direction of 'market socialism' (or as the Chinese prefer to call it, a 'socialist commodity economy')? What implications do the reforms have for the character and role of the state as a developmental agent and for its relations with the economy?

Maoism and the Socialist Developmental State

Chinese politics and economics at the time of Mao's death was a confused and contradictory amalgam built up layer by layer since

21

the early 1950s. The bedrock was laid down during the period of the Soviet model in the mid-1950s, but volcanic eruptions during the Great Leap Forward and the Cultural Revolution overlaid it with two layers of Maoist political lava.

The two major streams of Maoism had different historical roots, theoretical assumptions and practical consequences.[1] The first form, *developmental Maoism*, which emerged during the mid-1950s, reflected to a considerable extent Mao's own diagnosis of defects in the imported Stalinist model. This was the ideology behind the massive, and ultimately disastrous, upsurge of the Great Leap Forward and the formation of 'rural people's communes' in 1958–9. This strain of Maoism drew on his experience in the 1930s and 1940s in the northern revolutionary base-area of Yan'an (Yenan) during the war against Japan (for a classic analysis of developmental Maoism, see Gray 1973).

It levelled a double critique at the Stalinist approach to development. First, in terms of development strategy, Soviet planners had given priority to industry over agriculture, heavy over light industry and capital-intensive over labour-intensive technology. By contrast, Mao argued in the mid-1950s that the state should give greater attention to agriculture and light industry, which were more appropriate for an underdeveloped country like China and which, over the longer term, would generate funds to be ploughed back into heavy industry. In choosing technology, Mao emphasised the need to 'walk on two legs' towards industrialisation, using intermediate and 'native' as well as advanced foreign technology, and encouraging (small-scale) industrialisation by local collectives as well as in the state sector, in the countryside as well as in the cities.

Second, in terms of political and economic institutions, Mao criticised the Soviet model for being over-centralised and 'top-down' and argued for greater decentralisation of power to local governments and collective institutions (notably the communes) according to the principles of local 'self-reliance' and 'two enthusiasms are better than one'. The distinctive role of the hegemonic Party was to galvanise the state's administrative machine and mobilise the population for developmental purposes through wave after wave of mass movements. This was a 'revolutionary' state in the sense that its role was to lead an 'uninterrupted revolution', a developmental process marked by

qualitative 'leaps forward' in a continuing struggle against economic backwardness. This mobilisational notion of the developmental
state, which fuses the political and economic aspects of the state,
bears comparison with the Soviet Union in the early years of Stalin
during the upheavals of the First Five-Year Plan in the early 1930s
and contrasts with the later phase of Soviet Stalinism when the
Party-government machine had settled and solidified into a rigid
and conservative edifice.

During the early and mid-1960s, however, Mao and a group of
radical intellectuals gradually developed a new paradigm of socialist
development, *radical Maoism*.[2] In this view, the 'socialist' society
already established in China, the Soviet Union and other 'socialist'
countries embodied certain vested interests and incipient class
forces which obstructed the advance of genuine socialism and
threatened a 'reversion to capitalism'. Thus institutions and people
needed continually to be transformed alongside economic technical
modernisation; otherwise, in one of the slogans imputed to the
radical Gang of Four, 'while the satellite goes up to the sky, the red
flag falls to the ground'. This transformation involves a prolonged
political struggle waged by a 'proletarian' Party, conducted under
the banner of 'the continuation of class struggle in socialist society'
in a process of 'continuing revolution' – this was the ideological
basis of the Great Proletarian Cultural Revolution which exploded
in 1966. Its primary targets were high-ranking Party-state leaders
who held opposing views – 'those in authority taking the capitalist
road' – and 'new bourgeois elements' allegedly emerging throughout society who threatened to turn the nation back to capitalism.
The Party had to be transformed into a radical force to counter
these trends by mobilising the 'masses' under the banner of the
'mass line'. At the ideological level, radical Maoism called for a
struggle against forms of Marxism–Leninism which allegedly
fostered capitalism, notably Soviet 'revisionism'; at the institutional level, the target was 'bureaucratism' which was to be
attacked through constant ideological education of officials, their
repeated involvement in manual labour or visits to the grass-roots
to practise the 'mass line', and their participation in institutions
which contained mass representatives (such as the 'revolutionary
committees' set up to run units during the Cultural Revolution, or
the 'three-in-one' innovation groups set up in factories which
combined workers, technicians and managers).

Radical Maoism offered a critique of Stalinist institutions and advocated ways to reform them. But, in the context of the early and mid-1960s, it also sought to defend them against those in the Soviet Union and other Eastern European countries who were moving falteringly in the direction of 'market socialism' (including the market-oriented Yugoslav 'self-management' model of socialism, in spite of its strong commitment to mass participation at the enterprise level). 'Revisionist' ideas about the need to encourage market mechanisms, provide economic incentives for workers and grant more autonomy to productive enterprises – elements of an embryonic version of what was later to become a more fully-fledged 'market socialist' paradigm – were current in China in the early 1960s and had attracted the interest of key leaders in the CCP. It was as much against this ideological trend than against the deficiencies of Stalinism that the Cultural Revolution was directed. Maoists were violently opposed to any hint of market socialism and vociferously denounced what they saw as 'bourgeois' innovations, such as individual material incentives to spur productivity, profits as an index of enterprise performance, the play of supply and demand as a stimulus to greater economic efficiency, and expanded links with capitalist economies abroad (except as an unavoidable way to acquire advanced technology).

Policy and ideology in the Cultural Revolution decade were a complex mixture of these two layers of Maoism. In their different ways, they envisaged a form of 'socialist development' which went far beyond mere economic improvement to include a wide range of social and political objectives, to be achieved through the pervasive intervention of an activist Party/state. But there was a huge amount of slippage between Maoist talk and action: for example, strategic economic priorities in the 1960s and 1970s continued to favour heavy industrialisation over all else, and popular living standards still came a poor second to the desire for high levels of capital accumulation and rapid growth rates. Part of the political failure of Maoism stems from the glaring gaps between pronouncement and practice (for an analysis of 'actually existing Maoism', see Walder 1987). Even where Maoist politics did succeed in introducing certain new elements into the traditional Soviet model of statist development (notably the emphasis on decentralisation to local governments), the institutional essentials of the old system not only remained, but were also protected against market-oriented reform alternatives which might have threatened them. There was still a hegemonic Party dominated by a single leader and ruled by a single ideological orthodoxy; the economy was still subject to direct control by state agencies (even though these might be organs of local rather than central government); and markets were diagnosed and treated as noxious 'carriers' of capitalism. Indeed, the Maoist experiment served to intensify these characteristics and take them to extreme lengths. In the economic sphere, instead of achieving 'leaps forward' in developing the human and material potential of the nation, Maoism served to restrain growth in productivity by stifling initiative and penalising excellence. In the political sphere, since it failed to shake off the institutional imprint of orthodox Marxism–Leninism, its real impact was a grotesquely distorted mirror-image of its proclaimed intentions: whereas the Party/state machine was supposed to become more responsive and democratic, it became more sluggish and authoritarian; whereas the 'mass line' was supposed to bring officials and citizens closer together, it widened the gap between state and society, particularly in the cities. As a project for the reconstitution of revolutionary socialism, Maoism was faulty in both its conception and in its implementation; the longer its political life was extended artificially (until the death of Mao himself), the deeper the grave it dug for itself.

The Demise of Maoism and the Rise of the Reformers

It is common to talk of the death of the 'Maoist model' after the death of Mao in September 1976. However, while the removal of the Shanghai 'Gang of Four' soon afterwards removed the main-stays of radical Maoism within the leadership, it did not bring about the immediate demise of Maoism as a whole, but of *one version*, radical Maoism. Indeed 1977–8 saw a resurgence of a moderate form of 'developmental Maoism' under the leadership of Mao's chosen successor, Hua Guofeng. This in turn was criticised and superseded during 1978–81 by a new approach to development, the paradigm of 'economic system reform', given force by the growing political predominance of Deng Xiaoping, and ratified by the Third Plenum of the CCP Central Committee in December 1978. The five years after Mao's death thus saw a major political reorientation at the top of the Party, with power moving between three groups of leaders, each of which had a distinctively different view of the nature of China's socialist development and the role of the state in this process (for detailed analysis of this period, see Gardner 1982 and Harding 1987).

After Hua Guofeng came to power as Party leader in October 1976, immediate steps were taken to reject the ideological foundations of radical Maoism, vilify its chief exponents (the Gang of Four), remove or suppress their main supporters at all levels and rescind many of their policies. This campaign was carried out with great vehemence and met with almost no concerted opposition or popular protest. On the contrary, as this author can testify on the basis of a visit to China in early 1977, it was apparently received well by most sectors of the population.

Hua Guofeng and his likeminded associates did not reject the Cultural Revolution, still less Mao himself; nor did they view the previous decade as a disaster. Indeed, they emphasised that, in spite of 'serious interference and sabotage' from Lin Biao and the Gang of Four, the previous development strategy had basically been correct and economic performance generally good. Although their thinking was confused, they seemed to be harking back to the era before the Cultural Revolution and searching for some kind of amalgam between the stability of the Soviet institutions introduced in the mid-1950s and a more sensible and controlled version of the Great Leap Forward. They still used the language of developmental Maoism, but sought to tone down or revise some of its central tenets.

Development was still seen in socio-political as well as economic terms – as a big push, a 'revolutionary' struggle against backwardness proceeding through Great Leaps, though Hua was careful to define the aim of 'revolution' as 'liberating the productive forces'.[3] Mao Zedong Thought, suitably bowdlerised, was maintained (along with Marxism–Leninism) as the ruling ideology. Developmental Maoist slogans of local and regional self-reliance were maintained, as was the political style of setting 'models' for nationwide emulation. The previous models of *Dazhai* (Tachai) production brigade (for agriculture) and *Daqing* (Tachai) oilfield (for industry) were retained, as was the 'Charter of the Anshan Iron and Steel Company' as a framework for industrial relations. The original 'general line' of the 1958–9 Great Leap

Forward – 'going all out, aiming high to achieve greater, faster, better and more economical results in building socialism' – was reiterated. An overly ambitious new Ten-Year Plan was introduced at the first session of the Fifth National People's Congress in early 1978.[4] The proclaimed objectives of the Plan reflected the Maoist style of setting unrealistically high goals and then mobilising the population to chase after them. The basic aims were to achieve 85 per cent mechanisation of all major processes of farmwork and complete the construction of 'an independent and fairly comprehensive industrial complex' by 1985. Agricultural output was scheduled to rise by 4.5 per cent per annum and industrial output by over 10 per cent. The planned rate of national accumulation was actually scheduled to rise still higher than the previous high rate (indeed it reached 36.5 per cent of national income in 1978, the highest since the Great Leap Forward). Over the eight years to 1985, capital investment by the state was to be equivalent to the total for the previous twenty-eight years. Although there was talk about the need to increase investment in light industry and agriculture, heavy industry was still to receive the lion's share of state funds. Overall, the new programme continued the strategic emphases of the past, with one major new element, a 'Great Leap Outward' towards the international economy which involved a huge increase in purchases of plant and equipment from abroad and an acceptance of the need to borrow abroad to finance imports.

These ambitious developmental goals continued to require an actively interventionist state. Hua continued to view the state as an instrument of political mobilisation, not just of control and administration. Development would still proceed through mass movements and the Party-government apparatus would still act as a political vanguard in this process. However, the scale and intensity of mass mobilisation was to be reduced, given the economic disruption and popular antipathy it had engendered previously. To the extent that political mobilisation continued, moreover, it was to be directed towards economic rather than political purposes. Henceforth, politics would not be allowed to 'brush aside or supersede economics'; political work was to respect the 'objective laws' of economic development.[5] The 'Gang of Four' were criticised for allegedly maintaining that 'it is all right for production to go down as long as we do a good job in revolution' and 'we would rather have a low socialist growth rate than a high capitalist one'.[6] Thus the radical Maoist attempt to transform institutions and attitudes was largely abandoned.

Indeed, the Hua programme was conservative in institutional terms. Not only was the dominance of the Party taken for granted, but the importance of the hierarchical system of economic administration laid down in the 1950s was strongly reiterated. Indeed, the stress now was on restoring the previous putative effectiveness of this framework through selective centralisation, more accurate macro-economic planning, tighter administrative controls and a higher degree of managerial responsibility in enterprises. However, the Maoist emphasis on the need for decentralisation of economic management to localities was still retained, with the ultimate intention of dividing the country into six relatively self-reliant economic regions. The previous system of productive institutions also stayed basically intact, in spite of some marginal reforms. In industry, though there was greater stress on the need for material incentives to motivate workers, moral incentives and 'socialist labour emulation' were still given precedence. In the rural sector, though there were some moves towards reviving the private sector and criticism of 'egalitarianism' in distributing income within production teams, the absolute predominance of collective institutions was emphasised along with the need to 'overcome spontaneous tendencies towards capitalism'. The latter reflected the Maoist abhorrence of markets and market-like institutions (such as the increased use of income differentials to provide incentives to effort and a larger role for the private sector). Even the Great Leap Outward towards the world economy and the major capitalist nations did not mean a positive view of the international market; rather it was seen as a shortcut towards achieving essentially unchanged national goals within an essentially unchanged framework of economic administration.

Thus the immediate post-Mao period was in effect a Great Leap Backwards, an attempt to create a harmonious synthesis of developmental aims and institutions dating from allegedly halcyon days before the Cultural Revolution. In the eyes of the emergent economic reformers within the Party leadership, this programme did not go far enough merely by removing the excesses of Cultural Revolution Maoism. The heritage of the 1950s and early 1960s also contained fundamental flaws which had be addressed and corrected if the Party were to regain its political prestige and China's economic performance were to be radically improved. Not only were the remnants of the Maoist mobilisational approach to development to be rooted out, but the previously unchallenged predominance of Soviet-style central planning had to be questioned.

This impetus towards more thorough-going reform grew stronger in the late 1970s with the rise of Deng Xiaoping and his allies, rallying under the slogan of 'practice as the sole criterion of truth'.[7] They dubbed residual Maoist leaders as 'whateverists', i.e. people who thought and did 'whatever Mao Zedong thought or did'. The latter were gradually weakened and isolated, eventually to be removed or forced to resign. By early 1981, only Hua Guofeng remained of the major developmental Maoist leaders, and he was finally demoted at the Sixth Plenum of the Party Central Committee in June of that year, to be replaced as Party Chairman by a reformist, Hu Yaobang.[8] These transitional years also saw the rise to public prominence of a new conception of socialist political economy which went beyond a mere attack on Maoism to include a thoroughgoing critique of China's developmental experience over the past three decades. This coalesced to lay a new basis for China's economic future, a process of 'economic structural reform' leading to a new model of the socialist developmental state, the socialist economy and the relations between them.

The Political Origins of Chinese Economic Reform

Official Chinese (and many foreign) analyses of the economic reforms attribute their necessity to problems inherent in the previous Soviet-derived (and Maoist-adapted) state-directed economic system. As such, they were interpreted as yet another attempt to rectify the economic deficiencies of excessive state intervention in the economy. At the beginning of the reform era at least, there was little new or original about these ideas. Not only had they been current in Eastern Europe over the past decade or more, but elements of the reformist critique had already appeared in China as early as the mid-1950s when Chen Yun, for example, had advocated greater use of indirect planning methods and a more market-oriented pricing policy. Economists such as Xue Muqiao and Sun Yefang had also aired pro-market proposals in the media at the same time and there were short-lived experiments to grant enterprises greater power to act as autonomous entities outside direct state controls. Similar policy proposals and practical experiments surfaced again in the wake of the Great Leap Forward in the early 1960s, but they were submerged by the rising political wave of radical Maoism which led to the Cultural Revolution.

In both earlier periods of reformist thinking, the economic problems identified by critics may have been real enough, but there was not enough political impetus to convert reformist ideas into sustainable policies. This was not the case in the post-Mao era and I wish to explore why, to understand the political pressures which both impelled and enabled leaders to convert ideas into policy. After all, the adoption of a radical reform programme posed serious risks for its political sponsors. As Deng Xiaoping himself remarked, this was a 'second revolution' which aimed at a radical redefinition of the theory and practice of socialist economic development. Changes of this scale would be politically disruptive in their very nature, would provoke opposition from supporters of the old system and, though largely confined to the economic sphere, had potential implications for the Leninist political system which were hard to foresee at the outset. Clearly, to be successful the reforms required a powerful political impetus which could concentrate the minds of Party leaders, provide an underpinning of popular consent and weaken or neutralise potential opposition.

The experience of China and other state socialist countries undergoing economic reform suggests that the character and force of this political impetus derives from three sets of factors: (i) *economic factors*, notably problems in economic performance stemming from the previous strategy of economic development, and the institutional structure of state economic planning and management; (ii) *political factors* to do with the operation and impact of the previous political system, notably problems concerning the viability of the reigning ideology, the institutional effectiveness of the Party and the nature of relations between state and citizen; (iii) *social factors*, notably the evolving nature of Chinese social structure and the impact of the previous strategy of development on different social groups and on relationships between state and society. I shall discuss each of these categories in the context of the mid–late 1970s when the crucial political transition from Maoism to reformism took place.

Economic Factors

The economic achievements of the previous system of directive state planning had not been negligible, notwithstanding the disruptions caused by political turmoil. Indeed, in comparison with economic performance in most of the developing world, they were impressive. China had achieved high rates of industrial growth (about 11 per cent per annum gross between 1952 and 1978) and creditable rates of agricultural growth (about 3 per cent per annum gross) and had been successful in establishing a reasonably comprehensive industrial and technical base while avoiding political or economic dependence on foreign countries (for data on the growth of agricultural and industrial output, see Tables 1.1 and 1.2). There had been significant structural change in the economy with industry's share of gross national product more than doubling between 1949 and 1977 (from 25 per cent to nearly 60 per cent). Certain strategic heavy industries had developed very rapidly, notably machine-building, metallurgy, petroleum, chemicals and electric power. Consumption had grown at a rate of about 2.2 per cent per person per year between 1952 and 1976 (see Table 1.3) and this, combined with measures to spread income more evenly and establish a basic floor of welfare provision, achieved significant success in alleviating poverty.

But Chinese economists are right to argue that these figures over-reported real economic performance and concealed basic problems which were worsening in the 1960s and 1970s. In macro-economic terms, the pace of economic advance was erratic, with periods of boom and slump; in the disastrous recession following the Great Leap Forward, for example, between 15 and 30 million people died from the effects of famine (Riskin 1987: p. 136). Excessive concentration on heavy industry starved other sectors of funds and retarded their growth (for example, the growth in agricultural output barely kept pace with China's expanding population). In terms of economic efficiency, marginal capital–output ratios in industry were deteriorating, which meant that high growth rates were being purchased at increasing capital cost (Ishikawa 1983); labour productivity in state industry was static or declining (Field 1983); and efforts to bring about a breakthrough in agricultural productivity had proven unsuccessful (output per unit of capital was declining in the 1960s and 1970s in spite of the massive

Table 1.1   *Agricultural Growth 1952–91: Indices of Growth in Gross
Output Value (overall and by sector)
Measure: preceding year = 100; based on comparable prices*

Year	Gross output value of agriculture	Farming	Forestry	Animal husbandry	Sideline production	Fishery
1952	115.2	115.7	138.1	121.6	122.8	130.0
1957	103.6	102.9	105.7	125.7	101.3	170.6
1965	108.3	107.8	115.4	109.0	107.0	109.8
1970	105.8	110.5	114.3	105.0	137.8	101.9
1975	103.1	103.0	102.2	103.5	106.2	103.2
1978	108.1	109.4	105.5	104.9	102.2	100.0
1979	107.5	107.2	101.4	114.6	96.5	96.6
1980	101.4	99.5	112.2	107.0	106.1	107.7
1981	105.8	105.9	104.1	105.9	124.0	104.4
1982	111.3	110.3	108.5	113.2	121.9	112.3
1983	107.8	108.3	110.2	103.9	111.6	108.6
1984	112.3	109.9	119.0	113.4	133.0	117.6
1985	103.4	98.0	104.5	117.2	120.6	118.9
1986	103.4	100.9	96.4	105.5	120.0	120.5
1987	105.8	105.3	99.7	103.2	115.4	118.1
1988	103.9	99.8	102.3	112.7	112.6	111.6
1989	103.1	101.8	100.4	105.6	106.0	107.2
1990	107.6	108.6	103.1	107.0	103.8	110.0
1991*	103.0	100.9	107.8	106.1	101.8	106.7

Sources: SSB 1991, p. 286; **NCNA* 28 February 1992.

infrastructural projects in which the Maoists took great pride, and
agricultural output per labourer only rose 5 per cent in real terms
over the whole period 1952 to 1978) (Nolan 1990: p. 11).

By the mid-1970s, the political costs of these economic deficiencies were mounting. The incomes of the mass of the population, in
both cities and countryside, were either stagnating or rising only
glacially (Nolan and White 1984), as were levels of real material
welfare, such as consumption of food and light industrial products,
or availability of housing (Nolan 1990: p. 11). This not only fuelled
social discontent but, more insidiously, created a vicious cycle
whereby lack of incentives led to economic passivity which held

Table 1.2   *Industrial Growth 1950–1991: Indices of Growth in Gross*
Output Value (overall and by ownership)
Measure: preceding year = 100; based on comparable prices

Year	Total	State owned	Collective owned	Individual owned	Other ownership
1950	136.38	129.92	214.29	156.21	
1951	137.81	143.47	226.67	119.48	
1952	130.28	130.75	329.41	117.47	
1953	130.21	131.40	154.46	121.95	
1954	116.26	116.15	160.12	107.90	
1955	105.58	106.74	150.18	87.30	
1956	128.23	135.02	288.70	10.23	
1957	111.41	109.21	124.23	78.31	
1958	154.83	171.61	85.76		
1959	136.15	135.20	143.98		
1960	111.19	113.76	91.29		
1961	61.78	60.35	75.50		
1962	83.41	82.74	88.56		
1963	108.45	110.33	94.89		
1964	119.65	119.94	117.28		
1965	126.35	127.10	119.93		
1966	120.96	121.11	119.65		
1967	86.20	84.56	101.33		
1968	94.96	94.93	95.23		
1969	134.28	134.72	130.91		
1970	132.60	130.96	145.55		
1971	114.68	114.02	119.32		
1972	106.88	105.59	114.70		
1973	109.48	108.38	115.67		
1974	100.61	98.68	110.77		
1975	115.49	113.71	123.87		
1976	102.44	98.89	117.68		
1977	114.60	112.70	121.48		
1978	113.55	114.44	110.58		
1979	108.81	108.88	108.57		
1980	109.27	105.61	119.24		
1981	104.29	102.53	109.01	234.57	131.60
1982	107.82	107.05	109.54	178.95	127.73
1983	111.19	109.39	115.53	220.59	133.90
1984	116.28	108.92	134.85	197.47	156.81
1985	121.39	112.94	132.69	1189.60	139.54
1986	111.67	106.18	117.97	167.57	134.16
1987	117.69	111.30	123.24	156.59	166.39
1988	120.79	112.61	128.16	147.34	161.53
1989	108.54	103.86	110.48	123.77	142.68
1990	107.76	102.96	109.02	121.11	139.33
1991*	114.2	108.4	118.00	124.00	155.8

*Source: SSB 1991, p. 357; *NCNA 28 February 1992.*

Table 1.3   *Indices of Per Capita Consumption, 1953–90*
(at comparable prices)

Year	Preceeding year = 100			1952 = 100		
	All residents	Agricultural residents	Non-agricultural residents	All residents	Agricultural residents	Non-agricultural residents
1953	107.7	103.1	115.0	107.7	103.1	115.0
1954	100.4	101.2	100.1	108.2	104.4	115.0
1955	106.4	108.6	102.5	115.1	113.4	117.9
1956	104.3	101.4	104.9	120.0	115.0	123.7
1957	102.4	101.8	102.1	122.9	117.0	126.3
1958	101.4	102.5	95.1	124.6	120.0	120.1
1959	90.1	78.9	100.8	112.3	94.6	121.1
1960	94.1	95.4	88.3	105.6	90.3	106.9
1961	94.0	101.8	87.3	99.4	91.9	93.3
1962	104.4	107.5	103.6	103.7	98.8	96.6
1963	110.3	108.0	117.7	114.4	106.8	113.6
1964	106.2	106.8	111.2	121.5	114.0	126.4
1965	109.2	109.8	108.2	132.7	125.2	136.7
1966	104.1	104.5	103.3	138.1	130.7	141.3
1967	103.5	104.2	102.9	142.9	136.2	145.3
1968	96.5	95.2	99.5	137.8	129.7	144.6
1969	102.6	103.0	102.9	141.4	133.5	148.7
1970	104.1	105.8	102.2	147.3	141.3	152.0
1971	101.1	100.6	102.8	148.9	142.1	156.2
1972	102.8	99.5	109.8	153.0	141.5	171.6
1973	105.3	106.1	103.7	161.1	150.2	177.9
1974	99.8	99.2	102.0	160.9	148.9	181.5
1975	101.9	101.4	103.0	163.8	151.0	187.0
1976	101.8	100.3	104.5	166.8	151.4	195.5
1977	101.0	99.7	103.0	168.5	151.0	201.3
1978	105.1	104.4	105.6	177.0	157.6	212.6
1979	106.7	106.9	104.2	188.8	168.6	221.5
1980	109.5	109.7	107.1	206.7	184.9	237.3
1981	106.9	107.9	108.6	221.1	199.4	257.7
1982	105.1	107.6	99.0	232.3	214.6	255.2
1983	106.8	109.1	101.9	248.2	234.2	260.0
1984	111.0	112.4	106.4	275.5	263.1	276.6
1985	113.2	113.9	108.7	311.8	299.6	300.7
1986	104.3	102.4	107.1	325.0	306.8	322.1
1987	105.7	104.2	109.3	343.6	319.6	352.1
1988	106.9	106.1	107.1	367.1	339.2	377.2
1989	98.7	98.7	97.4	362.2	334.7	367.2
1990	101.3	99.5	103.7	367.0	332.9	380.7

Note   The precise data categories and sources are unclear in these official statistics, so they should only be taken as rough indicators.

Source: SSB, 1991, p. 241.

back improvements in productivity which dampened growth in real incomes, and so on. Since the legitimacy of the CCP regime, even in the Maoist period, rested heavily on its ability to improve the living standards of the population, such disappointing performance posed a serious political challenge to the Party leadership.

This challenge was compounded by the international context of the late 1960s and 1970s. Developed capitalism had experienced a prolonged boom, Japan in particular turning in an exceptional growth performance (about 10 per cent per year in the late 1960s and early 1970s). Moreover, the dynamic growth performance of China's capitalist neighbours, the East Asian NICs was already apparent, particularly the 'Four Tigers' (South Korea, Taiwan, Singapore and Hong Kong). Japan was an old competitive reference point for Chinese leaderships both before and after the Communist revolution, so its meteoric success was clearly a challenge. But the success of Chinese communities in Taiwan, Hong Kong and Singapore was particularly galling – particularly Taiwan which was ruled by the CCP's old enemy, the Kuomintang – and posed a powerful demonstration effect which Chinese leaders could ignore at their peril. Moreover, the NICs were not only demonstrating the domestic benefits of opening to the international economy but also demonstrating an enviable capacity to compete effectively therein. This suggested strongly that Chinese conceptions of national 'self-reliance' needed to be rethought (for a comparison of China and the East Asian NICs, see White 1988).

Persistent poverty, technological backwardness and pervasive economic inefficiency, thrown into relief by the success of others, were a source of great concern to Deng and other senior leaders of the CCP and provided a good deal of their political motivation in supporting the proposals of reform economists. The reforms, by promising to accelerate economic performance, provided the key not merely for improvements in popular welfare but for an increase in national power, opening the door to the 'rich and strong' country which Chinese leaders had been seeking since the national humiliations of the nineteenth century. Though the symbols of humiliation might now be an American satellite or a Japanese colour TV rather than a British gunboat, their political impact was no less real. In sum, therefore, in economic terms the political appeal of market reform was as a recipe, in the eyes of significant sections of the Party élite at least, for recouping the Party's political credibility by demonstrating its capacity to raise living standards and achieve China's national aspirations.

At the deepest level, the economic imperfections of the pre-reform era reflected fundamental problems in the specific form of state-directed economic development which the CCP had adopted after 1949 and demonstrates the inextricability of the economic and political aspects of this system. Chinese development experience embodied a marked 'state bias' (Nolan and White 1984), which skewed resources in economically irrational and socially regressive ways. Ideologically, state-owned enterprises were defined as superior to other forms of production, and collective institutions in both industry and agriculture were pressured to aspire to this exalted status. In all spheres, the interests of the state were given precedence over those of the collective and the individual. Structurally, the network of Party and government organisations had extended more deeply into the economy than had ever been envisaged in the heyday of the 'Soviet model' in the early to mid-1950s. State organs at various levels not only directly managed state-owned enterprises, but also exerted administrative control over the nominally more autonomous collective enterprises, the larger of which were run as *de facto* state concerns. In the countryside, state and Party controls extended directly into the nominally 'collective' people's communes, forging an unbroken chain of politico-administrative authority down to the village level (Gray 1988). Comprehensively, therefore, most productive enterprises were locked into a framework of state control and enjoyed precious little formal operational autonomy.

This pervasive 'state bias' in part reflected the claim of a particularly ambitious form of developmental state to represent and act in pursuit of what it perceived as the wider, long-term interests of society as a whole. Even if we grant that political leaders and state officials might genuinely be striving for a 'general interest', however, this could only be part of the picture given the facts that the Chinese Leninist state was not accountable to its mass constituency in any institutionalised sense and there was little in the way of effective channels for the expression of diverse social interests. In part, 'state bias' represented a process whereby the Party-state nexus increasingly came to act 'for itself', to represent apparatchik interests rather than those of the workers and peasants whom it represented in the initial era of revolution. This transformation in the political nature of the Party/state creates a link between state interests and institutions on the one side and economic development strategy on the other; the continued well-being of the Party/state apparatus becomes entwined with a continuing commitment to rapid industrialisation and high levels of capital accumulation. The result is a 'state-biased' pattern of developmental priorities which allocates resources to privileged sectors (notably heavy industry), the state organs (the key economic ministries) which represent them and the employees who work in them. The rest of society (and in the Chinese case this is the vast majority) loses out.

There is a 'Catch 22' of the developmental state operating here. A pervasive and all-powerful state is established in the initial stage of industrialisation for reasons defensible at the time, but then outstays its historical welcome as a bastion of economic irrationality and political authoritarianism. The state increasingly takes on the character of a chrysalis which will not open to allow the butterfly to go free. Economic progress increasingly demands a transformation of the state itself and of the relationship between state and economy. At the same time, the escalating economic costs of maintaining the *status quo* – in terms of productivity, income and welfare foregone – provide much of the political impetus behind pressures for reform. This said, however, it would be difficult to argue that China was facing an 'economic crisis' in the mid-1970s. Economic problems in and of themselves were not the only, nor the decisive, factor in propelling Party leaders towards economic reform; we must look further, towards the impact of deficiencies in China's political ideas and institutions.

Political Factors

There were other factors which strengthened the appeal of economic reform, stemming from the nature and functioning of China's political institutions in the Maoist era. Indeed, to the extent that the turn to the market was in response to *crisis*, its causes are to be found primarily in political rather than economic malfunction. Like Brezhnev's Soviet Union, China could have limped along much longer with an economy performing below par. It was the *political* experience of the previous two decades which had wrought pervasive damage throughout society, impairing the effectiveness of all institutions, economic or otherwise. The economy may have been suffering from the familiar deficiencies of Soviet-style planning, but these had been greatly intensified by the political instability and conflict of the Maoist years.

In the pre-Cultural Revolution era, China was not free of the characteristic political problems of Leninist regimes, notably popular resentment of the pervasive power of the single party and frustration at the bureaucratisation of society and economy. These tensions found expression in the criticisms voiced during the Hundred Flowers Movement in 1956–7 and in the vast eruption of organised mass politics during the first part of the Cultural Revolution in 1966–68, when large sections of the urban population used the opportunity of the officially-sanctioned campaign against 'people in authority taking the capitalist road' to vent their spleen against their political and administrative masters.

However, before the disastrous split in the top leadership of the CCP which brought on the Cultural Revolution, the CCP regime did enjoy certain political advantages: a credible revolutionary heritage and a considerable degree of leadership consensus, organisational coherence and ideological consistency which eased the task of mobilising popular support. The CCP's authoritarian style of governance also fitted well with a Chinese traditional political culture deferential to authority. These advantages, however, were seriously weakened during ten years of Cultural Revolution: the Party was at war with itself; the official ideology became demystified, functioning less as a unifying creed and more as a political weapon for competing leaders; the organisational stability of the previous regime, which had at least offered a degree of regularity and predictability to members of state and society alike, gave way to a dangerous political game ruled by ambiguity, arbitrariness and systematic insincerity. This not only affected ordinary members of society, but also members of the Party and state officialdom, who always ran the risk, and often suffered the reality, of being branded a 'revisionist' or 'capitalist roader'. They had a strong interest in a cessation of hostilities and a normalisation of political and bureaucratic life.

In terms of the Party's position in society, it had rationalised its right to monocratic power in terms of the need for firm and consistent leadership of the nation; but it was clearly unable to provide either during the Cultural Revolution decade. Ideological principles and political institutions lost a good deal of their former meaning and authority. The radical Maoist principle of 'politics in command' brought wave after wave of political campaigns which disrupted everyday lives, set people against each other and created growing mass resentment. In spite of Maoist attacks on bureau-cratic élitism and self-seeking, state officials actually strengthened their position as a privileged stratum in an economic system in which power counted for more than money in gaining access to scarce goods. Popular attitudes to politics changed to cynicism, apathy or active opposition (the latter trait being a residue of the mass politics and 'great democracy' of the Cultural Revolution). At the deepest level, one can detect a growing antagonism between state and society. To the extent that the post-Mao economic reforms were a response to this increasing tension between state and society, they were in effect a revolt against the state.

In sum, an alarming process of 'political decay' had taken place in China's political and administrative institutions between 1966 and 1976, affecting their internal operation and their relations with society at large. The economic reforms might provide the key for repairing some of this political damage, but there would also be a need to rehabilitate these institutions if the authority of Chinese state socialism was to be restored.

Social Factors

We have concentrated so far on the role of political leaders and institutions in determining the route to policy reform. Yet these operated in a wider political environment, society as a whole, which exerted implicit and explicit pressures on the Party leadership and thereby provided part of the political constituency for reform. There was widespread social dissatisfaction with the Maoist system by the time of Mao's death; let us look at this briefly in terms of different sectors of society.

Although politically quiescent, even at the height of the Cultural Revolution, the *collective peasantry* were chafing under both the institutional restrictions of the commune system and the extra policy restrictions imposed by the radical Maoists (for example, limitations on private agricultural or sideline production, on local free markets, or on the ability to diversify collective production away from grain into more profitable crops; or strict controls over the ability of villagers to leave their homes and seek work in towns and cities; or corvée-like demands on peasants to work, largely without pay, on local infrastructural projects, such as irrigation works, landscaping or roads). On average, their incomes and living standards were not rising significantly (although there were of course wide inter- and intra-regional differences) and the terms of trade between agricultural and industrial goods had not moved sufficiently in their favour, in spite of Maoist promises to reduce the 'great difference' between city and countryside. Peasant discontent usually did not take dramatic forms; rather it manifested itself in passivity at work and evasion of state levies (for example, by under-reporting production or income), which led to slow productivity growth in agriculture and continuing tension between peasants and state procurement agencies.

In the cities, the main body of *manual workers* in state enterprises, though privileged compared to anyone working out-side the State sector, saw their real wages hardly increasing and faced irksome restrictions on their ability to earn more through greater effort or skill and to move upwards to more responsible and better paid jobs. Worker morale also suffered from the legacy of organised factions during the Cultural Revolution which had split the workforce and damaged the social fabric of the enterprise. At the same time, Chinese *enterprise managers* were caught between the often arbitrary demands of their bureaucratic superiors in state supervisory agencies and the intractability of their own work-forces. During the Cultural Revolution, their authority had been cast aside and their ability to impose any kind of discipline in the productive process had been impaired. They themselves had little incentive to make an effort to improve the efficiency of the enterprise; nor did they have much scope to offer productivity incentives to their own workforce. Where managers were not Party officials or members, moreover, their professional judgement was always subject to political intervention at the plant level. Though many if not most managers had learned to play the game and had worked out informal arrangements with their state superiors, enterprise Party officials and their own workers, there was frustration, particularly among younger, more educated managers, and a desire for greater authority and the ability to get on with the job without interference.

The educated *intelligentsia*, particularly those working in the fields of education, health, culture and mass communications, were the social stratum which had suffered most from the Cultural Revolution (when they were vilified as the 'stinking ninth' category of bad elements) and had most to gain from its demise. However, even *officials* in the government and Party bureaucracies were open to change since they too, as 'people in authority taking the capitalist road', had been targets of radical Maoist politics. In generational terms, Chinese *youth* who had grown up during the late 1960s and early 1970s resented (particularly in the cities) the personal restrictions imposed by the 'correct proletarian line', particularly the lack of educational and job opportunities and the policy of sending urban youth 'down to the countryside and up to the mountains' which condemned them to an ignominious life on the farm and made access to scarce opportunities for advancement (particularly college entrance) vastly more difficult.

Clearly there was a widespread social mandate for change. Perhaps this was largely a negative phenomenon in the sense that people were in favour of a move away from Maoism, rather than having a clear alternative conception of something they wished to move towards. Yet economic reform (plus political 'normalisation') may well have had a strong positive appeal. For everyone, there was a vague promise of a better standard of living, greater personal freedom and a generally quieter life. For different groups, there were more specific possibilities: for the peasantry it promised greater economic freedom and higher prices for their goods; for urban workers it promised higher wages and bonuses; for enterprise managers it meant less outside interference and more space to practice a more professional form of management; for the intelligentsia it offered greater intellectual and cultural freedom and more scope to develop their professional talents; for state officials it meant a more peaceful environment and the political (and personal) benefits of a more productive economy; for youth it opened up the possibility of more educational places and jobs, a more interesting lifestyle, and the ability to be judged on merit rather than on political criteria.

However, in the context of the late 1970s, the appeals of economic reform were still vague possibilities. This was because, though certain broad principles of the new economic order were being enunciated, the precise nature of economic reform was as yet unclear. To the extent that there was any clarity, moreover, the initial version of the economic reform programme as it began in

1979 was a moderate one which looked as if it could bring economic benefits across the board without anyone losing out or having their position in society put in jeopardy. As we shall see in the next chapter, the economic reforms became more radical as they went along; this was to pose a threat to certain 'vested interests', those groups and institutions which had benefited from the previous system of central state planning. Their obstruction and opposition was later to have a major effect on the conduct of the reform programme. Even among those groups who stood to gain from the reforms, some would gain more than others and the latter could thus perceive themselves as 'losing' in relative terms. It is important at this early stage of our analysis to envisage the economic reform process as involving a complex interaction of conflicting or co-operating interests which play a major role in determining the effectiveness of economic policies.

Given this diversity of interests, it is also important to recognise that the initial (and subsequent) meanings of economic reform varied among different sectors of Chinese society. While for the mass of the population it promised higher incomes, greater consumer choice and personal freedom, for reform economists it was the key to improved economic performance through its ability not only to offer incentives but also to impose market disciplines. There are clear possibilities for a conflict of aims between these two categories. Similarly, while for reformist Party leaders economic reform is a powerful tool for restoring the battered political fortunes of the CCP and Chinese 'socialism' generally, for dissident political elements markets are a path towards emancipation by dispersing social power more widely and undermining the hegemonic position of the Party-state bureaucracy. The conflicts between these different sets of expectations will become apparent in our discussion of the political dynamics of the reform programme after 1978.

The Economic Reform Paradigm

The new economic strategy which emerged over the next few years had two major policy thrusts, 'readjustment' and 'reform' (the latter is often called 'restructuring' in Chinese texts). Readjustment reflected an attempt to correct certain basic structural imbalances in the economy which, it was argued, originated from China's adoption of the Soviet model in the 1950s; Maoist leaders had either failed to correct them or had made them worse.[9] The main areas of imbalance were identified as follows. (i) The rate of overall capital accumulation had been too high: over the twenty-six years from 1953 to 1978, the share of accumulation in national income was over 30 per cent for thirteen years, reaching a high point of 43.8 per cent in 1959. In the future, argued reform economists, this should be kept down to 25 per cent or below, and correspondingly more attention should be paid to raising levels of personal consumption and social welfare.[10] By Chinese reckoning, per capita income was US$253 in 1979 and it was proposed to raise this to US$1000 by the year 2000.[11] (ii) State investment priorities were to be changed. Though heavy industry would still retain priority, the share going to light industry and agriculture should be increased. The previous situation wherein heavy industry had taken about three-quarters of total productive state investment was to be remedied. (iii) In the urban sector, the previous stress on large-scale, capital-intensive forms of production in state enterprises was to be amended by encouraging more labour-intensive collective industry outside the state sector. This rebalancing was at least in part an effort to address a serious and growing problem of urban unemployment which the Maoist strategy had failed to tackle except through the massively unpopular policy of sending unemployed urban youth to live in the countryside (Bernstein 1977).

These readjustments were to be accompanied by a thoroughgoing structural reform *of the system of economic planning and management* – this is the main focus of my analysis. The main elements of this structural reform programme are as follows.

A Redefinition of the Socialist Developmental State

In the previous system, the spheres of politics, administration and economics were intermeshed in practice: the state apparatus dominated the economy and the Party pervaded both. Reformers have regarded this situation as problematic, first, because direct politicisation of the state bureaucracy (through Party organisations) impedes the emergence of a more professional form of modern administration and, second, because excessive involvement by either the Party or the government administration in the affairs of productive enterprises is economically harmful. The intention, therefore, has been to separate out the institutional spheres of politics, administration and economics, to define their respective functions more precisely and to redefine the relationships between them.

There are three areas of separation here: between politics and administration, between politics and economics and between administration and the economy. The first of these relates to the question of political reform of the state apparatus and lies outside our main focus on economic reform (for in depth discussions, see Burns 1987 and Lee 1991). The second involves the attempt to depoliticise economic decision-making at all levels. Ideologically, reform spokespeople emphasised the need to treat 'politics' and 'economics' as distinct spheres and avoid subordinating the latter to the former. This separation has legitimised the revival of the academic study of economics and established economists as a group with considerable influence on policy making. At the institutional level, this separation implies a more limited role for the Party in everyday processes of economic management. The system of 'interlocking directorates', whereby Party officials 'wear two hats' by holding office as administrators or managers, should be reduced. Ultimately this means that Party organisations in economic bureaucracies and enterprises would either be removed or restricted to narrowly defined political work which does not involve them in the day-to-day operation of the unit. This implies greater role-specialisation, more autonomy for professional groups in their own areas of expertise, and changes in occupational recruitment criteria, from 'redness' to 'expertise'. Henceforth, there would be professional politicians, administrators, enterprise managers, accountants, technicians, academics, and so on, each with their own precise roles, their own area of autonomy and their own standards of professional competence. At the motivational level, there was far greater emphasis on the importance of economic as opposed to moral–ideological incentives in motivating labour. In practice this means a move away from Maoist-style 'egalitarianism', which stressed collective material incentives and restraint on income differentials, towards greater use of individual incentives and a positive view of income inequality as a way to stimulate effort.

The third area of separation was between government administration and the economy; the latter was to be 'de-bureaucratised'.

Previously, argued the reformers, the economy was run as an administrative system through a complex system of central ministries and local government departments. As such, it was prone to the characteristic problems of complex, centralised bureaucracies which systematically impaired economic performance. Nor was the problem merely one of administrative subordination; it was exacerbated by the fact that the enterprise's bureaucratic masters were neither uniform nor consistent: there were numerous higher organs, functional and regional, and their functions often overlapped, with the result that state enterprises were subject to 'too many mothers-in-law'. Economic management requires economic methods, argued the reformers; enterprises should be released from the grip of their 'superior departments'. While the state should still retain an important economic role, planning was henceforth to be based on 'guidance' rather than 'directive' methods and economic management was to be conducted largely by means of policy regulation rather than administrative fiat. Rather than abolishing the socialist developmental state, therefore, the reforms aimed at changing its character and functions, moving in the direction of the kind of economic regulation characteristic of capitalist 'mixed economies' while retaining basic socialist features, such as the predominance of public ownership.

Economic Decentralisation and the 'Socialist Commodity Economy'

This redefinition of the developmental state set the context for a programme to decentralise economic decision-making power and revive market-type relations between individuals and enterprises. Whereas the Maoists had sought to reform the planning system by decentralising power from central to local governments, the new thrust was to devolve power from any layer of government to the enterprise itself: this could be described as a transition from administrative to economic decentralisation. The Maoist emphasis on local 'self-reliance', it was argued, did reduce some of the problems of over-centralisation in Soviet-style planning, but only at considerable economic cost: for example, it tended to encourage local governments to establish irrationally comprehensive local industrial systems which violated the need for specialisation and exchange between areas. Moreover, it did not challenge the principle of administrative subordination of the enterprise; it merely relocated its source.

In the new system, the state would act to achieve its plan objectives by seeking to influence enterprise behaviour in certain directions, rather than by issuing administrative orders. This new relationship between state and enterprise would, it was argued, allow most micro-economic decisions to be taken at the enterprise level where they belonged.[12] The enterprise was to gain greater power in decisions about investment, output, wages and salaries, pricing, procurement and marketing and was to behave more directly in pursuit of its 'independent financial interests'. The new system meant a change in the nature of economic linkages, away from 'vertical' relationships between enterprises and the supervisory state organs above them, towards 'horizontal', market-type links between enterprises regulated by contracts and prices which reflected real conditions of supply and demand.

The underlying assumption behind this new type of economic system is that planning and markets are compatible principles: markets can be utilised to serve the aims of socialist development. Reform economists argue that a socialist economy, indeed any kind of economy, cannot operate without markets. Markets are an objective economic necessity, a response to the complexity of any economic system, the separation between economic actors within it and the differences in their economic interests. In the words of one reform text, 'the state plan can only reflect the needs of society in totality, but cannot reflect correctly and flexibly the kaleidoscopic needs of our economic life'.[13] The traditional form of planning could not hope to grasp the shifting dynamics of supply and demand, even in purely physical terms let alone in terms of the economic efficiency of transactions. Henceforth, production was to be 'for customers not for planning statistics'; enterprises would be expected to sell their products not merely to produce them and, to this end, would have greater powers over marketing, procurement and pricing. The resulting demand-led system would create competitive pressures which would require enterprises to become more efficient to survive. Since profitability was the best indicator of enterprise performance, this was to become the prime target for enterprise managers. To this end, production was to be rationalised through professionalisation of management, stricter financial accounting, tighter work discipline and more effective methods to link individual labour to payment in both agriculture and industry. Previous payment systems, it is argued, had been too egalitarian, encouraging workers to use 'an iron bowl to eat the rice cooked in a single large pan'.

While initial thinking about the need for markets focused mainly on product-markets, as the reforms progressed the argument was extended to include markets for capital, labour and land. In regard to capital, said the reform economists, the previous system for mobilising and allocating investment funds had been too cumbersome and monolithic; the financial system should be diversified and commercialised to promote a more flexible and productive flow of funds. This meant greater autonomy for state-owned banks and a wider range of financial institutions and assets, including the emergence of markets for bonds and shares. In regard to labour, the previous system of allocating jobs to workers in the urban-industrial sector had been dominated by state labour bureaux and the results had been systematic overstaffing and virtual job tenure for workers in state and 'large-collective' enterprises (the 'iron rice bowl'). A labour market was needed to promote a more flexible flow of labour and provide more freedom both for workers who wished to change jobs and for managers who wished to re-arrange their workforces in line with changing market conditions. In regard to land (in the event to be the most contentious issue), a market was seen as desirable because it allowed land to pass into the hands of the most efficient producers and encouraged diversification of the rural economy. For the more radical reformers, therefore, the ultimate character of the 'socialist commodity economy' was a fully-fledged market system in which a wide range of markets for all factors of production prevailed. But the desirable extent of 'marketisation' was to become a bone of contention between more conservative and more radical reformers as the reforms actually took their course.

Ownership

Reformers challenged the previous Stalinist/Maoist notion that economic entities undergo an inexorable transition from 'lower' (private, co-operative and collective) to 'higher' (state or 'whole people') levels of ownership in the process of socialist development. They argued that this contravenes the Marxian 'law' that the relations of production must conform with the level of productive forces. In other words, in China's conditions of economic under-development, large-scale state enterprises are often inappropriate, thus the role of private, small-scale co-operative/collective and various forms of hybrid or joint-ownership enterprises should be encouraged for the foreseeable future. At the same time, most reformers have tended to concede (publically at least) that state ownership should still remain dominant in the economy.

Rethinking on ownership has gone beyond mere support for diversity. Economic theorists have sought to make a distinction between ownership in the juridical or legal sense, and in the real sense of control over the use of economic assets. This means, for example, that the rural 'responsibility systems' which emerged in the early 1980s to replace the previous system of agricultural collectives and which devolved a good deal of real control over farming and the use of land to households, still operated within a legal context of collective ownership of land. Similarly, in industry where there has been an attempt to enlarge the operational autonomy of state enterprises, reformers have put forward a number of alternative arrangements which retain the form of 'state ownership', yet organise real control over production and responsibility for the enterprise's economic assets in different ways (for example, through holding companies owned jointly by a number of state institutions).

The Open Policy

Liberalisation of the domestic economy was to be accompanied by a greater openness to, and a wider range of linkages with, the international economy. The previous Maoist emphasis on national economic 'self-reliance' was condemned as a form of economic chauvinism which denied China the benefits of participation in the international division of labour through foreign trade and of infusions of foreign capital which could spur domestic development. Economic theorists reasserted the 'rational kernel' of Ricardo's theory of comparative advantage and argued that 'the international division of labour drives productive forces forward because it reduces social labour', citing success stories from Eastern Europe as evidence.[14] They advocated an increase in the ratio of foreign trade in the economy, the acceptance of foreign credits from both governmental and private sources, encouragement of direct foreign investment through wholly-owned or joint ventures, and the establishment of 'special economic zones' and 'open cities' to foster (and channel) foreign participation in the economy. This did not mean that the Chinese economy would be thrown completely open to, and dependent on, the outside world: the state would still play a crucial role in setting foreign trade policy and defining the terms of foreign participation to serve the broader interests of the national economy.

The above paradigm of economic reform has been abstracted from the reform process as it unfolded in the 1980s. When it began in 1978, many of these ideas were still embryonic and provided an initially easy basis of consensus among Party leaders who wanted to get rid of Maoism. There was no 'plan' of reform in the sense of a clear idea of some ultimate end-state and a series of steps or phases to reach it. Although CCP leaders could draw on experience of market reform in Eastern Europe to guide them (notably from Hungary and Yugoslavia), only part of this experience was positive and these were very different situations in any case (for an analysis of the Hungarian reforms by a prominent reformist intellectual, see Su Shaozhi 1983). Inevitably, therefore, when the CCP took the strategic decision to launch reform at its Third Plenum in 1978, they were venturing into uncharted territory and, as medieval maps used to tell the traveller, 'here lie dragons'. In practice, the reforms were to involve a constantly moving interaction between ideas, policies and practical results in a context of changing political alignments. Throughout this process, the scope of reform expanded and what seemed bold at the beginning became conventional wisdom later on. Indeed, it was this expansion of the ambit of reform which sparked the bitter leadership disputes which emerged in the mid–late 1980s.

Although there was no initial reform plan, however, the reform project which emerged in the late 1970s did have a clear strategic political goal, to re-establish the hegemony of the CCP and its version of state socialism. But the reform project carried within it a basic asymmetry from the start: while economically progressive, it was to be politically conservative; economic reform was to outrun political reform. The underlying thesis, which in retrospect at least seems suspect, was that the economic system could be changed in major ways while keeping the basic institutions of Leninism/ Stalinism intact. This is why the Chinese reform experiment has been dubbed, by political critics in China and elsewhere, 'market Stalinism' rather than 'market socialism'. This term, though no doubt intended as a term of abuse, is useful intellectually because it highlights the asymmetry between economic and political change. The term 'market socialism' would seem to be best reserved for a reform project which not only sets out to change the nature of a socialist economy by introducing markets, but also to recast the 'socialist' system in its political and institutional aspects. In the analysis that follows, we shall be interested in tracing the practical impact of this basic contradiction between economic change and political immobility which lay at the heart of the post-Mao reforms.

2

The Political Dynamics of Chinese Economic Reform: An Overview

The Third Plenum of the CCP Central Committee, held in December 1978, announced a decisive shift in the Party's developmental purpose. This had two main components. First, it rejected the previous Maoist definition of the Party's historical role as waging a political 'class struggle'; henceforth the main objective was to be economic modernisation. Second, in pursuit of this aim the traditional approach to economic development, based on the system of directive central planning inherited from the 'Soviet model' of the 1950s, was to be reformed both in terms of its strategy and its organisation. We have already introduced the main elements of the economic reform paradigm; here we shall analyse the political dynamics of implementing the reforms and assess the extent of their success, as of the early 1990s, in redefining the Chinese developmental state and economy along 'market socialist' lines.

An Overview of Reform from 1979 on

This brief historical overview of the reforms mainly covers the period between two crucial events: from their official launch at the Third Plenum in December 1978, to the crisis of Tiananmen and the Beijing Massacre of June 1989 (also referred to as the June 4 Incident or just June 4). I do not wish to duplicate other accounts by giving a detailed description of specific reforms or statistical assessment of their economic impact. Rather I shall use a broad brush, identifying the main elements of the reforms and the main phases in their evolution between 1979 and 1989. My main aim is to understand the political dynamics of these radical changes in economic policy and institutions, the ways in which politics have shaped their character and the political repercussions they have brought in their train.

The economic reform decade from 1979–89 can be divided into two main phases, each with its own fluctuations and sub-phases. The first ran from the Third Plenum (of the 11th Central Committee hereafter XI) held in December 1978, to the Third Plenum (of the 12th Central Committee hereafter XII) held in October 1984. The second phase ran from late 1984 to the Tiananmen trauma of June 1989. This began a third phase when Party conservatives attempted to consolidate their pyrrhic victory in June by seeking to limit the pace and scope of the economic reform and eliminate its (to them) unacceptable political and social repercussions, a course of action ratified at the Party's Fifth Plenum (XIII) in November 1989. I shall concentrate here on the first two phases. Broadly speaking, the first was dominated by a sweeping transformation of rural economic institutions; in the second an attempt was made to accelerate reform in the urban-industrial sector, but the reform process as a whole ran into increasing problems as the economy ran out of control, popular discontent mounted and consensus among the reform leadership disintegrated, culminating in the upheaval and repression of mid-1989.

1979–84: The Era of Agricultural Reform

The Third Plenum (XI) of December 1978 pushed forward a steady reorganisation of the top CCP leadership which gradually reduced the power of residual 'developmental Maoists', consolidated Deng Xiaoping's overall pre-eminence and created a leadership with a high degree of consensus on the need for economic reform. At the Third Session of the Fifth National People's Congress in the autumn of 1980, Hua Guofeng, Mao's chosen successor was replaced as state Premier by an ardent advocate of reform, Zhao Ziyang, who had pioneered early reform pilot projects in his native Sichuan province in 1978. At the Party's Sixth Plenum (XI) in June 1981 Hua was replaced as Party Chairman by another reformer, Hu

Yaobang, formerly head of the Young Communist League. Finally, at the Party's First Plenum (XII) in September 1982, he even lost his place on the Politburo. As the power of the 'whateverists' dwindled in the higher reaches of the Party and state, top posts were increasingly filled by protégés or colleagues of Deng Xiaoping who shared his view on the need for economic reform. At the same time, however, there were early signs of differences *within* the reform leadership, between those who favoured a more decisive move towards market socialism, such as Zhao Ziyang, and those, like Politburo Standing Committee member, Chen Yun, who wanted to retain basic elements of the previous system of central planning and keep the market within bounds. There was also disagreement over political changes, notably over the issues of how to assess the historical role of Mao Zedong and how much of his political heritage to retain. The nature and pace of reform policy was increasingly to depend on the balance of power between these more conservative and radical wings of the reform leadership.

The major area of success in this early period of reform was in agriculture. I shall discuss this in detail in the next chapter so I shall be brief here. The new policies aimed to achieve a decisive breakthrough in agricultural output and productivity by directing more resources into agriculture, providing more production incentives for peasant households and creating an economic environment generally more conducive to effort and entrepreneurship among the rural population. A sweeping series of *institutional reforms* dismantled the previous three-tiered commune system of collective agriculture and brought a reversion to *de facto* private agriculture based on 'responsibility systems' in which the peasant household (and not, as before, the production team) was responsible for production. The communes themselves were abolished and replaced by a basic-level of local government, the *xiang* (usually translated as 'township'); the former production brigade became a 'village' (*cun*), run by an elected 'villagers' committee' and the former production team either lapsed or was replaced by various kinds of co-operative unit with a much reduced role in production. The main collective institution remaining was the village; its role was also reduced, but it retained certain functions, such as supervising production contracts with its constituent households, providing productive services (for example, maintaining local irrigation works) and organising welfare facilities. The basic rationale of the 'responsibility system' was the perceived need to devolve responsibility for agricultural production to its most efficient level and to increase work incentives by establishing a clear link between individual/small-group effort and income, a link which had been weak under the commune system. Responsibility systems based on the household were very popular with the peasantry and by 1983, virtually all agricultural production (outside the relatively small state farm sector) was conducted on this basis. Thus the years 1979 to 1983 saw a programme of agricultural decollectivisation which, in reverse, was as sweeping a transformation as had been its predecessor, the collectivisation movement in the mid-1950s.

Along with these institutional reforms came *changes in macro-economic policy* designed to increase production incentives and set the context for a more market-oriented agriculture. Though the previous system of state procurement of agricultural produce remained in place, procurement prices were raised substantially, by an average of 31 per cent between 1978 and 1980 and an additional 13 per cent between 1980 and 1983. These increases reduced the 'price scissors' or the ratio between the prices of agricultural and industrial goods (both producer and consumer) which had previously acted as a brake on rural incomes. The previous Maoist emphasis on across-the-board grain production was repudiated and agricultural diversification was encouraged, for example through incentive prices to increase cash crops such as cotton. Commercialisation of agriculture was encouraged by increasing the share of agricultural output which peasant households could sell outside the planned quotas, fostering the expansion of local markets and rural–urban trade, and accelerating the emergence of 'specialised households' which were engaged in specialised lines of production exclusively for the market (such as keeping bees or rearing rabbits, mink or poultry).

The economic impact of these changes was gratifyingly favourable. Between 1979 and 1983, rural per capita income increased by about 70 per cent and the gross value of agricultural output increased at an annual average of about 7 per cent between 1980 and 1984, with growth in certain cash crops such as cotton being particularly dramatic. In 1984 agricultural performance was truly outstanding. By contrast, reforms in the urban-industrial sector during this first phase were more tentative and far less successful.

They reflected the basic principles of economic reform discussed earlier: a more flexible relationship between state agencies and their subordinate enterprises through a reduction in mandatory targets and a gradual move away from 'directive' towards 'guidance' methods of planning; a general encouragement of 'market regulation' whereby state enterprises would gradually become more independent and increase the share of their products sold on the market; measures to make flows of capital and labour more flexible and multi-channelled; an effort to diversify the economic system by encouraging the growth of private and co-operative enterprises and of those sectors which had fared poorly under Maoism, notably urban commerce and services; and an intensification of economic ties with the outside world through an 'open policy' which fostered foreign trade and investment and the absorption of foreign technology and management expertise.

Common to each of these areas of reform in the urban-industrial economy is the emphasis on the introduction of market mechanisms. It is thus convenient to discuss them under the heading of *three types of market* – for commodities, capital and labour. In *commodity* markets, there was some degree of relaxation of state controls over the supply of basic industrial raw materials (particularly for materials such as certain steel products which were deemed to be in good supply); state enterprises were allowed to sell a portion of their output independently (this proportion had reached 15 per cent on average by 1983); state commercial agencies were now able to exercise more discretion in handling the output of state industry instead of being forced as in the past to accept output, regardless of quality or specification, and then get rid of it willy-nilly. There was also a rapid expansion of co-operative and private businesses; by the end of 1984 these types of business were handling about half the nation's total retail sales (urban and rural). In the crucial and sensitive area of price reform, there was some cautious movement towards granting greater power over price regulation to local governments in order to introduce more flexibility into the national pricing system. More important, the number of goods subject to fixed prices decreased significantly; in tandem, an increasing number of goods were allowed to circulate either at 'floating' or 'negotiated' prices (varying within a range specified by the state) or at market prices. The last category applied particularly to less important consumer items, but in the case of producer goods, movement towards more flexible prices was more cautious, being mainly confined to selected experimental sectors (for example, certain types of electrical machinery and electrical goods under the First Ministry of Machine Building). Summarising, some limited progress was made between 1979 and 1984 in the direction of establishing commodity markets, but the heart of a commodity system of exchange – the price mechanism – was still subject to heavy controls by the state.

On the subject of *capital*, it was still rather bold in this early period to argue for the establishment of fully-fledged money and capital markets comparable to those in a capitalist economy, i.e. based on a wide range of financial assets (including shares and bonds) and operating through a wide range of financial institutions, many of them private. Financial reforms were more modest in this early period, but important none the less; they concentrated mainly on changes in the state banking system and in relations between state financial organs and enterprises. First, there was an attempt to impose market-like disciplines on state enterprises by moving away from the previous practice of supplying all of their fixed and much of their working capital as interest-free budgetary grants from the state treasury. Under the new system, an increasing proportion of capital advances were in the form of repayable bank loans, carrying a cost in terms of interest. In consequence, the role of the state banking system began to change, from acting mainly as an adjunct of the state fiscal authorities and a mechanism for implementing the state plan, to a supplier of credit to the economy on terms which were to become increasingly commercial. It was hoped that this would bring about a more efficient allocation of capital at the macro-economic level, and at the micro-economic level that it would exert pressure on state enterprises to improve their efficiency (or become less 'bankable'). In 1984, the People's Bank of China took on the role of a Central Bank in charge of overall monetary policy and financial regulation. Most of its commercial functions were transferred to specialised banks, most notably in the state sector a new Industrial and Commercial Bank responsible for providing credit to enterprises.

A second important area of financial reform was the move to devolve greater financial powers to state enterprises, by allowing them to retain a certain proportion of their net revenue which previously would have gone into state coffers as fiscal revenue. This was achieved either by some agreed ratio of retained profits, or by a specific rate of tax on profits. 'Retained funds' or post-tax revenue could be used for new investment, welfare benefits or bonuses, basically at the discretion of enterprise management but within certain official guidelines. It was anticipated that enterprises would wish to use 'their own' funds more productively than they had the funds previously supplied by the state.

To the extent that the role of credit money was expanded, sources of investment finance diversified and investment decisions decentralised, a certain amount of flexibility was introduced into the system of capital provision, but this fell far short of anything that could be called a capital market. The impact of certain key mechanisms of a true capital market – notably variable interest rates reflecting supply and demand conditions, the vetting of loans on commercial criteria and legally enforceable contracts – was still marginal. In spite of this, however, by 1984 a major change had taken place in the Chinese financial system since there had been a major dispersion of power over financial resources away from the central state fiscal authorities and towards banks, local governments, enterprises, administrative departments, and households. This reduced the ability of the central authorities to control the expansion and allocation of financial resources, at least unless a new set of financial control instruments could be set in place.

In the area of *labour* reform, the new policies sought to change the previous situation in which state labour bureaux had allocated workers directly to state and 'big collective' enterprises, leaving the latter very little say in decisions over labour recruitment. Reformers wished to encourage 'spontaneous' labour mobility to meet the needs of an increasingly dynamic and market-oriented urban/ industrial economy. State labour agencies were instructed to use administrative controls more selectively, enterprises were granted more power over hiring and firing, the 'iron rice-bowl' of state workers was threatened by the proposed introduction of a labour contract system, and individuals were encouraged either to find or create their own jobs instead of relying on the state. But labour reforms were politically sensitive to the extent that they strengthened the power of management over workers and threatened the status of state workers who were a crucial part of the Party's political base. It is not surprising, therefore, that the reformers moved cautiously in this early stage and that the overall impact of the reforms was very limited. There was little movement, in the state sector at least, towards what any Western economist would recognise as a 'labour market'. This was not the case in the urban non-state sector, however, where workers were changing jobs more frequently and setting up their own businesses and, in general, enjoyed less job security than their counterparts in state enterprises.

Though the impact of urban/industrial reforms varied across these three areas, in overall terms the effects of this first stage – in terms of moving decisively in the direction of a 'socialist market economy' – were fairly superficial. By contrast, moves towards greater participation in the *international market* in capital and commodities were more far-reaching. In the realm of foreign trade, there was a move away from a system of centralised state controls by increasing the number of agencies empowered to conduct foreign trade. This began with a grant of partial powers over foreign trade to several provinces and cities in 1979 and was extended to include the commercialisation of state trading companies and the right of enterprises to retain part of their foreign exchange earnings. Trade apart, international economic links diversified, to include direct foreign investment, loans from a wide variety of sources (including foreign governments, commercial banks and international organisations such as the World Bank) and credits from foreign firms. The most ambitious, and characteristically Chinese innovation was the establishment of four Special Economic Zones (SEZs) – Shenzhen, Zhuhai, Shantou and Xiamen – on the coast of the south-eastern provinces of Guangdong and Fujian, areas with a long tradition of overseas economic ties. These areas were expected to be points of contact with the international economy in terms of trade and investment and also test-beds for more radical economic reforms before they were implemented across the rest of China. SEZs were followed by the declaration of fourteen 'open cities' which, along with Hainan island off the southern coast, were given greater powers in 1984 to open their economies to foreign investment.

The results of the Open Policy were dramatic: the amount of foreign investment increased year by year, reaching nearly $1.5 billion in 1984; gross loans had reached $13 billion by the end of 1984 and the ratio of foreign trade to GNP rose from 5.6 per cent in 1978 to 10.3 per cent in 1984. However, this dramatic expansion brought problems. A relaxation of central control over trade and financial flows led to trade deficits and a rapidly growing indebtedness. This in turn led to concern among central policy-makers and efforts to correct imbalances; the resulting policy cycle became a repeated feature of the reform decade. This created a new experience for Chinese policy-makers, the need to include fluctuating and only partly controllable foreign balances in their macro-economic calculations, and made the task of macro-economic management that much more difficult. To that extent, foreign economic relations were exerting an increasing influence on the domestic trajectory of reform. It is not surprising, therefore, that the Open Policy was not equally popular with all members of the reform leadership. Conservative leaders such as Yao Yilin and Chen Yun pointed, for example, to the disappointing economic results of the SEZs, their excessive costs to the national exchequer and their baleful influence in introducing 'unhealthy' cultural and ideological currents.

Overall, this first phase of the reforms, from 1979 to 1984, provided early evidence of the difficulties which faced CCP leaders in managing the reform process. There was clear evidence of a 'stop-go' or cyclical rhythm to the policy process, each cycle characterised by an initial push forward with reform measures, the appearance of certain problems and a consequent attempt to pull on the reins to stabilise the situation. The first cycle began in early 1979 after the Third Plenum, gained momentum during 1980 amid escalating economic problems and culminated in a sharp retrenchment from the end of 1980. A second began with a gradual relaxation of controls beginning in late 1981, leading to an 'over-investment crisis' in 1982 which provoked a strong effort to reimpose central controls in July 1983.

There is a politico-economic dynamic here which is endemic to the reform process. The basic elements are as follows: economic liberalisation leads to a dispersion of power over economic resources; in fiscal terms, this tends to reduce government revenue, create a budgetary deficit and increase government borrowing; in financial terms, in the context of a continuing 'shortage economy' characterised by 'investment hunger' and an impetus for expansion at all levels (Kornai 1985), there is a surge in investment and imports which fuel economic activity but quickly lead to overheating, reflected in inflation; this is intensified in turn by the tendency of enterprise managers to assuage worker discontent through inflationary wage increases. This leads to popular discontent at rising prices and the government reacts by introducing retrenchment measures, attempting to control monetary expansion, wages and prices through a partial reassertion of previous administrative controls. These measures bring their own politico-economic problems in turn since the resulting economic downturn reduces flows of credit, squeezes enterprise profits, restrains the growth in workers' incomes and creates real or feared unemployment; these problems generate pressures for a renewal of liberalisation policies. This rhythm, which continues into the next phase (and into the post-Tiananmen phase), reflects a complex intermeshing of political and economic processes which lie at the heart of the reform experience.

In spite of these problems, however, the first phase of reforms did make significant progress in achieving its aims; indeed, the agricultural reforms could be counted a resounding success. This created considerable optimism among reform leaders, particularly the more radical among them, and they attempted to follow up their success in agriculture by accelerating reform of the urban/ industrial economy. However, this decision, ratified at the Party's Third Plenum (XII) in September 1984, was to lead to increasing disagreement between more conservative and radical reformers over the conduct and ultimate objectives of the reforms.

Phase II: The Reform Unravels – October 1984 to the Beijing Massacre of June 1989

The Third Plenum (XII) decision called for a further reduction in the scope of mandatory planning and increased use of 'guidance planning', a further increase in the powers of enterprise managers and a cautious yet concerted effort to reform the price system by reducing administrative controls still further and allowing prices to find their own levels. The Open Policy was also to be extended by enlarging the powers of localities to conduct foreign economic relations and increasing the number of 'open' areas and 'development zones'. In agriculture, moreover, the long-standing system of state procurement was formally abolished in January 1985, as part of the next stage of rural reforms which aimed to deepen the process of agricultural commercialisation and rural economic diversification.

Even by early 1985, however, there was clear evidence of yet another reform cycle taking shape. The growth rate accelerated alarmingly, the money supply expanded likewise, bottlenecks developed in key sectors (notably transport, energy and basic raw materials) and inflationary pressures grew stronger. This cycle was distinctive in that one of its most alarming aspects was a yawning balance of payments deficit, indicating both the growing importance of the foreign trade sector in the economy as a whole and the intensifying links between domestic reform and the Open Policy. In mid-1985, the brakes were applied through the introduction of controls over credit and currency and efforts to stem the flood of imports (for example, the independence of the fourteen new open coastal cities was curtailed) and an attempt was made to cut back on excessive state investment projects. Price reform was also shelved for the foreseeable future. Reining in the economy proved very difficult, however, and the CCP leaders were increasingly taking on the appearance of a rodeo rider trying to control a bucking bronco.

These problems intensified the emerging split between the reform leadership and led to an increasing polarisation of approaches to the pace and depth of the reforms. This was not just a question of disagreements over how the reforms should be managed. The further the reforms reached, the more they revealed differences within the leadership about how far they should be allowed to go. In part, this reflected a generational difference between revolutionary veterans such as Chen Yun, Bo Yibo, Peng Zhen and Wang Zhen, who were more conservative in their attitudes to economic reforms, and a younger generation symbolised by Hu Yaobang and Zhao Ziyang who were prepared to follow the evolving economic and political logic of the reform process as it unfolded. To the extent that power within the Party was gradually shifting towards the latter, the former had increasing cause for alarm.

'Conservatives' and 'Reformers' in the CCP Leadership

The reform consensus within the CCP leadership thus began to break up into two broad groups, usually called the 'conservatives' and the 'reformers'. This is a misnomer because both sides of the argument were 'reformers' insofar as they saw the need to change the old system of central planning and give more scope to market mechanisms. While 'planners' and 'marketeers' might be a more accurate description of the two groups in terms of their attitudes to economic questions (indeed prominent 'conservatives' have been dubbed the 'planning faction' in China), differences between them extend beyond economics to politics, so broader labels are needed. 'Conservative' and 'radical' are also unacceptable since I have used the term 'radical' earlier to describe one of the Maoist tendencies; 'moderate (reformers)' and 'radical (reformers)' are rejected on the same grounds and also because it is hard to see the perpetrators of the Beijing Massacre of June 1989 as 'moderates'. Moreover, though certain leaders might be more radical in their reform aims, the real 'radicals' who favour a decisive transformation of Chinese society (combining a market economy based on private ownership with a liberal democratic polity) lie outside the Party leadership, among the Party membership and the general population. Though it is less than satisfactory, therefore, I shall use the conventional distinction between 'conservatives' and 'reformers', but with the clear understanding that for the most part these labels denote differences among reformers.

Two more points before we proceed to clarify the content of this new 'struggle between two lines'. First, talking in terms of two groupings is an over-simplification since each grouping has its own internal shades of opinion (for example, the post-Tiananmen 'conservative' leadership was internally heterogeneous, ranging from residual Maoists such as Wang Zhen to reform-leaning figures such as Li Ruihuan and Zhu Rongji). There are also uncommitted people who cannot be easily identified with either broad category. It is more sensible to see these two terms as referring to broad 'tendencies' or attitudes to the reforms, held to greater or lesser degrees by individual leaders, rather than to well-defined groups with some internal coherence and a shared programme. The dominant leadership group at any given time will include a particular mix of these tendencies. However, this simple dichotomy is helpful analytically in that it enables us to put our finger on the key points of disagreement over the conduct and aims of the reforms.

Second, our analysis only deals with differences within a relatively narrow spectrum of political opinion within the Party élite. Both within the Party and in society at large, there is a far broader spectrum of economic and political views, ranging from diehard radical and developmental Maoists on one side to out and out 'bourgeois liberals' on the other. Third, these are not static categories. As the reforms have proceeded, and dramatic events have interceded, positions on both sides appear to have hardened and the gap between them has widened. In the early 1980s, for example, reformers like Zhao Ziyang and Hu Yaobang were clearly impressed by the dramatic success of the first wave of economic reforms, and were emboldened to take them further than originally anticipated. Conservatives like Chen Yun, on the other hand, were becoming increasingly concerned about the unanticipated consequences of economic reform, notably macro-economic instability, and trends such as corruption within the Party/state and ideological 'contamination' within the population at large, particularly as a result of the Open Policy. Particularly crucial were the traumatic events in Beijing in 1989, when Deng Xiaoping himself was driven into the conservative camp, while Party reformers were radicalised by the experience.

Differences between 'conservatives' and 'reformers' in the CCP leadership are rooted in their attitudes to economic change, to political change and to the relations between the two. An individual's views on economic reform may differ from his/her views on political reform. Some leaders such as Zhao Ziyang or Hu Yaobang have been prepared to see these two aspects of reform march forward in tandem; others, such as Deng Xiaoping or Li Ruihuan, have been willing to countenance substantial economic reform *without* significant political reform. Moreover, certain leaders have tended to 'specialise' in either economics or politics. Deng Xiaoping has himself claimed to be 'a layman in economics'[1] while the late CCP General Secretary, Hu Yaobang, did not involve himself too deeply in economic matters. Similarly, former General Secretary Zhao Ziyang paid greater attention to economic affairs, a source of weakness when faced with the demands for political reform during the Beijing Spring of 1989; similarly on the conservative side, Chen Yun has been mainly concerned with the economic issues raised by reform, notably the need to maintain macro-economic stability and adequate levels of grain production.

Let us first discuss 'conservative' and 'reformist' *attitudes to economic reform*. They differed in their views on four key questions: planning, markets, ownership and the overall character of the post-reform 'socialist commodity economy'. The conservative view was that planning (both directive or 'guidance') is a fundamental defining characteristic of 'socialism' and should retain a dominant role in the economy. Though willing to admit that the previous planning system had shortcomings, they have tended to downplay these, arguing that 'real' planning had been bedevilled by Maoist political experiments and by a tendency to try to plan too much of the economy. In their view, central planning was both desirable and feasible. Reform of the planning system was possible – by increasing the scope of 'guidance' planning, particularly through the use of fiscal and financial controls to achieve macro-economic balance; by reducing the scope of directive planning to concentrate more precisely on key sectors; by improving the quality of information and personnel; by devising better incentive systems and the like. Markets, on the other hand, are seen as potentially anarchic and destabilising; they are incapable in themselves of achieving the aims of a socialist economy, but have certain benefits in balancing supply and demand and creating pressures for greater efficiency at the firm level. The market can thus play a valuable role in a socialist economy, therefore, but a role which is supplementary to the plan. As for the international market, conservatives were willing to recognise the economic benefits of foreign trade and finance, but again saw this largely as a useful supplement to a basically 'self-reliant' economic strategy and were reluctant to allow the Chinese economy to become too dependent on the outside, especially given the fact that the Open Door let in 'unhealthy' cultural and political influences. In terms of the system of owner-ship, moreover, conservatives have insisted that the public (state or collective) sector should remain dominant in the economy, although admitting that private and other 'non-socialist' sectors could play a valuable supplementary role, particularly in providing services and non-basic consumer goods.

For the conservatives, therefore, there are certain points beyond which market-oriented economic reforms cannot go. Their picture of the ultimate 'socialist commodity economy', to the extent that they have one, would seem to be of an essentially dual economy: central planning (still operating partially along directive lines) would dominate over a market sector. The operation of markets would be kept within tight limits – Chen Yun has likened the plan-market relationship in such a system to a bird in a cage – and would largely be confined to commodities. Markets in capital, labour and land threaten to undermine the very bases of a 'socialist' economy and have to be treated with great caution. This model is an amended form of the traditional Stalinist model (which also grudgingly allowed for a market sector); though the market sector has been enlarged and institutionalised as a long-term component of a 'socialist' economy (unlike the Stalinist view which emphasised the need gradually to displace markets).[2] As such, there are important institutional continuities between the old and the new models.

By contrast, the reformist model seeks a more radical break with the past. Rather than a central pillar of socialism, it is argued, centralised directive planning is an impediment to socialist development since it is incompatible with economic efficiency; economic institutions should be defined as 'socialist' to the extent that they contribute to 'developing the productive forces'. In an advanced economy, only markets are capable of guaranteeing a rational allocation of economic resources and they should become the prime mover of the economy. The traditional planning system should be dismantled and, to the extent that state planning remains (to achieve long-term national objectives or correct certain negative effects of the market), it should be redefined mainly in terms of a regulatory framework of macro-economic policy, operating through 'economic levers' such as interest rates, taxation and tariffs. In the words of Zhao Ziyang, whose report to the Thirteenth Congress of the CCP in 1987 was the classic official statement of the reformers' position, 'the state regulates the market and the market guides enterprises'.[3] The exchange of commodities would largely be governed by a competitive price system, and markets would gradually emerge for basic factors of production – capital, labour and land – leading to comprehensive 'marketisation' of an economy which would also become extensively integrated into the international economy. Since private and other non-socialist forms of ownership were dynamic and efficient, they should be encouraged and not fettered by politically inspired restrictions; moreover, traditional forms of state and collective ownership should be fundamentally reformed. The end-point of the reforms would be very different from the conservative model – it would essentially be a market (and probably private enterprise) economy, though perhaps one with a relatively large residual public sector and substantial state regulation of the economy. Whether this would in any way be 'socialist' or differ significantly from a familiar

Western capitalist 'mixed economy' would depend on the political environment of such a system – it is to the question of politics that we now turn.

Given the crushing constraints on open political discussion in China, it is more difficult to identify the clear points of difference between CCP leaders on issues of *political reform*. Although the conservative position is clear, since it was enunciated by Deng Xiaoping in a 1980 speech, reform leaders such as Hu Yaobang and Zhao Ziyang did not come up with a coherent alternative. There are two main axes of disagreement: first, over relations between political and economic reform and, second, over the nature and extent of political reform.

In their attitudes to the relationship between political and economic reform, CCP leaders share certain common positions. At least until the dramatic events of 1989, all have tended to stay within the parameters defined by Deng Xiaoping in March 1979 in terms of the 'Four Basic Principles' which ruled out sweeping changes in the political system.[4] This means, first, that debates about political reform have mainly been couched in terms of the needs of economic reform, rather than taking political reform as an issue in its own right. Second, both conservatives and reformers recognise that a clearer distinction must be made, in both theory and practice, between the political and economic systems. Political conservatives like Deng recognised that the Party had become too heavily involved in the everyday running of the economy and could improve its effectiveness and credibility by withdrawing to a less interventionist role. Reformers would wish to push the principle further (for example, by decisively reducing or abolishing the power of Party committees in factories). In spite of this common emphasis, however, both conservatives and reformers have continued to be imbued with the traditional state socialist view that politics (and therefore political leaders and state officials) have a key role in structuring and stimulating the economy. While this was more pronounced in the case of a political conservative like Deng Xiaoping, who is obsessed with rapid growth and the role of the Party-state in achieving it, similar impulses could also be detected in reformist leaders such as Zhao Ziyang and Hu Yaobang.

As the economic reforms deepened in the mid-1980s, however, this basic consensus on the question of political reform began to disintegrate as conservative and reform leaders increasingly diverged in their responses to the effects of economic reform. They differed in their reactions to the political effects of the spread of markets, particularly in the context of the Special Economic Zones. They could agree on the evils of rampant consumerism, corruption and the mindless aping of Western culture and on the need for some kind of socialist 'spiritual civilisation'. But the conservatives found these phenomena more alarming and they launched successive political campaigns against 'spiritual pollution' and 'bourgeois contamination'. On the other hand, reformers like Zhao Ziyang were more ready to dismiss them as inevitable transitional evils outweighed by the beneficial effects of economic reform – such as greater cultural freedom and intellectual diversity, more effective incentives to hard work and initiative, and greater openness to new ideas.

While such fears reinforced the caution of conservatives over political reform and led them to re-assert the political values of the old order, the reformers were undergoing a sea-change in their attitude to political change. Reformist leaders (and much more so their advisers) were moving to a recognition that more radical economic reforms would be obstructed by the Party-state apparatus and their conservative representatives in the Central Committee. There was a pressing need, therefore, to undermine this opposition through more thoroughgoing changes in the political and administrative systems. This shift is visible in Zhao Ziyang's report to the Thirteenth Party Congress in October 1987, in which he stressed the crucial importance of 'building democratic socialist politics' and the need 'to put political reform on the agenda for the whole Party'.[5] However, Zhao's own prescriptions for political reform in no way constituted a radical attack on the political orthodoxy defined by Deng. The most important thrust, to separate the Party from both government and economy, was in keeping with Deng's own stated preference. Where Zhao differed was in his determination to push reform forward in the teeth of opposition and in his tolerance for more political diversity and dissent, both within the Party and without. Even as late as June 1989, there is no evidence that Zhao and his reformist colleagues in the central leadership had a vision of an alternative political model. While they were willing to take political reform further than the conservatives, they continued to maintain that the needs of economic reform took precedence. Thus rapid, root-and-branch 'democratisation' would not be desirable because it would undermine economic reform by weakening the authority and diverting the policy thrust of a reformist government. However limited his own intentions, however, Zhao was willing to tolerate, indeed encourage, discussion of more radical political reform; as in the case of Hu Yaobang before him, this antagonised more conservative leaders who saw it as fostering 'bourgeois liberalisation'. Reformist leaders were to fall not so much for what they did themselves, but what they allowed others to do.

The Background to the June 4 Incident: Conflict and Crisis

These differences between more conservative and radical reformers widened as they encountered increasing problems in managing economic reforms from 1985 onwards and as major problems appeared in the sector which had hitherto been so successful – agriculture. The conservatives saw these problems – such as inflation, over-investment, budgetary deficits and spiralling corruption – as evidence that the reforms were being pushed too quickly and there was a need to stabilise the situation before proceeding further. The reformers, on the other hand, were more willing to accept these problems as an inevitable accompaniment of the reform process and were suspicious of conservative intentions in proposing retrenchment measures. Moreover, they were more likely to diagnose the macro-economic problems as continuing evidence of the irrationalities of a 'shortage economy' which could only be solved by deepening rather than stalling the reform process, in the political as well as the economic sphere. If these more radical initiatives could be essayed, it was worthwhile trying to ride out the storm.

Consequently, while reform leaders postponed significant deepening of the economic reforms during early 1986 until some semblance of macro-economic stability had been restored, they moved the policy debate on to new terrain. On the one side, 1985–87 saw the emergence of a wave of more radical proposals for economic reform; on the other side, there was greater emphasis on the need for deeper-going political reforms. In the economic sphere, the key proposals were as follows: advocacy of a much more rapid run-down of the directive planning system; extension of markets in commodities to markets in labour, capital and land; radical reform of the ownership system in the state sector, either through outright privatisation or a fundamental redefinition of the relationship between state agencies and enterprises which would grant the latter far greater real autonomy while retaining state ownership in legal terms; a comprehensive reform of the price system which would drastically reduce state price controls and allow prices to find their 'real' levels through the operation of the market; and a further extension of the Open Policy by declaring more 'open' areas and intensifying the interdependence between the national and international economies. In the political sphere, reformers pressed the argument that political changes were urgently needed – particularly a reduction in the socio-economic role of the Party, limited democratisation through more competitive elections and a more significant role for the system of elected people's congresses, greater scope for the organisation and expression of different social interests and more press freedom. Without these, the economic reforms would founder.

With the initial support of Deng Xiaoping, demands for 'political structural reform' to complement 'economic structural reform' grew louder and a nationwide debate ensued in mid–late 1986, led by several key members of the Party's reformist wing, notably state Vice-Premier Wan Li and Zhu Houze, head of the Party's propaganda department. But this shift in the terms of policy discussion among the Party leadership sparked off a much more wide-ranging and radical debate about political reform both inside and outside the Party. This worried Deng himself and other Party veterans and ideologues who had already been concerned about the political and ideological consequences of the economic reforms and were not about to compound the problem by countenancing political reforms as well. Thus, the split between reformers and conservatives in the CCP leadership became sharper. Seizing the political opportunity provided by large-scale student demonstrations in major cities in December, 1986, organised to advocate political reform and support reformist leaders, the conservatives unseated the highest-ranking advocate of political reform, Party Secretary-General, Hu Yaobang, in January, 1987. The period between then and the strategically important Thirteenth Party Congress in October 1987 was one in which the Party's factions jockeyed for power, beginning with a conservative offensive through a political campaign against 'bourgeois liberalisation' and ending with a partial reassertion of the power of reformers, notably Premier Zhao Ziyang, who replaced Hu as Party Secretary-General.

The official line of the Thirteenth Party Congress reiterated the need for further economic reforms and attempted to provide an over-arching ideological justification of the whole reform process through the notion of 'the initial stage of socialism'. Though the Congress' demand for political reform was restrained by the need for compromise among the leadership, it was none the less significant, particularly in the emphasis on the need to separate the Party from government administration, which would allow the emergence of a more professional and technocratic breed of state functionary and restrict the Party's role to one of making policy and monitoring rather than directing its implementation.

On the basis of the compromise reached at the Thirteenth Congress, which leaned heavily in the reformers' direction, three significant reforms were introduced in the spring of 1988: a free market in land-use rights to leased land in agriculture, a proposal to accelerate the development of China's coastal provinces and cities (known as the Gold Coast strategy) along with further decentralisation of powers to conduct foreign economic transactions, and a further bite at the bitter cherry of price reform. These in turn generated a fresh round of contention between conservatives and reformers which came to a head at the Third Plenum (XIII) in late September 1988 when the Party's opposing groups locked horns. The result was a decision in favour of comprehensive retrenchment through action to stabilise the economy by reimposing central controls and to postpone potentially destabilising measures, most notably price reform.

Though the arm of the conservatives had been strengthened by the persistence of the familiar macro-economic problems of the reform cycle, the vehemence of the struggle among the Party leadership in the autumn of 1988 and the clearly unstable nature of the compromise which emerged from the Third Plenum in September also reflected deeper causes of political frustration. It is not without reason that foreign scholars could describe the Chinese leadership as being on a 'rollercoaster' during 1987 and 1988. As the economy became more complex and dynamic and as power over economic resources became increasingly dispersed, the central leadership was increasingly losing its capacity to control events. The problem increased with each cycle, with each expansion more likely to get out of hand and each attempt to reassert control more difficult to implement. The CCP and government élite were looking less like economic managers and more like an economic fire-brigade.

This problem of managerial control over the reform process had reached alarming proportions by late 1988 and it was at that point that an even more alarming phenomenon emerged. Social unrest had been building up throughout the year with increasing resentment against economic trends and official corruption and tell-tale signs such as outbreaks of panic buying, rising crime rates, scattered strikes and social disturbances such as a football riot in Sichuan and a student protest in June in Beijing. This widespread popular dissatisfaction, particularly evident in, but not confined to, the cities, coincided with a growing political discontent among urban élites, notably the urban intelligentsia inside and outside the Party, over the continued power of the Party conservatives and with a growing feeling among reformers that further economic reform was impossible without more decisive moves towards political reform.

These currents, which overlapped with and reinforced the conflict within the CCP leadership, precipitated the events of April to June 1989, and their tragic culmination in the Beijing massacre on June 4. In the aftermath of this event, the new leadership, under Premier Li Peng and the new Party Secretary-General Jiang Zemin , attempted to slow the pace of economic reform yet found it difficult to do so and found themselves dragged along by the social, economic and political forces which the reforms had unleashed. They also tried to turn the political clock back without the authority necessary to do so; while they ruled political reform decisively off the agenda, they did so in a context in which their own political bankruptcy made it all the more necessary. By the early 1990s, the economic reform programme, indeed China's very future itself, was in limbo and, in the light of the collapse of communism in Eastern Europe and the Soviet Union, the viability of the Chinese strategy of 'market socialism', in either its conservative or reformist forms, seemed increasingly in question.

The Effects of Reform on the Relations between State and Economy

Most Western evaluations of the economic achievements of the reforms are more or less positive, although they admit that, after the astounding success of the first phase up to 1984, particularly in agriculture, serious economic problems emerged in the late 1980s to cloud the picture, notably macro-economic instability, a lagging agricultural sector, a sluggish state industrial sector, and growing inequalities between regions and groups. GDP rose by about 10 per cent a year during the 1980s, impressive even by the high standards of East Asia and even more so when compared with the depressing picture of uneven growth or stagnation in much of the rest of the developing world. Real levels of consumption more than doubled, with particularly dramatic increases in the acquisition of consumer durables such as bicycles, watches and TVs. The impact of these economic improvements was sufficiently widespread to bring about a dramatic decrease in the number of people under the poverty line, an effect which was particularly rapid during the first phase (the World Bank estimates, for example, that the percentage of the rural population with a food intake of less than 2185 kcals. a day decreased from 31 per cent to 13 per cent between 1979 and 1982 (World Bank 1986: p. 30).

The structure of the economy also changed substantially. The previous pattern of sectoral growth shifted in favour of agriculture (which expanded at an average annual rate more than double that of the Maoist period) and light industry (which grew at about 14 per cent per annum compared with heavy industry which decreased to about 10 per cent). While the overall economic structure did not change significantly in terms of quantitative shares of industrial and agricultural output in GNP, the distribution of the labour force did, as people moved into the rapidly expanding labour-intensive industries and services in both urban and rural areas (Riskin 1990: p. 45). For example, employment in urban collective enterprises rose from 20.5 million in 1978 to 35.5 million in 1990 and the workforce of rural 'township and village enterprises' expanded from 24 million in 1980 to nearly 90 million by 1990. In terms of productivity, there was an overall improvement in the efficiency with which capital investment was being used in both agriculture and industry (Wood 1991: p. 18; Nolan 1991: p. 120). China's relationship with the international economy also changed: exports grew rapidly (at an average annual growth rate of 16.7 per cent between 1979 and 1990) and their ratio to GNP increased from 5 per cent in 1978 to 13 per cent in 1987 while China's share of global trade increased from 0.8 per cent in 1978 to 1.7 per cent in

Table 2.1 *China's Foreign Trade, 1978–1991*
(total value in US$ billion)

Year	Total	Exports	Imports	Balance
1978	20.64	9.75	10.89	−1.14
1979	29.34	13.66	15.68	−2.02
1980	38.14	18.12	20.02	−1.90
1981	44.03	22.01	22.02	−0.01
1982	41.61	22.32	19.29	3.03
1983	43.62	22.23	21.39	0.84
1984	53.55	26.14	27.41	−1.27
1985	69.60	27.35	42.25	−14.90
1986	73.85	30.94	42.91	−11.97
1987	82.65	39.44	43.21	−3.77
1988	102.79	47.52	55.27	−7.75
1989	111.68	52.54	59.14	−6.60
1990	115.44	62.09	53.35	8.75
1991*	135.7	71.9	63.8	8.10

Note Figures before 1980 are from Ministry of Foreign Trade, and figures since 1989 are from Customs Statistics.

Sources: SSB, 1991, p. 554; **NCNA* 28 February 1992.

1987 (Nolan 1990: p. 19) (for an overview of China's foreign trade performance, see Table 2.1).

Since we are interested here in the extent to which the reforms have brought about changes in the nature of the Chinese developmental state, we need to look at their impact on state economic institutions and on the relationship between state and economy. We can do this under four headings: the pattern of ownership, the nature of productive institutions, the relationship between state planning and markets, and the economic role of state organisations. The *ownership structure* changed to some extent as the predominance of the state sector proper declined. In both rural and urban areas, a 'second economy' blossomed, composed of collective enterprises, economic 'associations' and private capitalist, household and individual businesses. New hybrid forms of ownership emerged in the domestic economy (a notable example was the Stone Computer Company in Beijing) and various types of joint Chinese-foreign or wholly-owned foreign enterprises flourished, particularly in the Special Economic Zones. The number of people employed in the urban private sector rose from a mere 150 000 in 1978 to 7.04 million in 1991 (*NCNA* 28 February) the non-state share of total industrial output rose from 21.5 per cent in 1979 to 44 per cent in 1990 (*SSB* 1991: p. 353); and in certain sectors, such as construction, retailing and household services, the state share dropped below half. However, given the fact that the 'non-state' collective sector was still directly or indirectly controlled by local governments and the private and 'mixed' sectors (including foreign-Chinese joint ventures) only accounted for about 5.7 per cent of urban employment as of 1990 (*SSB* 1991: p. 76) the state sector was still overwhelmingly dominant in the non-agricultural economy. In the rural sector, non-state enterprises of a bewildering variety enjoyed more freedom than their urban counterparts, but here also they were subject to regulation and control by county township and village governments.

Turning to the nature of *productive institutions*, the effect of the reforms was uneven. Changes in agriculture were relatively thoroughgoing as the introduction of 'responsibility systems' brought about a reversion to household farming. In industry, however, the state enterprise failed to change in its fundamentals, both in terms of its continuing subordination to state agencies and its internal organisation. Overall, if we take into consideration that the state continued to subject the peasant household to mandatory claims on its output and the nexus of collective and Party institutions still continued to operate at the village level, there had been no decisive change in the character of basic units of production.

There were, however, substantial changes in *the balance between state planning and markets*. On the one side, the scope of direct administrative controls over the economy shrank substantially, but was kept fully in place for certain important investment projects and key raw materials and energy inputs; on the other side, the range of goods and services available on free markets expanded substantially, as any visit to a Chinese city or rural town in the early 1990s would visibly demonstrate, but this was largely confined to non-basic consumer goods. Between these two lies a large 'mixed' sector which combines elements of both market and plan. This is most visible in the so-called 'dual-track system' in which, say, part of the output of an enterprise or a peasant household is still subject to direct controls (in terms of output, inputs, price and destination); for the other part of its output, the terms of exchange can vary (for example, the state may offer to buy the output at higher incentive prices, or the enterprise may set their own prices and seek their own markets, or it may be free to do so subject to certain limits imposed by the state (for example, a maximum price). Although the exact proportion of these three sectors is hard to determine, Wood (1991: p. 9) argues that, as of 1990, 'the majority of goods and services in terms of value' were in the 'mixed' sector, 'subject to some mixture of plan, market and negotiation'. While this change in the balance between plan and market is significant, it applies more decisively to goods and services. There has been less movement towards commoditising the basic factors of production – capital, labour and land but even here there was substantial movement, at least until June 4, after the pace of change slowed. Moreover, the degree of competition in markets for goods and services varies a great deal between sectors, because of local protectionism and oligopolistic domination of particular markets by large enterprises.

Finally, there have been concomitant changes in the *economic role and behaviour of state agencies*. In terms of the balance of power between state economic organs and productive units (enterprises, households and firms), it has shifted substantially in favour of the latter. This is a consequence of the processes discussed above: diversification of the ownership system, greater autonomy for enterprises in the public sector and the rapid spread of market relations throughout the economy. For example, an economist from the central State Planning Commission complained in late 1989 that 'the government now has under its control only 60 per cent of national construction, mostly basic industries, while the other 40 per cent, mostly processing industries, are running wild in the hands of collectives and private business people'.[6] This meant that the ability of the central government to enforce its economic will by administrative or political fiat had declined.

There was also a major shift of economic power *within* the state: vertically from the central government to local governments at the provincial level and below (Oksenberg and Tong 1991; Unger 1987 and Wong 1987), and horizontally within each layer of government towards individual administrative departments. This was partly the result of conscious policy, for example, by devolving powers to conduct foreign trade or by granting greater financial autonomy to localities through revised revenue-sharing arrangements. It was also partly a result of the enhanced ability of specific institutions within the state machine to act in an 'entrepreneurial' way to exploit the opportunities for economic self-aggrandisement offered by the reforms (notably by generating 'extra-budgetary revenue', or going into business on their own) (for the phenomenon of 'state entrepreneurship', see Blecher 1991 and White 1991a). Moreover, changes in the structure of the economy – from heavy to light industry and from state to collective/private enterprises – have also served to strengthen local governments which are mainly respon-sible for the latter sectors. By the early 1990s, the power of the central government was visibly dwindling and the Chinese economy was beginning to look more like a patchwork of 'independent kingdoms' (sometimes called 'economic fiefdoms') than an inte-grated national economy under central control.

In spite of these substantial changes, however, as of the early 1990s, while it can be said that China's economic reformers have been successful in launching a programme of potentially funda-mental reform, with many areas of achievement to their credit, they have not yet been able to achieve a decisive breakthrough to a new form of developmental state, a new type of economy and a new relationship between state and economy. While they might have been on the brink in 1986–7, the key policy nettles were not grasped (notably reform of the price and ownership systems) and the Beijing massacre led to a partial reimposition of the old system. While the autonomy of state enterprises has increased, they are still to varying degrees subordinate to their state 'minders' and the traditional institutions of central planning are still in place. The main trend has been towards a 'dual' economy composed of a relatively sluggish state sector and a relatively dynamic collective, private and hybrid sector (though it should be noted that the state sector has also been making gains in productivity – for evidence see see Jefferson *et al.* 1992). This structural divide intensified in the late 1980s, and began to take on political significance: many reformers saw the state sector as a conservative force and looked to the non-state sector as a potentially powerful stimulus for more radical reform. Yet the latter is still subject to control by local governments, so the state/ non-state distinction is partly a distinction between different locations of state control. Much of the power accruing to local governments, moreover, continued to be exercised in traditional directive ways, though as Blecher (1991) and Shue (1989) have shown, this varies immensely from locality to locality.

So, at the beginning of the 1990s, the overall picture after more than a decade of reform was mixed, substantial change coexisting with substantial continuity. At best, this was a 'half-way house' in which the new and old developmental states and economic systems intertwined. From an optimistic point of view, this marked substantial progress and augured well for further reform (for example, Wood 1991: p. 21); from a more pessimistic point of view, this hybrid produces 'a worse result than either Stalinism or genuinely competitive markets' (Nolan 1991: p. 117). This author is more inclined to see some economic virtue in this dualism, yet recognises that the 'half-way house' is not necessarily just a staging-point in a continuing process of managed reform; rather it is a political deadlock, reflecting serious contradictions which lie at the roots of the 'market socialist' programme. It is to these political problems that we turn in our last section.

The Political Dynamics of Economic Reform

In spite of the economic problems which surfaced from the mid-1980s on, the reforms could still be considered an overall success in economic terms – in increasing output, raising productivity, and improving the material welfare of the population. Yet, as the Tiananmen tragedy of June 1989 dramatically highlighted, they culminated in political disaster. How do we explain this paradoxical combination of economic success and political decline? Why did economic reform knock even more nails into the CCP's coffin instead of reviving the corpse?

Part of the paradox can be explained in terms of the practical policy problems involved in handling such a fundamental economic transition. The scope of the task was vast, the policy territory was virtually unknown, the linkages between different areas of reform were complex, and the technical problems of designing new policies and institutions were a constant headache. Moreover, the reforms were being introduced into an economic context which continued to operate according to the logic of what the Hungarian economist Janos Kornai called a 'resource-constrained economy'. This type of economy systematically created excess demand for material and financial resources and, combined with a 'soft budget constraint' which encouraged financial irresponsibility on the part of enterprises, tended to push the economy towards overheating whenever administrative controls were relaxed (Kornai 1985). These basic tendencies within the previous economic system, which could only be removed by successful reform, were a major impediment to that very success.

But the problems inherent in the reform process go far beyond these practical issues of policy design and execution. We can identify certain basic *political constraints* (or, perhaps more accurately, conditioning factors since they can act to constrain or stimulate) which have shaped and ultimately bedevilled the reform programme. We can identify five types. The first in the *Ideological Constraint*. This refers to limits imposed on the reform process by deep-rooted political and ethical attitudes among sectors of the population able to influence the policy process. We can simplify this notion by discussing it at two levels; first, Ideology with a capital I – the official ruling ideology of Marxism–Leninism–Mao Zedong Thought – and ideology with a small i – the political, social and economic attitudes held by different sectors of the general population. The first level will be discussed in detail in Chapter 5. Suffice it to say here that, on the one hand, the pre-existing Ideology, through its influence on key policy-makers and executors in the Party, served to inhibit the reform process by preserving a definition of a 'socialist' economy which precluded more radical reforms – such as large-scale privatisation of public enterprises and the establishment of fully-fledged markets in land, labour and capital. On the other hand, the intellectual categories of the previous Ideology were so intractable as to preclude any attempt to redefine it in ways conducive to more radical reform.

By small-i ideology, we are referring to ingrained habits and expectations in the population which reflect the policies and institutions of the Maoist era. Most notable are the phenomena of 'egalitarianism' (opposition to wide income and status differentials), and the desire for an 'iron rice-bowl' in the form of guaranteed job security. Large sections of the population appear to regard these values as defining characteristics of 'socialism', yet both of them run counter to central tenets of the economic reform paradigm. For example, reformers have argued for greater wage differentials in industry and maintained that more enterprising or hard-working people should be encouraged to 'get rich first' as an incentive to themselves and an example to others. They have also attacked the 'iron rice-bowl mentality' as encouraging sloth and low productivity. Both these elements of popular ideology owe a lot to Maoist egalitarianism and the experience of previous institutions (notably state enterprises and rural collectives) which provided security for their members, albeit at considerable economic cost. These attitudes continued to be widespread in both the cities and countryside throughout the reform period and exerted a powerful braking influence on policies such as wage and labour reform.

At the same time, however, the reforms created (or unleashed) new sets of social attitudes which provided a psychological impetus to reform policies – notably a willingness to take economic risks and work hard in pursuit of material success and to accept any resulting inequality as ethically justifiable. The coexistence of the new and the old, in the realms of both Ideology and ideology, led to pervasive moral and cultural confusion which the Party leadership sought in vain to clarify. An attempt was made at the Sixth Plenum (XII) of the CCP Central Committee in September 1986 which published a Resolution intended to provide a definitive description of 'socialist ethics' in the new era.[7] But the document was an unconvincing hotchpotch which reflected both disagreement among the CCP leadership and the diversity of popular attitudes; as such, it merely compounded the problem. In terms of political and social morality, therefore, the reforms undermined the certainties of the previous order without providing a replacement. The result was both Ideological confusion within the political élite and ideological anomie among the population at large, especially among sectors particularly influenced by the new environment, such as urbanites and youth. While the 'old' attitudes impeded reform and the 'new' attitudes helped it along, the war between them created a psychological environment hardly conducive to orderly and peaceable change.

The second type is the *Systemic Constraint*. We refer here to the consequences of the fact that economic reform has far outrun political reform. The basic rules of the political game and the core political and administrative institutions of the Leninist order have persisted, limiting and distorting the emergence of a new economic system. In the early 1990s, the Communist Party was still the only source of political authority and it still maintained a pervasive presence, penetrating every office, school, factory and village. The ubiquitous government bureaucracy has actually become very much larger and more complex (White 1991a). The denizens of this Party-state apparatus have to prevent radical reforms which threaten their interests and to adapt more moderate reforms to their own requirements. The latter was the root of the pervasive official 'corruption' which intensified from the mid-1980s onwards. While part of this involved abuse of power by Party and state officials for their own benefit (we could call this 'personal corruption'), part was a systematic result of the coexistence of the old politico-adminis-trative set-up with the new economic system (we could call this 'systemic corruption'). Officials were well placed to take advantage of their increased economic autonomy to further not merely their own interests but those of their bailiwicks. For example, they used the system of 'dual-track pricing' to buy cheap and sell dear in the interests of their own enterprise, department or locality. These phenomena reflect a basic contradiction in the political and economic systems which, to be resolved, requires systemic changes in the political/administrative as well as the economic spheres. We shall return to this issue in the concluding chapter.

These ideological and systemic constraints are 'first-order' factors which define the overall political context within which the following three 'second-order' factors operate. Type three is the *Interest Constraint*. This involves the influence of the multifarious interests in Chinese society – of individuals, groups, strata, classes and institutions – on the reform policy process. The impact of any particular interest on the reforms is variable since it may be able to exert more or less influence, and it may be in opposition, in support or ambivalent. Moreover, as the reforms progressed, the balance of power between interests shifted and new interests were created. For example, within the state apparatus local governments have gained more power and wish to hold on to it. Moreover, the 'first wave' of state institutions created by the previous planning system has been joined by a 'second wave' created by the economic reforms: for example, new auditing bureaux to supervise government and enterprise budgets, new legal organs to adjudicate economic disputes and special organs established as part of the Open Policy, in the Special Economic Zones and elsewhere. The array of institutional interests within the Chinese state is far more complex than before and each may seek to further, obstruct or redefine specific reform policies to suit its own interests.

In society at large, the reforms have given more power to groups that were formerly subordinated. In the countryside, for example, the power of village cadres has declined and peasant households are now in a better position to bargain with the Party-state over issues such as cropping patterns, prices and taxes. Moreover, as the rural economy has diversified, the peasantry have become more differentiated in terms of income and occupation and their interests are correspondingly more diverse. In the economy as a whole, diversification has given rise to a vast number of new institutions and occupations, notably the rapid growth of non-state enterprises and the consequent rise of a new class of private or 'semi-private' business people, particularly in areas where the impact of the Open Policy has been more extensive.

This is a complex and dynamic picture in which interests are proliferating and realigning. To the extent that these interests are able to wield power over policy (and this ability varies enormously), the politics of economic policy has become more complex and conflictual. To the extent that there are powerful interests aligned on different sides of the issue of economic reform, the policy process has become a political battleground with uncertain outcomes.

The fourth type is the *Control Constraint*: The dual dispersion of economic decision-making power – within the Party-state itself and between state and economy – has reduced the power of the central government to implement economic policy, whether in a conservative or reformist direction. This not only means that the central government finds it more difficult to enforce policy down the long chain of bureaucratic command, but also to mobilise the revenue needed to underpin policy. The history of reform has been one of recurrent fiscal crises, with dwindling sources of revenue being counterposed against increasing demands on the treasury. The latter have arisen from increasingly vocal demands for extra resources from sectoral interests and the financial costs of trying to ensure social 'peace and stability', notably the escalating burden of subsidies designed to cushion urban consumers against increases in agricultural prices. As the power of the centre wanes, it becomes more difficult to exert the political pressure necessary to reverse this process (for example, by radically reducing subsidies to urban consumers) and a vicious circle is created which intensifies the political difficulties of managing reform.

We call our last constraint the '*Hard Policy Constraint*', drawing on Kornai's terminology. For all of the above four reasons, reform leaders have found it politically convenient to introduce relatively 'easy' policies and have been reluctant to grasp 'hard' policy nettles. One can distinguish 'easy' and 'hard' policies along three dimensions: first, the degree of conflict between a given policy and the core values of the official Ideology; second, the balance of interests pro and con a particular policy; and, third, the extent to which the results of a given policy are 'positive sum' (gains to all parties affected) or 'zero-sum' (gains to some, but actual or perceived losses to others). For example, the agricultural reforms of the early 1980s were relatively 'easy' in terms of these three dimensions. First, the introduction of 'responsibility systems' did not involve out-and-out decollectivisation because land still remained under collective ownership and a residual collective (and Party structure) was retained at the village level. Thus, the changes, sweeping though they were, could be portrayed as changes within rather than away from collective agriculture. Second, as we shall see in the next chapter, there was a large groundswell of support among the peasantry for the household responsibility system and, third, while local cadres were initially opposed, their opposition wilted as the economic benefits of the change became apparent and they were themselves able to take advantage of new economic opportunities. In the urban-industrial sector, however, policies were much 'harder'. First, some of the reforms conflicted with core Ideological principles: for example, the desire to introduce a labour market conflicted with the Marxist idea that a market in labour power was 'capitalist' and proposals for radical reform of the system of state ownership ran up against the idea that public ownership was a defining characteristic of a 'socialist' economy. Second, the balance of support and opposition weighed more towards the latter since not only was there a dense network of state institutions whose interests, indeed whose very survival, were threatened, but also the manual workforce in state enterprises felt threatened by any attempt to weaken their 'iron rice-bowls' or increase the powers of enterprise managers. Third, these groups thought that they would lose out from more radical reforms; though there were also potential benefits, these would be longer-term and there would be risks involved in securing them.

If we look at the link between the urban and rural sectors, the issue of how to manage the relationship between rural producers and urban consumers was also a hard one. While the government wished to encourage agricultural production through higher prices, it was reluctant to pass on the increase through higher retail prices in the cities for fear of unrest. The result was a crippling burden of price subsidies which intensified the fiscal difficulties of the state. The same kind of political fear pervaded official attitudes to the broader question of overall price reform.

Here we can see clearly the clash between the economic logic and the political logic of the reforms: 'harder' reforms – in the nature of state ownership, in the labour system, in the price system – recommended themselves as economically essential but proved politically intractable. On the other hand, some of the economic benefits of politically 'easier' policies, such as the financial reforms of the early 1980s which devolved financial powers to localities, banks, government departments and enterprises, were ambiguous to say the least (Bowles and White 1989). Indeed, looking at the reform era as a whole, one can differentiate its two phases in terms of an 'easy' stage of success in the agricultural sector up to 1984 and a 'hard' phase from 1984 onwards which tried to tackle the more intractable urban-industrial sector and ran up against mounting problems in agriculture which defied an easy solution. The political difficulties of the latter 'hard' phase go some distance towards explaining the growing conflict among the Party leadership and the more general socio-political stresses and strains which set the context for the Beijing massacre.

This emphasis on the importance of political constraints leads one to pessimism about the future of reform. One approach would be to try to bring in the 'harder' reforms in a piecemeal fashion, an approach which the post-Tiananmen leadership is using in regard to price and ownership reform. But the reform potential of the Jiang Zemin-Li Peng leadership is undermined by its lack of political authority, and by its own conservative definition of the limits to economic reform. As such, it is prone to all the above five conditioning factors, particularly the ideological and the systemic. The future of a more radical view of economic reform would seem to depend on tackling the first two constraints head on; this would require a change of heart on the part of the current leadership or a shift of power in favour of the reformers within the CCP. Alternatively, it might require more far-reaching changes in the political institutions of Leninist state socialism, an issue to which we return in the last chapter.

3

The Politics of Agrarian Reform

At the beginning of the reform era, China was still a predominantly agrarian society. In 1978, 82 per cent of the population (790 million people) lived in rural areas; of the total labour force then, about 76 per cent worked in the countryside, mostly in agricultu.e.[1] Despite substantial progress towards industrialisation over the past four decades, and despite rapid diversification of the rural economy during the reform era, agriculture still remains the foundation of the Chinese economy. The performance of agriculture continues to underpin the fortunes of the national economy as a whole and improvements in popular living standards. Success in reforming agriculture is also essential for success in the reforms as a whole.

Agriculture is also important for our analysis of the post-Mao era because it is in this sector that the impact of the reforms, in terms of social and institutional change, have been the most profound. The dismantling of the communes was a massive political *volte face* and we need to understand why and how it happened. Our concern, as throughout this book, is in the political dynamics of this change: what were the political factors which prompted policy-makers to move decisively away from collective agriculture; what was the political process surrounding the introduction of these momentous new policies and what has been their political impact? At a broader analytical level, we are interested in the 'politics of agriculture' more broadly: the nature of the interplay of political forces which, at the macro level, operate to condition national policy towards agriculture and, at the micro level, influence the impact of policy and the operation of economic institutions at the village level. We will begin with a brief description of our framework of analysis.

A Framework for Analysing the Politics of Agricultural Policy

The politics of Chinese agricultural policy is one arena within the wider political process outlined in Chapter 1, involving a specific set of actors and interests involved in the formulation and implementation of agricultural policy. To facilitate analysis, I shall make a simple distinction between macro (national) and micro (village) levels, in full recognition of the fact that the reality is far more complex in view of the complex institutional layering in between. The intermediate or meso levels become increasingly important in the second phase of the reforms when agricultural policy becomes one element of the increasing tension between the centre and the provinces; we shall bring this into our analysis where relevant.

The Macro-Political Environment of Agricultural Policy

From the point of view of Chinese farmers, the 'macro-level' constitutes the total political environment of the village. This has three major components: (a) major policy-makers in the higher reaches of the CCP; (b) the institutional nexus of the Party-state, and (c) the overall pattern of social groups and interests.

(a) At the *leadership* level, there are certain common objectives which underlie policy differences between conservative and reformist leaders. They all recognise the fundamental role of agriculture in the economy, as a guarantee of food security (particularly against the possibility of famine), as a source of inputs for industry and of foreign exchange through exports and, in political terms, as an important guarantee of social stability in both countryside and cities. However, there have been important differences on agricultural questions. The reformers have been eager to press ahead with more radical reforms to privatise agriculture and reduce state controls over production and marketing; conservatives have been concerned about the undermining of 'socialist' institutions and, in the early 1990s, some were contemplating a return to collective agriculture. Reformers have favoured rapid diversification of the rural economy, whereas conservatives (such as Chen Yun) have sought to maintain grain production as a prime priority and expressed doubts about an overly rapid expansion of rural industry. Reformers (such as Zhao Ziyang) have been more willing to let regional inequalities rip (particularly through his 'Gold Coast' strategy launched in 1988 to accelerate growth in the coastal provinces) and solve any resulting problems in the supply of agricultural goods through inter-regional and foreign trade; conservatives have worried about the economic risks involved in an increasing division of labour between provinces or an increasing reliance on foreign trade. These differences became more apparent from 1985 onwards when serious problems began to emerge in agriculture, and since then the balance of power between leaders has had increasing influence on prevailing policies towards agriculture.

(b) *the Party/state apparatus* defines the overall institutional context of agricultural politics. Agriculture is one of the six main organisational 'systems' (*xitong*), a vertical institutional sector in which Party and state organisations intertwine (Barnett 1967). The *Party* is the core of this system. Party cadres at all levels are involved in implementing agricultural policy and they disagree in ways similar to their superiors at the centre. The Party operates through a system of Rural Work departments or committees which play a role in both defining agricultural policy and supervising its implementation. At the centre, there is a Rural Group within the Central Committee's Policy Research Centre. Party committees at each level tend to have one or more officials who 'specialise' in agriculture.

Turning to the *state or governmental* apparatus, the institutions involved in the agricultural policy process are manifold, as we can see from Figure 3.1 which was compiled by two experts from the Chinese Academy of Agricultural Sciences (Zhu and Tian 1989: p. 164). Each of these agencies operates at the central level and has subordinate agencies at each lower level within the state hierarchy. To simplify the picture, one can distinguish, first, agencies which have a more general co-ordinating role (such as the State Council which is the supreme government cabinet, the State Planning Commission, or regulating agencies such as the Ministry of Finance and the People's Bank of China) and agencies with more specialised roles, notably the specific ministries listed. Second, one can distinguish institutions by the extent to which they have whole or partial, direct or indirect involvement in agriculture. The agencies most centrally involved are the Ministries of Agriculture, Water Conservancy and Forestry, but other ministries are heavily involved in specific aspects of agriculture (for example, the Ministry

Figure 3.1 *State Level Organisational Arrangements for the Administration of Rural Policy*

	State Council		
OVERALL MANAGEMENT	State Planning Commission Ministry of Finance People's Bank of China State Price Bureau Agricultural Bank of China		
FUNCTIONAL MANAGEMENT	**Ministry of Commerce** -Supply and Marketing Cooperatives -Department of Means of Agricultural Production **Ministry of Foreign Economic Relations and Trade** -Specialised Import/Export Corporations **Ministry of Water Conservancy** **Ministry of Agriculture** -Agricultural and Animal Husbandry Machine Corporation -Corporation of Plant Protection -Corporation of Seeds -National State for Agricultural Technical Extension **Ministry of the Machinery Industry** -Bureau of Construction and Agricultural Industry **Ministry of Energy** **Ministry of Chemical Industry** **Chinese Corporation of Petroleum and Chemical Products** **Ministry of Building Material Industry**	**Ministry of Agriculture** -Planning Bureau -Bureau of Agriculture -Bureau of Animal Husbandry -Bureau of Aquatic Products -Bureau of Land Reclamation -Bureau of Rural Enterprise Administration Ministry of Forestry	**Ministry of Commerce** -Supply and Marketing Cooperatives -Grain Department -Department for Aquatic Products **Ministry of Forestry** **Ministry of Light Industry** -Food Processing Department **Chinese Corporation of Tobacco** **Ministry of Foreign Relations and Trade** -Specialised Import-Export Corporations
	INPUTS SUPPLY	PRODUCTION	OUTPUT MARKETING

Source: Zhu and Tian (1989), p. 164.

of Commerce is responsible for supplying inputs to agriculture and marketing its produce domestically and the Ministry of Foreign Economic Relations and Trade plays a similar role with regard to imports and exports).

In addition to these political and bureaucratic agencies, there are *intellectual institutions* such as research and consultancy units which generate information about agriculture, shape policy alternatives and offer advice to officials. The number and significance of these organisations has increased considerably during the reform era. The Ministry of Agriculture has its own Policy Research Centre and there have been successive rural development research units under the State Council. The most important of these was the Rural Development Research Centre (RDRC), established in 1982 under Du Runsheng, a former vice-minister of the State Agricultural Commission (forerunner of the Ministry of Agriculture), in order 'to make suggestions on major rural issues and offer consulting services to the CCP Central Committee, the State Council and other leading departments'.[2] This Centre played an influential role as a 'brains trust' for Zhao Ziyang and other reformers in defining and introducing agricultural reforms in the early 1980s. Similar units can be found in academic institutions: for example, the Chinese Academy of Agricultural Sciences, and Institutes for Rural Development or Agricultural Economics in the Chinese Academy of Social Sciences. There is also a quasi-independent Chinese Agricultural Economics Society which holds symposia on agricultural issues involving experts from a wide range of institutions across the country. An even more independent research capacity was developed within the non-governmental Beijing Social and Economic Sciences Research Institute in the shape of a group known as Fupin, dedicated to research and practical action to alleviate rural poverty (Whiting 1989: p. 42). In general, the influence of these intellectual organisations has varied according to their proximity to official power, the most important by far being the Rural Development Research Centre given its access to top reformist leaders. However, political influence also means political vulnerability: for example, the RDRC was disbanded after the 4 June Incident in 1989 because, it was alleged, it had given aid and comfort to the Democracy Movement.

Another source of political pressure on agricultural issues, which only emerged during the reform era, was the *media*, in particular the

Peasants' Daily (Nongmin Ribao) which increasingly took on the
role of advocating rural/agricultural interests, particularly from the
mid-1980s onwards as the condition of agriculture deteriorated.
Perhaps because there was a view among Party conservatives that
state policy had been neglecting agriculture, the newspaper was able
to continue this role to a degree after the Tiananmen events.

Last, one should mention the role of *foreign agencies* which
became increasingly important as China opened its economy to
international advice and assistance in the 1980s. These include a
wide variety of organisations, notably the major international
institutions such as the World Bank and the United Nations Food
and Agriculture Organisation, the aid agencies of individual foreign
nations, foundations such as Ford and Winrock and a plethora of
non-government organisations (NGOs). By making assistance
conditional on or targeted towards certain policies or institutions,
some of these foreign agencies have exerted significant influence on
Chinese policies towards agriculture, as in other sectors.

The agricultural policy process at the national level involves these
different individual and institutional actors and the politics of
agricultural policy reflects their interaction, their motivations and
their relative influence. They interact in certain formal meetings
which are forums for debate and decision. The most important
domestic forum is the annual National Rural Work Conference,
convened by the CCP Central Committee and the State Council.
This meeting draws together officials concerned with agricultural
matters from both Party and government, central and local levels,
as well as agricultural economists and other experts. The formal
purpose of the conferences is to monitor progress in rural
development, identify and diagnose problems and, where appropriate, come up with policy remedies. The Rural Work Conference
also plays an informal political role by providing a context in which
competing interests and perspectives can be expressed. There are
also one-off meetings to discuss particular policies or problems. For
example, the National Symposium on Agricultural Economic
Problems, convened in August 1981, played a significant role in
smoothing the process of introducing the new 'responsibility
systems' (Zweig 1987: p. 267). In November 1989, there was a
National Meeting for the Exchange of Experiences in the Comprehensive Development of Agriculture which turned out to be a
forum in which provincial vice-governors put forward their views

on agricultural issues.[3] Formal meetings aside, there is also a process of ongoing (and often informal) consultation and co-ordination between departments (for example, between the Ministries of Agriculture and Commerce) and agencies may co-operate to send a joint policy proposal to the State Council for consideration and approval (Zhu and Tian 1989: p. 163).

While the major co-ordinating agencies, such as the Party's central leadership, the State Planning Commission and the State Council, are there to oversee this complex process, they are subject to claims from other constituencies (such as industry or the military) which may limit the amount of resources they are willing to commit to agriculture. The power of these countervailing pressures is partly responsible for the fact that, in spite of a declared commitment to increase state investment in agriculture, it has actually declined in percentage terms during the reform period from an annual average of 10.5 per cent of total state investment in capital constructions between 1976 and 1980 to 3.9 per cent in 1990 (*SSB* 1990: p. 133). Moreover, decision-makers must deal with the competing sectional interests of the institutional participants within the arena of agricultural policy, each of which, as Oksenberg has suggested (1982: p. 181; cf. Lampton 1987: p. 14), tends to have 'its own "organisational ideology", its own sense of mission and purpose' with its own constituency to satisfy. Therefore, while agricultural policy does reflect the intention of central politicians and planners, it is shaped (both in the making and the implementing) by these institutional actors. Thus gaps may develop between policy intent and policy results. As Zhu and Tian (1989: p. 169) point out, 'provincial and local governments and state commercial and administrative agencies may alter the control signals of the central government through implementing their own preferred measures which may speed up or retard the achievement of central goals'.

As this quotation suggests, the political picture (and the problems faced by central politicians and planners) are further complicated by the relationship between the centre and regional/local agencies. On the one hand, local officials exert influence on national decision-making through their participation in national conferences and their multitudinous formal and informal ties with individuals and institutions at the centre. On the other hand, the centre must rely upon local agencies to implement its policies and to provide some of the resources necessary to do so. But local governments and Party organs have their own specific priorities which may or may not coincide with those of the centre (or each other). Each region has its own specific economic and ecological situation which conditions the demands of its representatives: for example, provinces which are richer or poorer, grain-deficient or grain-surplus, more or less industrialised, or more or less oriented to foreign trade. The resulting political pressures surfaced, for example, at the meeting on the Comprehensive Development of Agriculture in late 1989. While grain-producing provinces such as Anhui, Shanxi and Shandong were pushing for higher grain prices, Qinghai (a large grain-importer from other provinces) stood to lose out from an increase in the grain price because it was forced to subsidise retail sales.

Local officials are strongly motivated to pursue local interests, partly because of an underlying bureaucratic imperative towards maintaining and expanding their bailiwicks, partly because local politicians wish to minimise local discontent and expand their patronage base, partly because of a sense of local 'patriotism' and partly because each assumes that other localities are operating along similar lines. The result is a tug of war between centre and provinces and between localities, each seeking to influence the behaviour of, and extract resources from, each other's territorial unit.

(c) The macro-politics of agriculture is also shaped by the overall configuration of *social groups and classes* the most important of which is the divide between rural and urban populations. To the extent that the urban–rural distinction embodies both a distinction between industry (notably state-owned industry) and agriculture, and between 'unproductive' and productive enterprise (the former reflecting a concentration of service, administrative and welfare activities in the cities), it provides the basis for a basic divergence in material interests. Moreover, the cities, and the state institutions rooted in them, are nuclei of superior power which seek to exert dominance over the countryside while at the same time being forced to bargain with it. One can detect three political imperatives behind this impetus towards urban dominance: (i) the *control* imperative whereby urban-based political and administrative élites, in pursuit of national or sectional objectives, seek to influence the nature and level of agricultural output and control the agricultural surplus. At its broadest level, this reflects the strategic desire of developmental élites in both socialist and capitalist systems to harness agriculture to serve the prime priority of rapid industrialisation (for a comparable analysis of Taiwan, see Moore 1988). At a more specific level, it involves, for example, the desire of individual industrial sectors (and the state institutions which bestride and 'represent' them) to control sources of inputs (such as cotton or sugar). (ii) The *cheapness* imperative reflects the desire of urban-based élites not only to control the agricultural surplus, but also to acquire it 'cheaply', i.e. at a price lower than that set by a hypothetical free market. State economic managers want to obtain cheap raw materials for their industries and to keep down the cost of wage-goods, notably food, for the urban labour force. (iii) The *political interest* imperative reflects the need for urban political and administrative élites to attend to the interests of their urban constituencies. The latter can exert pressure on urban governments expressing their discontent if food prices increase at rates beyond their real wages or if their jobs are threatened by an influx of rural job-seekers. This imperative lies behind the 'urban bias' which has been diagnosed as a structural feature of development policy-making in other Third World contexts, notably India (Lipton 1977). In general, however, there are serious limits to the ability of urban/state élites to enforce these three imperatives on the countryside and the rural–urban political relationship cannot but rely on some degree of reciprocity and bargaining.

To summarise, this nexus of leaders, institutions and social forces constitutes the macro-political environment of agriculture, that network of political forces which surrounds and shapes Chinese village communities and rural life more generally.

The Micro-political Environment of Agricultural Policy

In keeping with our broad analytical framework, we can think of politics at the village in terms of leadership, institutions and groups. First, village *leaders* – Party or non-Party, in the former brigades and teams or in the new villagers' committees – are a crucial bridge between the Party-state and the peasantry, the last link in the chain of political and administrative command emanating from Beijing. Their political role, as an intermediary between state and peasants, is ambiguous and often difficult. While they are an important instrument of state power, they are also subject to pressures from their own village constituencies. The particular way in which each set of village leaders handles this contradiction has considerable influence on the varying ways in which state policies actually impinge on the rural population.

The reforms have had two major effects on village leaders. First, the dissolution of the brigades and teams and the introduction of responsibility systems has weakened their power in the village and made the task of leadership more complex and difficult. Second, the reforms have encouraged the emergence of a new type of leader: unlike the political mobiliser of the past, the new leader is more business-oriented and entrepreneurial. After over a decade of rural reform, the village leadership cadre is thus very heterogeneous: in some cases, the old leaders are still in place and retain a commitment to collective institutions; in others, younger leaders have emerged to manage the village as a mini-corporation operating entrepreneurially in the more commercialised rural economy; in others, they have jumped on the bandwagon of self-enrichment and operate a *laissez-faire* regime within the village. Given these two trends, it is likely that the state is having an increasingly difficult time in enforcing its writ at the village level and that the actual impact of state policies varies widely.

Village-level *institutions* – political, administrative and economic – provide the matrix of micro-political activity. The Chinese village is still, to varying degrees, integrated into the wider political-administrative system, through the power of township governments over villagers' committees and township Party organs over village Party branches. This institutional matrix has changed significantly in the reform era and we shall be probing the political implications of these changes.

The nature of village politics also depends on the specific *socio-economic profile* of its inhabitants: for example, the amount of inequality between households and groups; the specific pattern of economic activity; the degree of solidarity of the village as a natural unit; or its degree of openness or 'porousness' in relation to the outside world. The reforms have changed the socio-economic character of many village communities in major ways, and this has important micro-political repercussions.

Having sketched the macro and micro dimensions of agricultural politics, let us look finally at the relationship between them. The

state, on the one side, places certain demands o‹
terms of output, sales, investment and social b
family size) and exerts pressures to secure
operating through its agents at the village level.
their side, have an interest in minimising state cl
the net transfer of resources from the state and in general securing a
(real if not formal) policy environment amicable to their interests
(Oi 1989). There are certain key points of interaction. The most
important of these are the annual struggles over the procurement of
agricultural produce which take place after each harvest. While
these struggles are intermittent, there are more continuing engage-
ments, such as the pressure on rural households to restrict their
families to one or two children, to send recruits to the armed forces,
to pay taxes and contribute financially to local services, or to
provide labour for local infrastructural projects. Each of these
interactions between macro and micro levels involve clashes of
interest which give rise to a continuing political struggle characterised by stand-offs, bargaining and conflict as each side
mobilises the political resources at its disposal to achieve its aims.

To summarise, this first section has been largely a simplified
cross-section of agricultural politics, a static photographic image
without dynamics or change. It is intended as a rough guide to the
historical analysis which follows. Our main aim from now on is to
trace the impact of the post-Mao rural reforms on the political
environment and character of the agricultural policy process.

The Political Background of Rural Reform: The Commune System

The commune system had emerged during the Great Leap Forward
and its aftermath and had remained unchanged in its essentials since
the early 1960s. It consisted of three nested layers: the commune
itself, the production brigade and the production team. The
commune was divided into brigades (on average about 9 to 13 per
commune) and the brigades were divided into teams (averaging
about 7 to 8 per brigade) – each level was subordinate to the one
above. The *communes* were large units, averaging about 15 000
members each as of 1980 and were often composed of a small
market town with its surrounding villages. They were multi-
functional, responsible for local government, Party affairs, social

elfare (such as secondary education and hospitals), economic planning, culture and communications, public security, rural investment projects (such as land improvement and irrigation works), local industry and commerce, and technical extension services. The *production brigade* was responsible for small-scale rural infrastructure and industry, and social welfare (elementary schools and clinics); it was also the site of the lowest branch of the Party. The *production team* comprised between 20 and 40 neighbouring households and operated as the basic unit of agricultural production.

Formally speaking, the team owned the land cultivated by its members and was the basic 'unit of account': in other words, it calculated revenues and expenditures and distributed income to team members in cash and kind according to quantity and type of labour. The income of each working member was a share of the team's net income available for distribution after paying taxes and debts and reserving certain funds for productive investment and social welfare. Remuneration was measured in terms of 'workpoints', awarded to each worker on the basis of time or task. Incomes varied each year depending on harvests, on the amount creamed off for collective investment and welfare and on the level of procurement prices and subsidies set by the state.

The village (i.e. a brigade or several teams) was encapsulated in a hierarchical network of political, governmental and economic institutions. The commune had a dual role: as a 'collective' institution theoretically responsible to its members and as a representative of the state, acting in effect as the lowest level of state administration. Though brigade and team leaders were outside the state system, they were subordinate to the commune leadership; similarly Party organs in the brigades were subordinate to Party organs at the commune level and above. In consequence, the political autonomy of the communes, brigades and teams was heavily circumscribed and they were under constant pressure to comply with prevailing state policies.

State policies towards agriculture in turn were not designed to encourage rural development merely for its own sake, but to link agriculture and other sectors of the rural economy into an overall economic strategy which benefited industrialisation. This was not only a national priority, but also the goal of provincial and local governments who have tended to think of regional development in terms of replicating the pattern of national development. To these ends, the state sought to control agricultural output through a system of mandatory procurement whereby agricultural collectives were obliged to meet annual output targets, the produce being sold to the state at fixed prices. Since the state wished to hold down the cost of food and other wage-goods to spur industrialisation and avoid urban discontent, it endeavoured to keep procurement prices low. Moreover, since the bulk of state investment resources went into industry, agriculture was starved of funds. As a counterweight, the state imposed pressured rural collectives to reserve a large proportion of their revenue for local investment; this meant that less funds were available to improve peasant living standards.

In this system, politics was authoritarian in three senses: (i) formal authority was hierarchically organised, with strict subordination between levels; (ii) flows of power and information within this structure of authority were predominantly top-down, with weak channels for communicating upwards the views of the peasant population; (iii) the triad of Party, state and commune exercised a political monopoly, preventing the formation of independent power centres. This was a 'fused' system of rural organisation in the sense that there was little separation between the political, social and economic spheres. Politics ran like a red thread through all aspects of rural life.

This triad of Party, government and collectives was organised to secure peasant compliance with official policy; the formal political role of ordinary peasants was largely confined to powerless participation in political 'movements' emanating from above. Though decision-making within the basic unit, the production team, was often reasonably democratic (Blecher 1978), its political significance was very limited since important decisions had already been taken above their heads. However, in spite of the 'top-down' nature of this system, there was some scope for the collectives to defend and express the interests of local populations against the state, thereby continuing the traditional cat-and-mouse game between state and peasantry which has been a perennial feature of Chinese history. Village leaders often suffered from political schizophrenia. If their formal authority was insufficient to induce peasants to meet the demands of their bureaucratic superiors, they resorted to informal clientelism (through 'relationships' or *guanxi*) (Oi 1989). Peasants could also use informal methods to resist the demands of village officials.

This institutional matrix well suited *the substance of rural politics* which was rooted in a triple subordination of the short-term interests of the peasant household: subordination to the over-riding priority of national (and regional) industrialisation, through mandatory procurement quotas at unfavourable prices; subordination to the primacy of accumulation over current consumption at both national and local levels, enforced by the commune's high-investment regime; subordination of household to collective accumulation, enforced by the basic accounting units, the production teams (Nolan and White 1984).

This triple subordination of village to state defined *the specific issues of rural politics* during the Maoist period. As we saw in Chapter 1, peasants nursed a good many grievances: they resented the disruptions caused by successive political movements, or pressure from local officials to work on construction projects during the slack season, usually without adequate recompense. There was also dissatisfaction with key national policies, such as the movement to send urban youth to live in the countryside (peasants often saw them as a costly nuisance), or to force the basic unit of account upwards from the team to the larger and more cumbersome production brigade. Peasants resented the superior lifestyle of urbanites and felt that the latter were favoured by the government. Locally, many yearned to move out of agriculture into industry or trade, and the feeling grew that agriculture was a mug's game at the very bottom of the social totem-pole. They also chafed at the many restrictions on their economic freedom: they were confined to their village by a system of household registration (*hukou*) and could not go to the cities or richer regions in search of work; private production was discouraged through limitations on private plots and potentially lucrative household sidelines (such as poultry, pigs and handicrafts); private exchange was kept in bounds through the banning or strict control of local free markets; they were forced to grow grain instead of more ecologically appropriate and profitable cash crops; and they could not use as much of their collective income for private consumption as they would have wished. These discontents lowered morale and dampened productivity.

This gradually worsening political and economic situation posed serious problems for the CCP leadership. Growth in agricultural output was sluggish and there is evidence that the state was losing out in the battle for the agricultural surplus: *per capita* net procurement of grain dropped from .063 tons/person in 1966 to .054 tons/person in 1978 (Oi 1989: p. 63). Given the cardinal role of agriculture in the national economy, the post-Mao Party leadership and their academic advisers came to realise that urgent changes were required in both policies and institutions (Zhang Yulin 1982). In terms of policy, the mandatory procurement system was too rigid and impeded a more productive use of agricultural resources; procurement prices were too low and offered little incentive for increased productivity; and restrictions on private production and marketing dampened the natural dynamism of local rural economies. In institutional terms, criticisms were levelled at the commune system itself: it could not organise production efficiently; it did not provide effective incentives for effort; and it stifled economic initiatives on the part of both collectives and peasant households. In consequence, the struggle between the state and peasantry over the agricultural surplus had become a relentless, wearisome game in which both sides expended a lot of unproductive effort. Mao Zedong had once criticised Stalin for 'draining the pond to catch the fish' in just such a context; the better way was to tickle the trout out of the water and it was to this new approach to state–peasantry relations that the economic reformers were to apply from 1978 onwards.

The Politics of Decollectivisation

Our concern here is to describe the new policies in detail, and to analyse the political processes involved in their introduction and their political impact. Who opposed or supported the changes and how did these political alignments affect the nature and pace of rural reform? What effect have they had on the relationship between state and peasantry and on the nature of village-level politics?

Agricultural Reform Policies and their Impact on the Countryside

As we have seen, measures were taken after the Third Plenum (XI) to improve the policy environment of agriculture by raising procurement prices and granting more economic freedom to peasant households. Overall, there was a move away from direct state controls over agriculture (operating through procurement quotas) towards more flexible, market-oriented methods of regulating agriculture: by means of pricing policy, a diversification of purchase and sales channels and the replacement of procurement quotas with voluntary contracts signed between peasant producers and state grain departments.

At the micro level, the reforms set in train a *de facto* decollectivisation of agriculture through the introduction of 'production responsibility systems' (*shengchan zirenzhi*) (for overviews, see Hartford 1985 and Shue 1984). This dramatic transformation went through several stages, each marking a further step away from collective agriculture. At first, the contracting unit was a small group within the team in a system called 'contracting output to the group'. In late 1979, however, official permission was given for contracting to individual households. At first, the CCP leadership envisaged this as a concessionary measure appropriate only to poorer communes, but it became virtually universal over the next few years.

It took two basic forms, a more moderate 'contracting output to the household' (*bao chan dao hu*) and a more radical 'contracting work to the household' (*bao gan dao hu*, also translated as 'comprehensive contracting to the household'). In the former, a household was allocated a piece of land (or rather a number of small parcels of land of different quality) and a specified proportion of its output was handed over to the team in return for an agreed number of workpoints. Current inputs such as seeds, pesticides and fertiliser were provided by the team or by both partners. Production planning, services such as irrigation and major means of production, such as machines or draft animals, were still handled by the team. The latter form, 'contracting work to the household', which spread across the country from 1981 onwards and involved 98 per cent of peasant households by the end of 1983 was, in effect, a return to household agriculture. This is usually referred to as the 'household responsibility system' or often just 'the responsibility system'. Households are now responsible for both production and the distribution of net revenue (workpoints distributed by the teams are now obsolete); they also control means of agricultural production such as tools, draft animals and mechanical equipment. As long as the mandatory procurement system is still in operation (formally or informally), the household is still obliged to deliver a certain amount of output to the state; it must also pay state agricultural tax and a contribution to the upkeep of the village collective. After meeting these responsibilities, it is free to dispose of its extra output as it wishes (consume it, sell it on the local free market, or sell it to the state at higher-than-quota prices).

In terms of production, this is a kind of tenantry system with the household paying a 'rent' to the collective 'landlord'. Though the initial period of the contract was only a year, it was gradually extended to give the household *de facto* ownership over its allocated land and, though a formal market in land has not yet been revived, subcontracting of land-use rights is now widespread, particularly in areas where there are opportunities for off-farm employment. In terms of exchange, this is still a 'mixed' system in the sense that, though the peasant household is far more involved in markets than before, it is still harnessed to the requirements of state procurement. Although the latter was scheduled for abolition in 1985, by the beginning of the 1990s, it was still in force *de facto*.

The new system of rural institutions is also 'mixed' in the sense that collectives, while by and large removed from the management of day-to-day production, still retain a significant economic role (Wang *et al.* 1985: pp. 62–68). At the village level, the 'villagers' committee' is responsible for maintaining welfare services formerly handled by the brigade, organising technical services and rural works, overseeing contracts and managing (directly or indirectly) village industry. In this last case, the reforms have led to a contracting out of most of the enterprises formerly run by the brigade; enterprise assets are leased temporarily to individuals or groups in return for a cash payment to the village. At the level of the former commune, the township (*xiang*) government still plays a powerful role, not only in handling the routine business of government (public security, legal affairs, taxation, etc.), but also in encouraging the development of local industry, whether public (run directly by the township), private or mixed. The township government is also crucial as a means to maintain state controls over the countryside, both directly and indirectly through its supervision of village organisations. The Party apparatus is still largely intact in the countryside though its effectiveness has waned in many areas.

The last point raises the issue of regional variations which needs to be stressed. The Chinese rural scene is very complex and the concrete situation varies greatly from place to place. In some areas, the previous institutional triad – collective, Party and government – remains as dominant as before the reforms. In other areas, collective institutions at the village level have atrophied and rural Party branches have been weakened as Party cadres have defected to business, lost ideological heart, or succumbed to corruption. This has left the township government alone with the task of getting its locality to conform with state policies, a difficult job when the chain of authority has snapped at the village level.

In general, however, from the perspective of the early 1990s, much has changed on the rural institutional scene. Agricultural production is now undertaken largely by peasant households and the private sector has expanded greatly (into transportation, finance, trading and services as well as industry). The economic power of the collectives has declined and the grip of the state over agriculture has relaxed to some extent, allowing farmers greater say about what to produce, where to sell and on what terms. Overall, there has been a very significant redistribution of economic power away from the collective/state and towards individuals/households. There has been substantial progress towards freeing the peasantry from the 'triple subordination' of the commune era.

On the other hand, there are important continuities. The collectives have retained significant economic, political and social functions in many areas. Though the grip of the Party and state has relaxed, the apparatus of authority and control is still in place. Though the market has expanded rapidly in the countryside, it is still far from being the dominant element in China's rural economy. Though the private sector has expanded enormously, it is still ancillary to the public sector in most areas, though in some areas, such as Wenzhou in the eastern province of Jiangsu, it has become dominant (Nolan and Dong 1990). As in the reform process as a whole, therefore, Chinese agriculture has reached a half-way-house situation.

The Politics of Reform

We now turn to an analysis of the political factors which promoted both change and continuity. As in the reforms as a whole, rural reform has passed through two basic phases: the first, from 1979 to 1984, was one of rapid change and economic success; in the second, from 1985 until the early 1990s, the reforms – and Chinese agriculture generally – have run into serious problems. The two phases also mark different stages in the content of reform policies: the first period concentrated on agricultural decollectivisation at the micro level while the second attempted a broader process of rural commercialisation. In consequence, the politics of the two periods are quite different and we shall divide our analysis accordingly.

Phase I: Nothing Succeeds Like Success (1979–84)

In the first phase, the main policy issues concerned the extent of institutional reform at the commune level and below. There was concern among officials at all levels of the institutional hierarchy involved in agriculture about the Ideological significance and socio-political effects of moving from collective to household agriculture. There were those who felt that collective agriculture was a hallmark of 'socialism' and the reforms were politically regressive; there was also concern that they might lead to a class 'polarisation' between rich and poor peasants, or might undermine the authority of the Party State in the countryside.[4] Those arguing for sweeping re-forms, on the other hand, argued that the new 'responsibility systems' did not deviate from socialist principles (particularly since land was to remain in collective hands) and the continuance of collective and Party/state organisations in the countryside would more than suffice to prevent any undesirable social repercussions.[5]

It was in agriculture that reform leaders chose to launch their first offensive, not the least because the impediments to change were less densely concentrated in the countryside than in the cities which were honeycombed with state institutions and state enterprises. A pioneering role was played by Zhao Ziyang and Wan Li who, as early as 1977 had initiated reform experiments in Sichuan and Anhui provinces where they were first Party secretaries (Walker 1984: pp. 786–7). In spite of this early political initiative, however, the process of reforming the communes was an incremental process covering more than five years (from 1978 to 1983). It passed through a series of stages, each punctuated by official meetings and/or documents, and each widening the scope of reform (Zweig 1983 and 1987).

How do we account for this policy process which was incremental in its execution yet radical in its consequences? Certainly there was an element of trial and error involved, as reform ideas were first tested in one or more localities before being submitted for official ratification and wider implementation. However, this explanation is inadequate by itself since the rural reforms were carried much further than even the more radical reformist leaders had initially anticipated and were implemented in the teeth of initially powerful opposition. A political analysis is necessary to understand what was happening.

Let us begin by looking at the opposition. Apart from a more general Ideological scepticism pervading the Party/state which waned as the power balance at the top shifted, many officials dealing with agriculture at the local level (prefecture, county, commune and brigade) were particularly vocal in their opposition to radical change since they had made careers in creating and maintaining the previous system and stood to lose power and status (Zweig 1983; Travers 1985; Perry 1985: pp. 186–9). In the initial stages, moreover, when different kinds of responsibility systems were admissible, provincial leaders differed in their views on which forms were appropriate to their own conditions. Certain provinces which had acquired a Maoist reputation previously (such as Hunan, Mao's birthplace, and Shanxi, the site of the Maoist agricultural model of Dazhai), were ideologically hostile at first. But there were also economic reasons for different provincial reactions. This was visible, for example, during a meeting convened by the CCP Central Secretariat in September 1980 which brought together the first secretaries of all provincial and municipal level Party committees to discuss agricultural responsibility systems. The Secretariat maintained that 'airing different opinions helps the centre to make decisions on principle and policy'. Party leaders from poor provinces, such as Gansu, Henan and Yunnan supported contracting to households, while more developed regions, such as Jilin and Shanghai, rejected the system as inappropriate to their conditions.[6] Work by Jon Unger in Guangdong suggests that there were also widely varying reactions among villages within a province (Unger 1985–6).

On the other hand, there was substantial support from different quarters for the notion of household contracting. Leaders in impoverished regions were more likely to seize upon it as a way to invigorate stagnating collectives. More generally, in both richer and poorer areas, there was a groundswell of support among ordinary peasants who welcomed the increased economic freedom it provided. This pressure from below was very significant during the crucial transitional stage of 1980–81 when it was still unclear how far reforms of the collectives could be taken. One can detect an implicit political alliance between central reformist leaders and the 'masses' which outflanked and weakened the position of local and basic-level officials who resisted household contracting. In fact, central leaders explicitly used the fact of widespread peasant enthusiasm to strengthen their hand. Deng Liqun, for example, in a speech to a national conference on ideological–political work in rural areas in late 1982, said that the rural reforms were the 'result of peasant initiative', contrasting this with the bad old days of the Cultural Revolution when 'everything was done top-down by compulsion'.[7] The reformers' line was that, if the masses wanted change, then it was all right and local officials should accede to their wishes (Bernstein 1984).

This political alliance between reform leaders and peasants was crucial in tipping the policy balance, not merely in favour of household as opposed to group contracting but also towards the more radical option of 'contracting work to the household'. This policy shift created a different political environment from when different areas had been encouraged to experiment with alternative methods. Household contracting now became orthodoxy and officials who had reservations and dragged their feet could be accused of 'Leftist' obstruction. The result was a revival of the Maoist tendency to impose a policy across the board with scant regard for local variations. Unger documents this process well in the case of Guangdong province In his words, 'whatever the leadership believed, in very few villages was (complete decollectivisation) voluntarily undertaken by the peasantry; and had the choice been the peasants' to make, not every village would have completely decollectivised' (Unger 1985–6: p. 593).

As rural reform gathered momentum, therefore, it produced results which were in certain ways contrary to the aims of both the reform leaders and their peasant constituency. There was still a tendency to convert the process of implementing policy into a one-dimensional political movement which carried all before it. In spite of attempts by the reformers to encourage a more liberal climate of ideas, political discourse was still couched in terms of ideological orthodoxy; whereas in the past, cadres had been afraid of being accused of 'rightism', now the situation was reversed. This does not mean that widespread adoption of the household contract system was economically or politically unwise; merely that, if the rhetoric of the reformers about the need for experimentation, local diversity and popular choice had been realised, the extent of decollectivisation would have been less and the rural institutional scene far more diverse. Moreover, some of the problems which emerged later, which were at least partially a consequence of hasty, across-the-board decollectivisation, might not have been so serious.

Let us draw some conclusions about the politics of agricultural policy in this first phase of rural reform. As of 1978, even a seasoned observer could not have foreseen the sweeping changes which were to take place over the next five years. The commune system seemed to be entrenched, despite its acknowledged deficiencies, and the ideological commitment to collective agriculture still seemed firm. Yet the reformers were able to carry through a radical programme of institutional reform without encountering any major political difficulties. Indeed, they themselves were swept along by the tide of events and the reforms which actually took place were more radical than they had originally intended. This is a reversal of the common experience of large shortfalls between policy intention and result so characteristic of attempts at radical economic reform in Eastern Europe. Instead of the usual question 'What went wrong?', we are obliged to ask 'What went right?'.

Clearly the key political underpinning of policy success was the fact that reform leaders at the centre and the mass of the peasantry both shared the desire for institutional change at the village level. But there were also new actors in the policy process (notably the new specialised research and consultancy agencies at the disposal of the reformers), and these were beginning to acquire influence through their links with key leaders. Though the forces of opposition, particularly officials in local governments and communes, were initially strong, they found themselves caught in political pincers and forced to climb aboard the policy bandwagon. The potential for political conflict over agricultural reform, which had initially seemed great, was thus reduced. This process was greatly assisted by the emergence of a general consensus on the need for reform among the central Party leadership, as the remaining Maoists were removed or neutralised and the overall ideological and political atmosphere changed as a result. The removal of their sponsors at the centre weakened the position of recalcitrant officials throughout the Party/state apparatus.

This felicitous political trend was strengthened by the economic success of the reforms, visible in the explosion of rural house construction and the spread of consumer durables (such as bicycles and TVs) across the countryside (for the effects on rural incomes, see Travers 1985). This not only vindicated reform policies, but also provided an expansion of resources which benefited nearly everybody, regardless of whether they were enthusiastic or sceptical about reform. For example, state grain-procurement departments could increase their 'take' along with the dramatic rise in agricultural output; local governments found their resource-base expanding as agricultural production took off; and poor peasants who had been afraid of losing the protection of the collective suddenly found a new vista of economic opportunities opening before them.

At the end of the first phase of successful reform, not only had the institutional context of Chinese agriculture changed, but so also had the political context of agricultural policy. The establishment of the household responsibility system had brought about a seemingly irrevocable redistribution of power in favour of the peasant household, both in terms of its relationship with the state and in relation with the collective cadres who had formerly ruled the roost in the village. From now on, power could not be exercised, either by the state or by grass-roots cadres, in the old direct ways; henceforth political relationships were inescapably to involve a degree of bargaining and persuasion. The state's grasp over the agricultural surplus had relaxed and officials now had to resort to more flexible means (notably price inducements) to obtain their economic objectives. Similarly, within the village, the successors to team and brigade cadres did not have the same range of control over their fellow-villagers as in the past, and were forced to find new ways of securing peasant co-operation.

Phase II: Economic Slow-down and Political Divergence (1985 on)

The first phase of agricultural reform ended with a bumper harvest in 1984 when everything seemed to be going so well. Little wonder, therefore, that the CCP leadership became, in Stalin's words about the Soviet collectivisation campaign, 'dizzy with success'. They embarked upon an optimistic strategy which, on the one hand, assumed that agriculture could look after itself for a while and merited less attention and resources and, on the other hand, decided to press ahead with a further wave of market-oriented rural reforms in the expectation that they might enjoy the same success as the first wave.

The new programme aimed at a comprehensive spread of market relations throughout the countryside. This had several key components. First, the system of mandatory state procurement for agricultural produce was abolished by Document No. 1, 1985, issued by the CCP Central Committee and State Council on 1 January 1985.[8] Henceforth, the role of the state as monopsonist would decline and the role of markets would increase. To the extent that the state continued to procure agricultural goods (notably grain and cotton), it would do so through contracts rather than obligatory quotas, a methods referred to as 'commercial planning'. The result would be a 'two-track system' which combined state regulation through contracts with free markets. Prices in the former would be set by the state but flexibly with an eye to the market prices which emerged in the latter. Second, the freeing of markets for commodities was to be followed by an expansion of markets in labour, finance and land (whether freehold or leasehold). Since the resulting economy was still to be 'socialist', co-operative institutions of all kinds were still to be encouraged, but unlike the communes they would be of the kind which fostered rather than hindered the commercialisation of agriculture.

Third, agricultural production was to become more specialised as farmers moved away from multi-faceted subsistence production and concentrated on commercial crops in which they had a comparative advantage. Fourth, the pace of rural economic diversification was to be accelerated, both within agriculture (away from crop farming towards other branches such as animal husbandry, forestry and aquaculture), and away from agriculture towards other sectors such as industry, commerce and services. These sectors would absorb the rural surplus labour which would be released from agriculture as it became more efficient and technically advanced.[9] However, though these policy changes flowed naturally from the reforms that had gone before, they were rooted in an over-optimistic view of the future of agriculture. As central leaders turned their attention to urban-industrial reform, this change in official priorities fed down through the chain of command, encouraging local governments to pay less attention to agriculture and to vie with each other in establishing a rural industrial base within their bailiwicks.

Such optimism proved ill-founded as agriculture ran into serious problems after the boom year of 1984. The average annual growth rate dropped by nearly a half between 1985 and 1991 compared with 1979 to 1984. Output of grain was a particular headache: from a base of 318.7kgs/pn. in 1978, it had only risen to only 364.3 kgs/pn. by 1989, an increase of only 14.3 per cent over a decade. This was partly the result of farmers deserting grain production for more lucrative cash crops or leaving agriculture for jobs in local industry. There was also concern that the rural infrastructure (particular irrigation works) built up during the commune period was deteriorating because the collective institutions which had built and maintained it had been weakened by the reforms. For example, the area of land under irrigation fell from 45m. hectares in 1979 to 44.5m. in 1988. Concern was also voiced about the ecological consequences of the new stress on household agriculture and market exchange (a decline in soil quality caused by 'mining' the soil for short-term profit, invasion and destruction of forests, and pollution by unregulated rural industries). Some Chinese econo-mists felt that the early years of spectacular economic progress had been to a considerable degree 'one-off', i.e. the result of institutional and policy changes in the early 1980s which increased output dramatically but temporarily, and which had relied heavily on an accumulated stock of rural capital built up over the previous two decades.[10] After this spurt, agriculture was now facing the same massive underlying constraints as before: a dwindling area of arable land, increasing population pressure as the 'one-child family' policy was proving increasingly ineffective in the countryside, and low levels of investment and technology.

Some of these economic problems were the result of Party policies. Since agriculture was no longer such a priority, the ratio of state investment funds spent on it declined substantially and the rural reforms had not yet reached a point (particularly in terms of guaranteeing ownership rights over land) whereby peasant house-holds themselves were investing at a satisfactorily high level. The central government was also reluctant to raise procurement prices since its financial status was parlous. This, combined with the restrictions on credit imposed from 1988 onwards meant that by 1989 grain procurement departments could not secure the funds necessary to pay peasants for their produce and the latter had to accept IOUs or 'white slips' in lieu of cash. The budgetary losses of state procurement agencies had been mounting and the burden of retail price subsidies had been imposing an increasing burden on state coffers (Sicular 1988: p. 691). The centre had also exhibited a tendency to 'oversteer' agriculture, first by underestimating the effect of policy changes (such as price rises) and then reacting with new policies which over-compensated. This created an environment of uncertainty, particularly in regard to the relative prices of different crops. Farmers were having difficulty coping with fluctuating markets and official prices; they were also caught in an increasingly serious 'scissors' situation as the prices of inputs such as fertiliser, plastic sheeting and pesticides rose rapidly while prices for their output were only rising slowly if at all.

The years 1986 onwards saw a rising chorus of peasant complaints and the relationship between state and peasantry became strained as the former sought to maintain supplies of essential goods such as grain and edible oil by retaining mandatory output quotas under the guise of 'contracts', and the latter strove to avoid these impositions or improve the terms of trade. Some of this discontent was captured in surveys of peasant opinion. For example, the Ministry of Agriculture carried out a national survey of 3200 households in 1988 and the newspaper *Nongmin Ribao* (*Peasants' Daily*) played an important role in disseminating the results of this and other surveys. The targets of peasant criticisms were not only official policies towards agriculture, but also the unacceptable behaviour of local government and village-level cadres.[11] Reporters from *Nongmin Ribao* also made their own investigations of peasant opinion and the results, sometimes very hardhitting, were published in considerable detail.[12]

While these problems increasingly forced themselves on the attention of central policy-makers in the mid-1980s, they found it hard to tackle them because of certain intractable political problems. First of all, the onset of inflation, which had escalated to worrying proportions by 1988, created widespread discontent in the cities and made it difficult to increase official prices for agricultural products without incurring ruinous costs in terms of state subsidies to urban consumers. Second, there was now less room for manoeuvre in designing and enforcing agricultural policies. State control over the peasantry was no longer so sure and a new policy could run into serious trouble if peasants chose to ignore or oppose it. There were official complaints, for example, that peasants no longer queued up to deliver public grain; instead local cadres were going from village to village to persuade peasants to deliver grain. In Wuxi prefecture in Jiangsu province, for example, peasants were refusing to sell grain to the state for a number of reasons: because they thought the prices of agricultural inputs were too high; because they were aware that some of the rice they sold to local procurement agencies at fixed prices was being resold by those same agencies at 2.5 times the original price; because they were not being paid in cash but partly in IOUs in the form of one-month fixed bank deposits; and because they had decided to store grain to wait for a better price later. Clearly, 'education' by local cadres no longer had the desired effect; only a change in prices could persuade them to sell.[13]

At the same time, the central government was having increasing difficulty in imposing its will on its own machinery of policy implementation. Particularly important was the shift in the balance of power between central and local governments during the reform years. As provincial, county and municipal governments acquired increasing powers, particularly financial, to define their own developmental priorities, they could increasingly pick and choose whether or how to implement Beijing's policies. One of the academic magazines specialising in agriculture pointed out this problem in late 1990: 'Some policies are perfectly good in and of themselves, but when various regions and departments come at them from their own interest orientations, or when they arbitrarily alter these policies or even come up with their own "counter-policies", the result is that policies are defeated by counter-policies'.[14] Local governments had strong motivations to favour industry (including rural industry) over agriculture: partly because policy signals from the centre had encouraged and therefore licensed them to do so; partly because economic returns from investment in industry were greater and quicker than from agriculture; and partly because industry could be placed more firmly under their control to become the goose that laid 'golden eggs' to swell their coffers. Thus, when central leaders began to complain about a bias towards industry in local investment and a corresponding neglect of agriculture, local governments had powerful reasons to turn a deaf ear.

An even more pervasive shift in state behaviour, which affected Party and government agencies at all levels involved the phenomenon of what we have called the 'entrepreneurial state', whereby individual departments use their power to exploit economic opportunities for their own corporate advantage. In the agricultural context, departments charged with supplying inputs or marketing output were now able to manipulate the 'dual-track' pricing system introduced in the mid-1980s to their own advantage (and to the detriment of the state as a whole and their rural clients and suppliers). The *People's Daily* complained in mid-1989 that, as the economy became more market-oriented, all sectors of the state involved in the rural economy were pursuing their own special interests at the expense of agriculture: departments in charge of capital investment or materials supply diverted resources to projects from which they could reap quick and huge profits; some commercial departments raised the prices of farm inputs arbitrarily, or sold them elsewhere for a profit or foisted sub-standard products on farmers. The central government was also a loser: 'the gap between what farming needs and what is actually supplied has to be made up by the central government and this has become an unbearable burden'.[15] Some of this bureaucratic arbitrage was conducted across provincial boundaries. One example involved transactions in silkworm cocoons, across the borders of three provinces – Hubei, Anhui and Jiangsu. In 1988, Luotian county in Hubei increased cocoon prices to export departments and bought them cheaper in Jinzhai county, Anhui; meanwhile, Langxi county in Anhui increased its own prices and bought in cheaper cocoons from Liyang county in Jiangsu. The matter was investigated by the State Council which instructed Luotian to compensate Jinzhai and Langxi to compensate Liyang. Any profits made in these transactions were to be paid to the state treasury.[16] In such cases, the finger of suspicion was pointed at local governments for failing to take the necessary action to control these phenomena: 'Some production and business departments take advantage of loopholes in the law to raise prices. In order to raise revenue, some local governments turn a blind eye to violations of price policy.'[17] Such condemnations were useless since the phenomena described were the predictable outcome of the intersection between the opportunities offered by a more flexible price system and the desire of local governments to increase their own revenue.

As the problems of agriculture mounted (Party spokesmen were calling the situation 'grim' by 1988), the Party leadership was facing an increasing political deadlock and divisions emerged in the leadership over how to tackle the issue. In terms of development strategy, there was disagreement over the relative importance of agriculture in the national economy. In late 1988, an editorial in the *People's Daily*, which contained a résumé of the Rural Work Conference held in November, criticised 'certain comrades' as follows: 'Although (they) know that agriculture is important and that without agriculture . . . reforms and construction would be out of the question, and while they also shout that agriculture is the foundation, they are in fact only enthusiastic about the industrial growth rate.' The editorial also criticised the view that 'industry produces cash quickly and agriculture slowly'.[18] While these criticisms were no doubt directed against local officials who were rapidly extending their industrial base, there was probably also an implicit criticism of central reformers, such as Zhao Ziyang, who could be accused of encouraging such behaviour if not actually advocating it. The post-4 June 1989 conservative leadership attempted to re-assert the importance of agriculture in relation to industry, both urban and rural. Some policy-makers, including Premier Li Peng, Minister of Agriculture He Kang and Party General-Secretary Jiang Zemin expressed reservations about the headlong rush towards local industry which gathered momentum in the mid-1980s. However, the supporters of local industry, particularly but not exclusively in local governments, fought back and by 1990 the central leadership was forced to take a more conciliatory line.

There was also a disagreement over the relationship between agriculture and foreign trade. Some reformers, reflecting a notion of the 'Great International Circle' attributed to Zhao Ziyang, argued that some problems in agriculture (such as faltering grain production) could be remedied at least partially through imports. The view attributed to Chen Yun, which was echoed by the post-4 June leadership, was that economic and political stability depends crucially on agriculture and that the key question of agriculture is grain. Without a secure foundation of domestic grain production adequate to supply the needs of the whole population, the economic (and implicitly the political) system would be vulnerable. This implied that means must be found to prevent too many people moving too rapidly out of grain production and agriculture generally, and that China should aim for basic national self-sufficiency in grain, with imports only playing a relatively marginal role.[19]

There was also disagreement about the extent to which the rural economy should be regulated by markets or should still be subject to state controls of various kinds. The conservative response to the agricultural problems of the mid–late 1980s involved a partial reversion to administrative controls combined with selective price incentives and an increase in state investment in agriculture. Both the latter measures were compatible with the reimposition of controls since price policies could be varied within a continuing framework of mandatory sales to the state (even if these were now putatively based on contracts). Moreover, any planned increase in state investment would be implemented by state agencies, as opposed, say, to an approach favoured by the reformers which sought to increase investment by the peasantry themselves by stabilising *de facto* ownership over land and allowing a *de facto* market in land).

Several features of the conservative approach demonstrated their unwillingness, at least in the short term, to bring about a fundamental change in the rural economic system. In the area of commodity exchange, effective procurement quotas were reimposed; in order to stimulate production, a given supply of inputs was bartered in return for a guaranteed amount of contracted output (as part of what came to be known as the 'three links' policy). In 1988, to counter problems of extortion and profiteering in the supply of inputs, state control over inputs was strengthened through a system of 'exclusive management'. Henceforth, the supply of chemical fertilisers, insecticides and vinyl mulch was to be handled by the China National Agricultural Production Means Corporation under the Ministry of Commerce, working through state-controlled supply and marketing co-operatives in the country-side. Certain key categories of these goods were to be distributed by planning commissions at central and local levels and the whole process of supply was to be subject to 'unified planning and management'.[20] In the countryside itself, the conservative emphasis was on concentrating land with the aim of 'managing agriculture on a larger scale' which sounded suspiciously like the beginnings of recollectivisation, in spite of attempts by individual central leaders to discourage this idea. In the aftermath of 4 June, this emphasis on large-scale production, along with an emphasis on strengthening co-operative services at the village level, the call for local governments to mobilise peasants for collective work on rural infrastructural projects during the slack season and an attempt to strengthen rural Party organisation, suggested an attempt to re-establish some of the institutional controls which had been undermined by the reforms. Whether or not these policies constituted an effective response to the agricultural problems of China in the early 1990s is a problem we turn to in our conclusion.

Conclusion: Changes in the Politics of Chinese 'Agriculture

The success or failure of the new policies only depends in part on whether they are addressing the problems of agriculture in economically defensible ways. The viability of policies towards agriculture depends on basic political and institutional factors. Changing economic policies without changing at least part of this matrix means that the results of policy will likely be at best disappointing and at worst self-defeating. This was as true at the beginning of the reform era as it is now. What, if anything, has changed?

To the extent that there are strong institutional and social continuities, both at the macro and micro levels, things have not changed. Agricultural policy-making at the centre is still constrained by the influential interplay of powerful institutional interests both in Beijing and the localities. There is still a contradiction between the interests of the rural and urban populations which policy-makers ignore at their peril. The current Party leadership still regards it as politically crucial to maintain its control over the peasantry, particularly in the light of the urban instability of the late 1980s.

In some ways, however, the agricultural policy process has improved markedly. Leaving aside innovations in policy content, one can argue that the policy process has become more 'rational' in the sense that there is a greater role for relevant expertise and information (though this still has a long way to go). The policy process has also become more 'transparent' in the sense that options are presented more openly and there is greater scope for discussion and debate. At the same time, it has become more complex (in terms of the actors and interests involved) and more decentralised in power terms. The result is that, from the point of view of decision-makers in Beijing at least, the policy process has become more difficult to manage. In institutional terms, the centre has lost power to the localities and must increasingly resort to bargaining and bluster to get its way. China's hybrid system – half state, half market, with its ambiguous pattern of institutional behaviour – part entrepreneurial, part bureaucratic, operates to distort the best intentioned and informed policies. The state (and its former agents, the village cadres) have lost a good deal of their former ability to determine the behaviour of the peasantry. As markets which have sprung up spread, the rural population themselves have become socio-economically more diverse and politically more vocal and there are now more channels for them to make their voices heard. To a very considerable extent, central policy-makers are the prisoners of this over-arching political network of social and institutional interests and pressures.

Clearly, for the fundamental problems of agriculture to be tackled at their roots, there has to be action not merely at the level of economic policy but also at the level of this political system of interests and institutions. Leadership disagreements over policy reflect deeper disagreements over system. Since the present hybrid system contains many of the deficiencies of both planning and market, particularly visible in the often grotesque phenomenon of bureaucratic entrepreneurship which acts to worsen the already problematic relationship between state and peasantry, there is a natural tendency for policy-makers to seek consistency between policy and system – either by moving backwards towards the old institutional system as the post-4 June leadership have done, or by moving forwards towards a more fully commercialised and open rural political economy as their reformist opponents had intended. It seems plausible that too much has changed – socially, economically, psychologically and politically – to make the former option viable over the longer term. To move decisively towards the latter option requires not merely changes in the Party leadership, but action at the institutional level to change the political matrix within which the agricultural policy operates. This would not merely involve reform in the structures of Party and government, but also a drastic reconsideration of their functions and their relations with the rural population. Economic institutions, such as the system of land ownership, and the role of collective/co-operative organisations would have to be redefined. The Party faces a dilemma here, as in other areas of society and policy. If it fails to move towards institutional reform, the contradictions between institutional stasis and socio-economic change will intensify. If it seeks institutional change, it may unleash forces which it will be hard-pressed to control, as in the first phase of the reform era when events at the grassroots outran intentions at the centre.

4

The Politics of Industrial Reform

The political territory of industrial reform differs substantially from that of agriculture. As Chinese commentators often point out, urban/industrial reform is more complex and thus politically more difficult than its rural counterpart. The term 'complex' here refers not only to diversity, but also to the threatened interests and potentially uncooperative attitudes of the denizens of this sector. The political significance of industrial reform is arguably much greater than that of agricultural reform. The political credibility of the regime depends heavily on industrial performance, both in enhancing national power and raising mass living standards. Moreover, state industry has become the material base of the Party/state itself, providing the main source of state revenues; in 1980, for example, 83 per cent of government revenue derived from industry and 82 per cent from the state sector (*SSB* 1990: pp. 209–11). Industry also creates the working class which, in both theory and practice, has constituted a crucial base of political support for the CCP.

A Framework for Analysing the Politics of Industrial Reform

As in the preceding chapter, I shall analyse industrial reforms as a political arena containing three sets of political actors, each with their own (internally differentiated) interests and (varying degrees of) influence on the policy process. First, political and governmental *leaders* at the centre and in the localities differ ideologically in their broad approach to industrial reform. Individuals or groups of

118

leaders also develop specific perspectives from their specific position or background in the Party/state apparatus. For example, they may have work experience in industry (such as Li Peng in the power industry or Yu Qiuli in the petroleum industry) which may lead them to favour the sector in general or their 'own' particular sector. Second is the complex nexus of institutions involved in industry. At the national level, there are the industrial ministries and their subordinate departments; and other state organs with an involvement in industry, such as the financial agencies which depend on revenue from state industrial enterprises, state banks charged with handling enterprise deposits and providing credit to industry, the commercial organs which manage industrial products, and foreign trade organs which handle industrial imports and exports (for a valuable study of the industrial bureaucracy, see Shirk 1989: pp. 342–5). Here again we can distinguish between institutions which have a broader co-ordinating role of which industry is but one part (such as the CCP itself, the State Planning Commission, the State Economic Commission, the Economic Structural Reform Commission, the State Science and Technology Commission, the Ministry of Finance and the People's Bank of China) and more specialised agencies (such as the industrial ministries, or the Industrial-Commercial Bank which is specifically engaged in financing industry). These institutions, together with their myriad counterparts at the regional-local levels, provide the institutional environment of the state enterprise.

Industrial enterprises are the base of this organisational pyramid. On the eve of the reforms in 1978, industry produced about 50 per cent of China's national income (*SSB* 1990: p. 26), and the overwhelming bulk of it was state-owned or state controlled (most of the larger 'collective' enterprises were in fact controlled by local state agencies). Industry employed 61 million people in 1978, about 15 per cent of the total social labour force (*SSB* 1990: p. 106). By 1989, there were just over 100 000 state industrial enterprises, of which approximately 12 per cent were classified as 'large and medium', and 38 per cent were in light and 35 per cent in heavy industry (*SSB* 1990: p. 390). State enterprises were controlled by different levels of government. In 1983, for example, Wong (1987: p. 388) calculates the breakdown as follows: 25 000 large enterprises controlled by the central government (producing 30–35 per cent of gross output); 30 000–40 000 medium–small enterprises controlled by provincial and city governments (25–30 per cent); and 40 000–50 000 enterprises run by prefectural or county governments (13–15 per cent). By 1990, local state enterprise employed 77 per cent of the total state industrial labour force (*SSB* 1991: p. 354). These figures do not include industrial enterprises at the town/township and village levels which were nominally 'collective' enterprises; by 1990 there were nearly a million of these (*SSB* 1991: p. 353). The external institutional environment of a state enterprise is often complex and ambiguous. Although each state enterprise had multiple relations with a number of state agencies (managers often complain of having too many 'mothers-in-law'), they were normally under the direct authority of an 'industrial department' (enterprise managers refer to these as 'our superior organ') which was itself subject to 'dual leadership' from a department at a higher level (on the vertical branch or *tiao* principle of administration) and a government at the same level (on the horizontal 'area' or *kuai* principle). There is a particularly close symbiotic relationship between the enterprise and its industrial department. While enterprise managers attempt to minimise the claims of their superior department and resist any untoward interference, they also depend on the latter's support in solving economic problems and resisting the claims of other state agencies. On their side, while industrial departments must exert pressure on their enterprises to meet planned targets, they have an interest in reaching a mutually beneficial *modus vivendi* with them: first, because their own institutional credibility in the eyes of their superiors depends on the performance (and therefore co-operation) of 'their' enterprises and, second, because the latter are also a source of 'extra-budgetary' revenue which can be used at the departments' discretion.

The state enterprise itself is a network of institutions which interact in politically significant ways: the most important are the Party branch and its committee, the director and his/her management committee, and organisations representing the workforce (notably the trade union branch and, during the reform era, the workers' representative congress). In the pre-reform period, power within the enterprise was highly centralised and hierarchical with the Party committee and its secretary ruling the roost. However, the role of formal institutions was limited since power was exercised to a considerable extent along informal, 'clientelist' lines, as Walder (1986) has shown.

The third type of political actors are certain *social groups*. First, Party and government functionaries in both the industrial bureaucracy and state enterprises; second, enterprise managers who play a double role, as agents of their bureaucratic superiors to whom they owe their jobs and as representatives of the enterprise with responsibilities to its workforce; third, enterprise 'staff and workers', a highly heterogeneous category including skilled and unskilled, manual and mental workers, with interests which, to the extent that they found expression in the pre-reform era, did so informally through ties (and implicit bargains) with their superiors within the enterprise.

The politics of industrial reform revolve around the interaction between these three types of actors. This complex interplay of political forces helps to explain why certain industrial reforms get onto the policy agenda, how much political impetus lies behind them and how much 'slippage' there is between intention and impact. To the extent that they are successful, moreover, industrial reforms change the previous constellation of political interests, by bringing about a redistribution of power and resources. This sparks off political conflict, resistance and accommodation, phenomena which we shall be highlighting in the analysis which follows.

Industrial reform involves a host of issues and we shall simplify analysis in two ways. First, as in the preceding chapter, we shall make a simple distinction between macro and micro politics: the political-institutional environment of the enterprise on the one side and the internal world of the enterprise on the other. Of course, the macro context contains its own levels, notably the distinction between the centre and the meso level of nested local governments and branch departments. Second, we shall focus on two specific areas of reform policy: the first, industrial finance, enables us to look at relations between the Party/state and the enterprise as a corporate entity; the second, labour reform, enables us to look at the interaction between the macro-political environment and the internal micro-political dynamics of the enterprise.

The Background to Industrial Reform

China's modern industrial sector was incorporated into a Soviet-style planning system in the mid-1950s during the First Five-Year

Plan. In this system (as it was supposed to operate, at least) central planners calculated overall economic balances and issued broad directives on industrial output and distribution; the industrial ministries at the centre and industrial departments at local levels would further specify and transmit these instructions to state-owned firms down a hierarchical chain of bureaucratic command. Though enterprises were formally independent accounting units responsible for their own profit and loss, in reality they were subordinate, being required to meet mandatory economic targets set by their administrative superiors. The number of plan targets varied from the mid-1950s on, but eight tended to endure: total output value, product mix, product quality, consumption of raw materials and energy, total wage bill, costs of production, profits (i.e. net revenue) and working capital. In the early years, managerial authority within the enterprise was vested in the director, a system based on the Soviet practice of 'one-man management'.

Markets played a marginal role in this system of industrial planning. The enterprise had very limited powers to determine the level and composition of its own output and its relationship with other enterprises was handled through administrative intermediaries. The pattern of industrial output was determined predominantly by state officials, not market demand; most prices were set administratively and were only marginally subject to conditions of supply and demand; capital was allocated to enterprises through the state fiscal system or through a centralised mono-bank; industrial manpower was allocated administratively by state labour bureaux; supplies of raw materials to industrial enterprises and purchase of their products were both handled by specialised state agencies (departments of materials allocation and commerce); and relations with international markets were mediated by a system of trade regulation operating through the Ministry of Foreign Trade and specialised state trading companies.

This description of pre-reform industrial planning is an ideal type. The Soviet model was not adopted in full and was modified by successive reforms in the Maoist era, notably during the Great Leap Forward and the Cultural Revolution. The main thrust of Maoist reforms was to decentralise industrial planning and administration from central to local governments. In consequence, though the principle of directive planning was retained, the Chinese system differed from the highly centralised Soviet model, combining central with strong elements of local control over industry. Maoism also sought to politicise the planning system by subjecting it to successive political campaigns and restructuring authority within the enterprise to give the Party branch predominance over professional managers.

On the eve of the reform era, therefore, the industrial planning system was a complex and often contradictory amalgam of institutions and procedures, which had grown, coral-like, over the preceding two-and-a-half decades. It could not be described as highly centralised nor was it particularly planned. Its capacity for framing and enforcing longer-term (more than annual) plans was weak and was further weakened by the political struggles of the 1960s and 1970s. The real as opposed to formal authority of the key central planning agencies (the State Planning Commission, SPC and the State Economic Commission, SEC) was very limited. One can distinguish two (ideal) types of planning: 'autonomous planning' whereby the planning agency bases its calculations on priorities defined by itself or by a superior political authority, and secures compliance from subordinate units; and 'dependent planning' where the agency's calculations are determined by those units which are theoretically the recipients of its instructions. Chinese planners were heavily dependent on functional departments, notably the ministries, which exerted considerable influence over choice of priorities and allocation of resources by intervening at each stage of the planning process, namely the definition of objectives, balancing and adjustment, implementation and monitoring (Barnett 1967: pp. 440–1).

Moreover, 'planning' took place in a variety of locations, not just in Beijing. Functional and regional governments, individual departments and state enterprises all drew up their own plans. Though plans at each level and in each sector were in theory supposed to be co-ordinated and integrated with national plan priorities, interrelations were loose in 'normal' times and grew looser in times of political conflict and economic instability. The resulting uncertainties prompted both administrative and productive institutions to seek to protect themselves by expanding their autonomous power and resources. At regional/local levels this took the form of 'independent kingdoms' or 'ducal economies' under local Party bosses (Shen and Dai 1990). At the level of individual governmental institutions it took the form of 'departmentalism' as each organisation strove to improve its position in the bureaucratic struggle for resources. At the enterprise level, managers made strenuous efforts to limit the claims of their bureaucratic superiors through bargaining and deception; they also sought to enlarge their room for manoeuvre by hoarding capital equipment, labour and materials which enabled them to meet and 'overfulfil' planning targets without undue exertion.

Clearly, this highly fragmented and conflictual system was very far from the model of 'central planning'. However, some of its economic deficiencies were remedied by informal means of adaptation which developed over the years to clear blockages and oil the cogs of the planning machine. There were complex networks of horizontal and vertical relationships based on personal 'connections' which crossed bureaucratic frontiers or linked bureaucrats with enterprise managers. Managers also made informal links with other enterprises: for example, 'purchasing staff' (in effect, 'fixers') ranged far and wide to secure scarce materials by purchase or barter. Temporary labour could be taken on through informal contracts with urban neighbourhood organisations, illegal labour gangs or nearby rural communes. The extent of this 'shadow economy' is impossible to estimate accurately, but without it the 'official economy' would have been in far worse trouble. Within enterprises, informal relationships and implicit understandings between managers and workforce underpinned the enterprise's ability to meet plan targets. These were disrupted by the political factionalism of the Cultural Revolution but demonstrated remarkable staying power none the less (Walder 1986). Industrial planning and management in the Maoist era was thus a complex mixture of administrative regulation, informal networking, political bargaining and 'grey' markets.

This system of industrial planning and management embodied a particular distribution of power and interests. If rapid industrialisation had been the original *raison d'être* of pervasive state planning, it was gradually converted into *raison d'état*, the means whereby the Party/state apparatus created its own basis of economic power. It established the overwhelming predominance of the state industrial sector and within this, of heavy industries which gulped down the lion's share of state investment. Once this strategic pattern was set and powerful institutions were established to press the interests of heavy industry, it created a lop-sided pattern of industrialisation which perpetuated itself to the detriment of other economic priorities. Regardless of sector, moreover, state organisations battened on to industrial enterprises which not only provided an overall 'material basis' for the state as a whole, but also for specific agencies which syphoned off their resources for use in the incessant process of inter-bureaucratic combat. This overall pattern of interests and relationships encapsulated a pattern of industrialisation which, in the eyes of economic reformers, made less and less economic sense. In seeking economic change, through 'readjustment and reform', however, they also threatened the political *status quo* in state industry.

The Reforms in Industrial Strategy and Structure

Though this chapter is preoccupied with issues of industrial planning and management, we need to look briefly at the question of industrial strategy and structure since the two areas of reform are interconnected. As we have seen, early efforts at economic 're-adjustment' aimed to redirect state investment priorities away from heavy towards light industry (and from industry to agriculture), and to diversify the ownership system by encouraging the non-state collective and private sectors. Both of these measures had major implications for industrial strategy and structure and the political interests embodied therein.

First, on the question of changing the priority in industrial investment, official statistics suggest that there was very little change over the decade from 1978 to 1988. While the share of light and heavy industry in total state funds for capital construction averaged 6.7 per cent and 45.9 per cent per annum respectively between 1976 and 1980, by 1988 the shares were 7.4 per cent and 44.8 per cent (*SSB* 1989: p. 415). The proportion had begun to change in the early reform years reaching 9.8 per cent and 39 per cent in 1981, but the previous pattern gradually reasserted itself. It is arguable that this continuity reflects certain political factors which have remained virtually unchanged. First, the CCP leadership has retained its commitment to rapid industrialisation and has been loath to preside over too drastic a redefinition of the state's strategic priorities (the real loser has been agriculture whose share of state capital construction funds dropped substantially, as we have seen). Second, the heavy industrial sector itself, and the provinces where it is concentrated, notably in the North East and interior provinces in the South West which were the location of a massive 'Third Front' investment programme in the 1960s and 1970s (Naughton 1988), exerted powerful pressure to maintain their share of state funds acting through their representatives, the industrial ministries (such as Metallurgy, Machine Building and Electronics) and certain provincial authorities, including Shaanxi, Sichuan, Guizhou and Hubei (Shirk 1985: pp. 210–16). Large industrial enterprises also organised themselves to apply pressure on central and local policy-makers. One example was a Shanghai meeting of 51 large enterprises in early 1988 which issued a list of policy changes 'which large enterprises expect'.[1] Third, since large-scale heavy industry tends to be the responsibility of central as opposed to regional/local government, it is a crucial factor in determining the power of the centre. For example, Lu Dong, Minister of the State Economic Commission, estimated in early 1985 that, although large and medium enterprises constituted less than 2 per cent of the total number of enterprises, they accounted for 66 per cent of the total taxes and profits turned over to the state.[2] The larger the enterprise, moreover, the greater the state 'take'; it was estimated in mid-1985, for example, that, whereas rural enterprises delivered 30 per cent of their profits to the state and urban collectives 50 per cent, large state enterprises delivered 80–90 per cent.[3]

But the relationship between large/medium state enterprises and the state is a problematic one. A considerable proportion of these enterprises are loss-makers, partly for policy reasons (they may have to sell their products at artificially low official prices) and partly because of technological or managerial deficiencies. This poor performance partly reflects their age. At the end of 1986, for example, it was estimated that, of 7500 large and medium state enterprises, 5500 had been built in the 1950s and 1960s.[4] This puts the state in a bind: on the one hand it is forced to subsidise loss-making enterprises and spend money on modernising their obsolete plant; on the other hand, it is reluctant to subject them to the rigours of throughgoing reform because they might well be economically unviable and the state cannot let them go bankrupt because they are a fundamental element of its political base.

The economic reforms have opened up a gap between these older and more sluggish large/medium state enterprises on the one side and more modern and dynamic non-state enterprises on the other (the latter including collective and private enterprises and joint ventures with foreign capital, particularly but not exclusively in the Special Economic Zones). This emerging industrial 'dualism' raises our second major issue, the diversification of industrial ownership. While the state sector's share of gross industrial output in 1978 was 78 per cent, the remaining 22 per cent produced by collective enterprises, by 1990 the picture had changed substantially. The state sector's share had dropped to 54.6 per cent and the collective sector (35.6 per cent) had been joined by private enterprise (5.4 per cent) and 'other ownership', including joint ventures (4.4 per cent) (*SSB* 1991: p. 353). Moreover, the secular growth trend of the non-state sector was far faster: the average annual growth rate of collective industry was 18.2 per cent between 1979 and 1990, outpacing the state sector's rate of 7.7 per cent (*SSB* 1991: p. 357). Particularly impressive was the surge in rural small-scale industry which increased at a phenomenal rate in the 1980s. By the mid and late 1980s, there were visible signs of intensifying conflict between the two sectors: state enterprises complaining that collective and other enterprises were poaching their markets or competing for scarce materials and energy; collective enterprises complaining that state enterprises were receiving priority in the allocation of finance and raw materials. Economic dualism was being translated into political conflict.

One should be careful not to draw too decisive a line between 'state' and 'non-state' sectors, since much of the collective sector is subject to direct or indirect state control. The differences are: first, that the collective sector is connected with local governments and thus its growing strength contributes to the gradual shift in the balance of power between centre and localities in favour of the latter; second, relations between state and enterprise are looser in the collective/private sectors, particularly in the case of private and joint Chinese-foreign enterprises which enjoy greater autonomy. This said, however, the shift in the sectoral balance within industry does have important political implications since it involves a gradual redistribution of power over industry away from the state in general and the centre in particular.

It is not surprising, therefore, to see the issue reflected in policy differences within the CCP leadership. More conservative leaders such as Li Peng (and the post-4 June leadership in general) have been concerned about the erosion of the dominance of state industry (particularly the large/medium firms) and have been unsympathetic to the political and economic claims of the collective sector, particularly rural industry. For example, they criticised the latter for developing too fast in an irrational manner which put intolerable strain on supplies of basic raw materials, energy and transport. Reformers like Zhao Ziyang, on the other hand, have been sympathetic to this 'second economy', welcoming it as evidence of the effectiveness of reform policies and arguing that it could set a good example for less dynamic state enterprises. This disagreement has been reflected in regional development policy: conservative leaders have been more concerned with those areas in the North East, centre and West of the country which had a concentration of large state enterprises; reformers such as Zhao Ziyang have explicitly favoured the coastal provinces in which the second sector was developing most rapidly (Yang 1990). Conversations with Chinese reformers, both in China and abroad, reveal a sensitivity to the political implications of the shifting balance of economic power between the first and second economies. One enterprise manager, in a conversation with the author in Beijing in 1987, likened the political relationship between the sectors (particularly between urban state industry and rural non-state industry) to Mao Zedong's theory of revolutionary victory by way of 'the countryside surrounding the city'. Indeed, the non-state sector does have the potential ability to 'crowd out' the state sector through superior productivity, forcing the latter to reform itself or face extinction. This strengthens the hand of reformist leaders and shifts the balance of industrial power in their favour.

Reforming Industrial Administration: Relations between State and Enterprises

In this section we shall be asking questions about the politics of industrial reform at the macro level, specifically the question of changing relationships between state organs and state enterprises. The bedrock principle of introducing market mechanisms into industry was to expand the autonomy of the industrial enterprise.

Ultimately it was to behave as an economic actor making its own decisions in the light of market signals within a framework of economic law and current government policy. While this autonomy involved increasing power over a wide range of economic decisions, I shall concentrate on one issue – financial relations between state and enterprise – to reveal some of the political dynamics of industrial reform at the macro level. Specifically, I shall concentrate on issues of *fiscal* reform: on the one hand, claims by the state as a whole and by its constituent parts on the net revenue of enterprises; on the other hand, claims by the enterprise on part of its own revenue and access to the budgetary and 'extra-budgetary' fiscal resources of the state. The central thrust of reform was to rectify a situation in which enterprise finances were controlled by state agencies which supplied expenditures and siphoned off net revenue, so as to allow enterprises to enjoy greater control over financial resources and display greater responsibility over their use. There was also an intention to put state-enterprise financial relations on a more regularised, depersonalised, 'hands-off' basis since the old system of financial relations involved a constant process of bargaining between state officials and enterprise managers over the levels of financial resources flowing into and out of the enterprise. These are economic issues in the sense that reformers have been seeking to change financial relations in ways which will enhance the autonomy and efficiency of industrial enterprises; these are political issues in the sense that readjustments in financial relations embody a potentially radical redistribution of power between state and industry, and thus engender conflicts of interest between key political actors in the process of reform. In this area of industrial reform policy, one can discern three major sets of institutional actors whose interests are engaged throughout – (central and local) state financial planners and fiscal authorities, state agencies of industrial planning and administration (the 'industrial departments') and the enterprises themselves. Ideally, if the industrial reforms were to be successful, they would affect the position and interest of those three sets of actors in different ways: first, *maintaining* the power of the state to generate revenue and regulate the financial system (though there will be potential clashes of interest between central and local levels of the state); second, *reducing* the power of industrial departments; and, third, *expanding* the power and autonomy of the enterprises.

The first phase of reforming industrial finance, from 1978 to 1983, saw the gradual introduction of a system of *profit-retention* whereby an enterprise could retain a certain proportion of its net revenue for discretionary spending on productive investment, social welfare and wage bonuses, subject to certain official guidelines. In theory, it was hoped that profit-retention would be both economically productive (by granting more financial initiative to the enterprise and reducing the practice of financial bargaining between enterprise managers and state officials) and politically acceptable (the fiscal authorities would accept it because the level of state revenue could be maintained or increase, the industrial departments would tolerate it since it did not represent a serious inroad on their power over enterprises, and enterprise managers would be happy with their enhanced financial power, so the interests of all sides would be served).

However, the profit retention system developed certain problems in practice. Economically, enterprise managers tended to pursue profit-seeking to the exclusion of other economic goals in order to maximise their retained profits; they also often used their discretionary funds unproductively (for example, on bonuses unrelated to productivity). But profit-retention also ran into political trouble. On the one side, enterprises gained considerably from the reform. There was a dramatic increase in their discretionary funds; overall, the state transferred about 28 billion *yuan* to enterprises in retained profits from 1979 to 1981. Though this could be seen as proof of a successful policy, it posed potentially serious problems for the state. First, though total enterprise profits and retained profits had increased, the state's 'take' had decreased, contributing to an emerging fiscal crisis visible in accelerating budget deficits in 1979 and 1980 and a rapid decline in the proportion of state fiscal revenue to national income (which dropped from 37.2 per cent in 1978 to 25.8 per cent in 1981 (*SSB 1989*: p. 47). Second, rather than putting relations between enterprises and their superior industrial departments on a different footing, the previous tradition of financial 'politicking' between managers and officials did not change since most forms of profit-retention still involved bargaining over the amount and uses of the retained funds. There were official regulations to define the ways in which enterprise funds could be spent and industrial departments often retained the power, if not the right, to veto each item of discretionary spending by enterprise managers. Thus, not only did industrial departments not significantly slacken their grip over 'their' enterprises, but they took the opportunity offered by the profit-retention system to siphon off more financial resources for their own use. The overall result was a dispersion of central control over financial resources, as 'extra-budgetary funds' accumulated in both the enterprises and their supervisory departments, reducing the state's ability to implement macro-economic policy. This situation caused great concern during 1979 and 1980 as the economy began to overheat, expenditures on capital investment ran out of control and the rate of inflation increased substantially. From then on, the centre's search for new policies to regulate financial relations between state and enterprise were guided by two basic political considerations: first, the desire to maintain or expand the level of budgetary revenues (which we may call the 'revenue imperative') and, second, the desire to maintain control over the financial system as a whole (which we may call the 'control imperative'). These are distinct from the 'efficiency imperative' which is the underlying economic motive of the reforms.

It was the efficiency imperative (and the economic deficiencies of the profit-retention system) which led the reformers to push changes in industrial finance still further when some semblance of macro-economic equilibrium had been restored. A second, more radical stage of reform, '(changing) tax for profit' (*ligaishui*), was introduced politically by Zhao Ziyang and intellectually by the economist Ma Hong, then a vice-president of the Chinese Academy of Social Sciences and head of its Institute of Industrial Economics. After earlier experiments, the new system was adopted officially in April 1983 when the Ministry of Finance issued 'Methods for Carrying Out the Substitution of Profits for Taxes in State Enterprises'.[5] This was to be introduced in two phases: an initial transitional period in which enterprise profits were to be subject to a 55 per cent tax, the remainder to be divided between the state and enterprises in the light of the latter's specific conditions and according to a variety of formulae; and a more mature, second phase in which the enterprise would pay a progressive income tax on all its profits. In terms of increasing the economic autonomy of enterprises, 'tax for profit' was seen as a great improvement on profit-retention: it would normalise financial relations between state and enterprise in a 'hands-off' way by creating a standardised regulatory framework (in the form of differential tax-rates), thereby removing the previous annual 'politicking' between state agencies and enterprises over rates of profit-retention and reducing the intermediary powers of the industrial departments in the process.

However, 'tax for profit' promised to meet the requirements of the control and revenue as well as the efficiency imperatives. The use of across the board taxes would, it was hoped, create a stable regulatory environment for the economy which would limit any tendencies towards macro-economic disequilibrium. Moreover, as Bachman (1987: p. 135) points out, since 'tax for profit' meant that local governments would no longer continue to receive profits from locally-owned enterprises but would only receive a relatively small share of tax revenues, it involved a partial recentralisation of fiscal power from localities to the centre. From a revenue point of view, moreover, it was hoped that this tax-based system would guarantee a steady and acceptably high flow of budgetary income for the state while still allowing enterprise managers to enjoy greater financial autonomy. The Ministry of Finance was at pains to ensure that the new industrial tax system was designed in such a way that, from annual increments in enterprise profits, 'the state should take the largest share, while the enterprise and the individual (i.e. workers) can only take the middle and the smallest share respectively'.[6] In overall political terms, therefore, 'tax for profit' appeared to offer benefits to both the central government (including both economic planners and financial controllers) and the enterprise, but carried a potential threat, at least in its second stage, to local governments and industrial departments, opening up the potential for an implicit political alliance between the latter.

The second stage of 'tax for profit', which would have achieved a key reform objective by allowing enterprises to retain all their after-tax profits and become fully responsible for their own profit and loss, was originally planned to begin in late 1984.[7] However, the transition between stage one and two made heavy weather during 1985–6 and was finally abandoned in the spring of 1987 when it was announced that financial relations between state and enterprise would henceforth be organised according to a 'contract responsibility system' (CRS). Though this took a variety of forms, its basic elements were as follows: the enterprise was to hand over a certain amount of taxes to the state each year; each year the enterprise also signed a profit contract with the state (which could include an agreed target for either profits or losses); the terms of specific contracts would depend on the specific conditions of the individual enterprise, both internal and external; and if the target were exceeded, the enterprise could retain a share of its extra profits or should reimburse a share of its extra losses.[8]

From the point of view of the industrial reform process, this was a regressive step. It marked both the failure of the attempt to introduce the second stage of 'changing taxes for profits' and a partial return to the spirit of profit-retention. Instead of introducing a universal standard (tax-rates) which would help to disengage the enterprise from its bureaucratic superiors, it perpetuated the previous bilateral, 'hands-on' type of relationship which left considerable discretionary powers over the enterprises in the hands of state industrial and financial departments, with the result that the fortunes of the enterprise still depended on its ability to bargain with its superiors and play the old cat-and-mouse game that masqueraded as 'industrial planning'. This policy reversal was of concern to many reformers,[9] but in the difficult context of the mid-1980s, reform leaders, including Zhao Ziyang himself, were apparently willing to accept the CRS as a temporary expedient.[10]

Why did this policy reversal come about? Again, it seems to have been the result of a complex interplay of economic and political factors. From the point of view of the efficiency imperative, there were criticisms of 'tax for profit', for example on the grounds that it had the effect of 'whipping the fast ox' by penalising profitable enterprises through an overly progressive tax system which meant that the more an enterprise earned, the less it could retain. Moreover, the macro-economic problems which accelerated in the mid-1980s made this kind of reform at the enterprise level problematic, since it threatened to undermine central control over the financial system. Other aspects of the reform programme were also lagging. The lack of a comprehensive price reform, for example, meant that the profitability of enterprises failed to reflect their economic performance and the resulting differentials still had to be evened out by means of a 'regulation tax' negotiated enterprise by enterprise. The lack of managerial and labour reforms within the enterprise meant that the enterprise's own funds were still being spent unproductively on ill-considered investment projects or welfare and bonus benefits to appease workforces worried about the effects of inflation on their real wages.

Intertwined with these economic problems were certain political problems which served to impede the reform of industrial finance. We can discuss these in terms of the three tiers of politics identified earlier: leadership, institutions and social groups. At the leadership level, consensus was beginning to break down. On the one hand, reformist leaders were sponsoring a series of more radical changes in industry. The proposed introduction of a 'factory director responsibility system' threatened the power of the Party within the enterprise. There was growing pressure in favour of a law to provide for the bankruptcy of state enterprises.[11] There were radical proposals to reform the ownership of state enterprises along the lines of some kind of shareholding system;[12] and there were indications that plans were afoot to establish *direct* relations between state co-ordinating agencies (such as the SPC and the SEC) and enterprises, thereby cutting out administrative 'middle-men', such as the industrial departments. On the other hand, more conservative figures were seeking to slow the pace of reform. The macro-economic problems of the time strengthened the hand of those, such as Chen Yun, who were concerned to maintain strong central control over the economy and were worried about the 'anarchic' potential of policies which granted too much financial autonomy to enterprises.

These conservative forces were supported by powerful institutional interests. At the centre, though the Ministry of Finance had been disappointed by the results of 'tax for profit', there was a steady decline in both profits and budgetary revenue from enterprises during 1985–6 (Zhang Yonggang 1990: p. 321). Moreover, there was substantial leakage of potential tax revenues into the extra-budgetary funds of local governments and individual departments, and through widespread tax evasion and avoidance (the apparatus of tax assessment and collection was relatively weak as yet). Advocates of the CRS sought the Ministry's support by arguing that in the past 'the money submitted by enterprises to the state was large yet unstable' and argued that the CRS would help to stabilise revenue flows.[13] The introduction of the CRS was also apparently favoured by the State Economic Commission which, Takahara argues, 'articulated the interests of production-oriented bureaucracies'[14] and was concerned that the chain of command necessary to implement planning objectives was being weakened by financial decentralisation.

Lower institutional levels, however, also had a strong vested interest in the reversion to a contract system. Local governments were also suffering from a drop in revenues which they linked with the introduction of 'tax for profit' and several (notably Guangdong, Jilin, Tianjin and Beijing) lobbied strongly for a change in policy.[15] The industrial departments also seem to have been both major proponents and major beneficiaries of the CRS. 'Tax for profit' threatened to remove much of their financial power by redirecting financial flows from the enterprises directly to state fiscal agencies rather than through them.[16] Indeed, some of the major 'models' for the CRS were powerful branch departments such as the Ministry of Metallurgy and the Ministry of Railways. For the industrial branch departments, this was a considerable political victory.

The conservative influence of these institutional interests was not sufficiently counterbalanced by pressures for change 'from below', from the enterprises which were intended to be the main beneficiaries of industrial reform. If this had been forthcoming, a winning coalition could have been forged between reformist leaders at the 'top' and enterprise managers at the 'bottom', comparable to that which gave impetus to the first wave of agricultural reforms. Most industrial managers in the mid-1980s owed their jobs to their bureaucratic superiors and had built up personal connections with them over the years. Furthermore, in the partly-reformed economy of the mid-1980s, managers faced serious economic problems which required the support of their superiors (Zhang and Zhang 1987). Industrial departments were useful not only in bailing 'their' enterprises out of financial trouble, but also in procuring raw materials and energy supplies and finding outlets for products. Moreover, many managers were not eager to be buffeted by the winds of market pressure, which promised a more stressful and potentially disastrous future. To a considerable extent, also, this sentiment was shared by members of their workforce, for whom the new bankruptcy law was a Sword of Damocles which threatened redundancy. There were indeed managers in tune with the reforms and central reformers encouraged them both to innovate at the plant level and to come together to voice their opinions. This led to a battle royal, particularly visible in the middle of 1986, when reformist managers were attacked from within and above the enterprise; a good number 'fell off their horse' in the face of 'very great resistance' and were dismissed or otherwise victimised, in spite of expressions of support from reform leaders and journals at the centre and in some provinces (such as Guangdong).[17]

Given increasing political deadlock and conflict at the centre, this political struggle over reforming industrial finance was an unequal one. The conservative coalition, which included central and local leaders, industrial departments, many enterprise managers and a significant proportion of the state workforce, won out on this occasion and brought about a policy reversion from 'tax for profit' to the 'contract responsibility system'. The forces of reform within state industry were increasing, particularly as managerial authority in the enterprise was strengthened by the introduction of the factory director responsibility system, as a more 'progressive' breed of manager was trained (called 'enterprisers', *qiyejia*), and as this new stratum increasingly began to organise themselves to exert pressure on policy-makers. However, in the mid-1980s, they were still politically weak in relation to the conservative institutional forces embedded in the previous system of industrial administration which was still largely intact.

Industrial Reform at the Enterprise Level

Our next case, attempted reform in the state labour system, enters the internal micro-political world of the enterprise to see how that has shaped the nature and impact of reform policies towards industrial labour.

Enterprise micro-politics revolves around two sets of relationships between key groups in the enterprise. First is the relationship between professional/specialised managers and Party officials. Although the initial system of enterprise management adopted in the mid-1950s, 'one man management', vested prime responsibility in the hands of the factory director, on the eve of reform in the late 1970s, the enterprise Party secretary was usually the dominant presence. The economist Ma Hong cites a phrase popular among workers to describe this situation: 'Under unified leadership the Party secretary is king, he has the final word on everything.'[18] This was a reflection at the plant level of the wider principle of the Party's 'unified leadership' over all economic institutions. Post-Mao reformers have sought to reduce the power of enterprise Party secretaries by introducing a 'factory director responsibility system' which vests supreme managerial authority in the hands of professionals and largely disengages the Party committee from economic decision-making within the enterprise, relegating it to some nebulous 'supervisory' role. The attempt to introduce this system in the mid-1980s led to virtual 'civil war' in many enterprises and in the aftermath of the 4 June Incident in 1989, the new CCP leadership took steps to strengthen the Party's position within the enterprise. The micro-politics of this process have been analysed in detail elsewhere so they will not be our main concern here (Chamberlain 1987; Chevrier 1990; Waldera 1989).

Second, there is the relationship between enterprise management (whether vested in professional managers or Party officials) and the workforce. In the pre-reform era, managers and workforce had succeeded in forging a *modus vivendi*, based on an implicit 'social contract' which traded workforce compliance with management objectives in return for certain material benefits and job security.[19] The post-Mao labour reforms threatened to disrupt this arrangement and their political consequences will be the object of our inquiry here.

During the 1980s, as we have seen, China's economic reformers have attempted to improve labour productivity in state industry by encouraging the emergence of a labour market and introducing more flexible terms of employment for enterprise workers and staff on the state payroll. At the macro (national) and meso (local/branch department) levels, this has involved measures to dismantle the previous system of administrative controls over industrial labour allocation. At the micro (enterprise) level, it has meant changes in the employment status of workers in state industrial enterprises which aim to weaken or abolish the previous system of *de facto* job tenure (the 'iron rice-bowl' for workers and 'iron armchair' for cadres) by employing staff and workers on a contract basis; also efforts to encourage employees to move between enterprises and give personnel managers greater powers to hire, fire and discipline their workforce.

As we shall see in the next chapter, the politics of labour reform are particularly sensitive since they involve fundamental ideological principles rooted in Marxist definitions of what constitutes the essential differences between a 'capitalist' and a 'socialist' mode of production. Labour reform has also challenged the traditional state socialist commitment to full employment and job security and has raised basic questions about the role of labour in a socialist economy. After all, the tepid term 'labour' refers to the industrial working class which, in theory at least, is the political bedrock of Chinese communism; it is in their interests and on their behalf that the CCP claims to exercise state power. The labour reforms embody changes in the social, economic and political status of Chinese industrial workers and, in particular, in the relationship between them and their managerial superiors. It is not surprising, therefore, that they encountered a good deal of scepticism and resistance.

Labour reforms have been the subject of acute disagreement and heated debate ever since their inception. Though much of this debate has remained hidden and the reform position has ruled the public media, the range of views has been wide, from those who want little or no change to radical reformers who lionise the alleged virtues of an unfettered labour market and the economic benefits of unemployment (for a review of the different positions, see White 1998a: pp. 172–7). Though the views of diehard opponents (such as some local labour bureaux officials and state workers) have been largely voiced behind the scenes, they have surfaced in the media sufficiently for one to gauge the force of their dissent. While central Party leaders have apparently agreed on the need for reform in the state labour system, they have disagreed over its pace and extent. Moreover, regardless of these disagreements, they have all had to face conflicting political priorities, that of achieving higher labour productivity on the one hand and of minimising urban unemployment on the other.

The issue of unemployment has been seized upon by opponents of thoroughgoing labour reform who have argued that full employment and job security are fundamental characteristics of 'socialism' and must be maintained, even if there are costs in terms of economic efficiency. The (unidentified) author of one rare public critique of the reform position, printed in a newspaper in Guangzhou, expressed the wish 'to cry out for the 'iron rice-bowl system' with a heavy heart' since 'many of our revolutionary comrades struggled all their lives so that the people of the whole country could each have an "iron rice-bowl"' (Yi Duming 1986). The author probably spoke for many, particularly Party/government cadres and state industrial workers, when he argued that job security was part of the 'superiority of socialism', and attempts to undermine it would lead to a system of capitalist wage-labour.

Similarly, the notion, espoused by certain reform economists, that unemployment is not such a bad thing since it promotes labour mobility and concentrates the minds of workers who are afraid of becoming redundant, has been vehemently contested throughout the reform era.[20] Critics also warned that labour reforms would be politically divisive and socially harmful: for example, they could lead to tensions and conflict between workers with secure and insecure jobs or between the employed and the unemployed; or they could lead to large-scale, open unemployment which could cause juvenile delinquency and a general decline in moral standards.[21]

Critics have also been concerned about the effects of labour reform on social relations of production within the enterprise. One can detect three mutually reinforcing themes here. First, there is a 'neo-traditional' attitude which views the firm as a family, inspiring quasi-kinship relations of obligation, loyalty and solidarity. From this viewpoint, changes which rupture this fabric by putting it on a more commercial or 'scientific management' basis would have both social and economic costs (Cheng 1986). Second, there is a recognition that lifelong job security appears to have been one reason behind the success of larger Japanese enterprises; if this was not incompatible with capitalism, why should it not be compatible with socialism? Third, there is a more directly political concern that a stable workforce is necessary to enable workers to exercise their rights within the enterprise in relation to management. For example, in the view of one noted industrial economist, Jiang Yiwei, former director of the CASS Institute of Industrial Economics, adoption of the labour contract system to counter the 'iron rice-bowl' would intensify an already significant shift of power within the enterprises in favour of managers, with the consequence that workers would become 'hired labourers' rather than 'masters' of the enterprise (Jiang 1985). This kind of view is reflected in statements by conservative post-4 June leaders, such Jiang Zemin and Li Peng, but it appears to be motivated less by support for workers' power within the enterprise, and more by a desire to placate workers in the wake of a political upheaval which could have been far more threatening if more industrial workers had participated in it. But leaders like Li Peng are cautious not to turn the balance too far in the favour of workers since they too are concerned about managerial efficiency within the enterprise.[22]

These views do not necessarily signify total opposition to reform policies – they often amount to no more than a counsel of caution and a call for political sensitivity in the implementation of policy. But some critics do suggest that the efficiency goals of the reformers can in fact be met by other means: by tightening labour discipline within the enterprise, introducing more effective wage and job-responsibility systems, improving training facilities, purchasing more advanced technology, and seeking better relations between managers and workers. However, these are not merely intellectual disagreements over the economic wisdom of labour reforms; they also reflect deeper political and economic interests which the latter threaten. To identify these interests, we need to look at the process of implementing labour system reforms at the enterprise level.

Viewing the experience of the 1980s as a whole, it is clear that labour reforms ran into a lot of trouble and did not get very far. In particular, attempts to break the 'iron rice-bowl' by putting state workers on fixed- (and relatively short-) term contracts made very slow headway. Although the policy was launched as early as 1982, only 8 per cent of the state industrial workforce were on contracts by mid-1988. While economists estimated that 15 to 20 million state workers were superfluous and thus candidates for retrenchment, very few were in fact being laid off. In the North-Eastern industrial city of Harbin, for example, a report in mid-1988 estimated that, though there were an estimated 100 000 under-employed and unqualified workers in the city, only ten had been dismissed during 1987.[23] Indeed the problem of 'unemployment on the job' seemed to become worse rather than better. There were shocking reports of workers playing cards and sleeping on the job because they had nothing to do. In one bizarre case, a chemical fertiliser factory in Shaanxi allegedly opened twenty doors to the plant and assigned 80 workers as door-keepers to keep redundant workers on the payroll. Unofficial estimates reckoned that working hours in many state factories were only 4–6 per day and, in the Shijiazhuang No. 1 Plastics Plant in Hebei, they were working only two and a half hours a day when the plant was working at full capacity.[24] Even the unimpressive statistics about the number of contract workers were misleading: although the length of contract preferred by the reformers was three to five years, many contracts were 'long-term' or even 'lifelong', not to mention 'false contracts' which no-one bothered to enforce.

How do we account for this signal lack of success? One important reason is that policy-makers themselves were afraid to grasp the political nettle and impose the new contracts on *all* state employees; they did not apply to enterprise cadres, nor to existing 'fixed' workers, only to new workers. Even in this watered down form, the contract system was highly unpopular. It ran into resistance from both the new contract workers themselves (who thought they were getting the short end of the stick just because they had come into employment too late and resented workers and cadres with 'iron' jobs); and from 'fixed' (i.e. tenured) workers who feared that the new policy was the thin end of the wedge and that they would be next. Nor were many managers enthusiastic about a reform which they regarded as managerially disruptive and administratively burdensome. They were reluctant to incur the resentment (and in some cases even physical retaliation) of laid-off workers, more general unease amongst other workers and the possibility of intervention by the enterprise trade union which found in the contract system a convenient opportunity to flex its muscles in a showdown with management.

While the labour contracts policy made little headway overall, however, its impact was uneven and it is important to understand why reforms were more successful in some areas than others. There are two important reasons. First, labour reform benefited from a strong political impetus given by reformist local leaders in some areas (such as Qingdao in Shandong province and Shenyang in Liaoning province) and their skill in managing the administrative complexities involved in introducing labour contracts. This also provided essential complementary measures, such as local labour exchanges, retraining and a dole for the temporarily unemployed. Because the repercussions of the policy were thought through in these cities and because they built certain 'cushions' into policy implementation, the process went more smoothly and local resistance was reduced. However, this could not be said of the national level where central policy-makers were aware of the potential opposition and decided to try to inject the policy in small doses rather than tackle the issue frontally. Thus the policy lacked political urgency and officials down the line of command could afford to ignore it or apply it in marginal ways. A second reason for the differential impact of labour reform was the nature of the local economic climate. If the local economy was expanding rapidly and there were plenty of attractive job opportunities in the private, collective or joint-venture sectors (or in other state enterprises), then state workers were more than willing to change jobs, policy or no policy. In fact, the problem facing enterprise managers in such areas was that of *keeping* rather than getting rid of workers. The most clear example was Guangzhou where, until 1988 at least, the non-state sectors of the economy were booming. As a reporter from the industrial newspaper *Workers' Daily* put it in late 1988, 'people in Guangzhou think the iron rice-bowl has no superiority at all and are trying their best to get rid of it'. He reported that some workers were deliberately violating enterprise discipline to get themselves sacked, while the city government was trying vainly to stem the outflow by decreeing that staff and workers who left their enterprise without getting a reference could not be re-employed in that district for a year.[25] Since the employment situation took a turn for the worse in 1989, some of these workers may have regretted leaving their 'iron rice-bowls'.

To a large extent, these two factors – a reformist local leadership and a booming local economy – appear to have coincided in a number of areas. In such cases, the politics of industrial reform was similar to the early stages of agricultural reform when there was an alliance between a dynamic reform leadership from above and an active support constituency from below (workers seeking better jobs in a favourable labour market), which allowed opposition 'in the middle' to be outflanked, whether this be from local labour officials or harassed enterprise managers. Looking at the nation as a whole, however, this was far from the norm; the disposition of political forces pro and con labour reform was far less favourable to reform. Even though central leaders sponsored the reform and relevant agencies, notably the Ministry of Labour or its equivalent, communicated the reform impulse downwards, there was simply too little political muscle behind the policy and too much obstruction below.

There is considerable evidence that a good deal of this resistance to labour reform came from officials in local labour bureaux (White 1988b). They were clearly reluctant to devolve anything but relatively minor powers to the enterprises. The stated principle of labour reform, indeed, proclaimed by both the Ministry of Labour and local bureaux, was 'to control the big things and decentralise the small'. Without sufficient countervailing power to the contrary, this is what they did. Once such a complex institutional network has been established and consolidated over several decades, it is difficult to shift it. However, the reasons for the demise of labour reform policies are more complex than any simple notion of 'bureaucratic vested interests' would allow. There was also scepticism and opposition within state enterprises themselves. Although managers resented the often unreasonable impositions of local labour bureaux, they were reluctant to push the issue of reform for danger of losing their best workers or disrupting hard-won under-standings. The 'social contract' between managers and workforce, whereby workers exchanged their co-operation for management guarantees of security and welfare, is a durable phenomenon and acts as a stumbling-block against labour reform.

This 'social contract' at the enterprise level underpins a broader 'social contract' at the macro-political level, which is also difficult to break. This is the Party's official commitment to maintain full employment which has yet to be officially repudiated in any decisive way. This commitment has created over the past two-and-a-half decades a kind of institutionalised patron–client relationship between the Chinese state and its industrial workers, mirroring a similar relationship between managers and workers in each enterprise. The state takes on the role of provider and workers come to depend on the state and expect its bounty. There is thus a mass constituency to retain state controls over, and guarantees to, labour, which coincides with and reinforces the institutional interests of state labour agencies.

While such a commitment to full employment is hard to honour even at the best of times, so much harder is it when the burden of surplus labour increases, as at the end of the 1980s when austerity policies forced many non-state enterprises to close and pressure built up in the big cities due to a mounting influx of job-seekers from the countryside and poor regions. State labour authorities are thus subject to two conflicting sets of political pressures: on the one hand, from reform leaders and their supporters at lower levels who are pursuing the elusive goal of greater labour productivity, the likely result of which is to turf under-employed employees out of state enterprises, thus worsening the unemployment situation; on the other hand, they are subject to political pressure from all sides to find a job for anyone who wants one. Since official labour policy, state labour agencies and the enterprises themselves all embody this basic contradiction, it is hardly surprising that progress towards significant reform in the state labour system has been slow and has remained so until 1992 when reformers gathered their forces to grasp the nettle yet again.

Conclusion: The Political Deadlock in Industrial Reform

Our two case studies of policy reform should have demonstrated the major political differences between reforming the countryside and reforming the cities. The policy process, and the political process which pervades it, is far more complex in the urban-industrial sector. This partly reflects the large number of actors involved in each policy arena, each of which must, to varying degrees, be accommodated politically to ensure that reform policies are actually carried out. It partly reflects the technical complexity of policy choices, such that a slight miscalculation or slippage between intent and impact may lead to damaging and unforeseen consequences. It partly reflects the dense interdependence of many areas of policy, which poses immense problems of co-ordinating between the wide range of institutions involved.

In political terms, there are inherent contradictions in both policy-making and policy implementation. Central policy-makers have had to grapple with a basic tension between economic and political goals. In the case of industrial finance, for example, the efficiency imperative which led to financial decentralisation was at war with the revenue and control imperatives which were crucial to the political credibility and effectiveness of the reform leadership. In the case of labour reform, the leadership were pushed in two opposing directions: towards the desire for greater labour productivity on the one side which would, in the short and medium term at least, have increased unemployment, and towards their commitment to full employment on the other side.

But the roots of the clash between economic and political rationality lie deeper, in the matrix of political forces which surround the process of policy reform. Unlike the rural context, CCP reform leaders have found it very difficult to build political coalitions to underpin their policies in the industrial context and these difficulties increased as the policies became more radical. For example, the attempt to introduce 'tax for profit' posed a major threat to the interests, indeed the very survival, of the industrial departments and they resisted in powerful ways, often with the support of their subordinates in state enterprises. This led to a policy compromise, the 'contract responsibility system' which was a step backwards in terms of the logic of economic reform, but had the political virtue of offering something to everybody. In the case of the labour contract system, opposition was even more generalised and vehement, including not only state labour agencies but also many industrial managers and a large section of the state industrial workforce. In this case, the centre had to settle for a much watered-down policy and a piecemeal approach to implementing it.

The political message here is that the balance of forces in the urban/industrial (with some regional exceptions) sector is stacked against thoroughgoing economic reform. This is one major reason why the reforms became deadlocked in the mid–late 1980s, producing an economic system which in some ways combined the worst of both the old world of central planning and the new world of the market. The disposition of political forces, at all levels, was such that it was difficult to move either forwards or backwards. The question is: how can this deadlock in urban/industrial reform be broken? If a radical change in the political system is not forth-coming, the longer-term political answer lies perhaps not within the state sector itself, but in the relationship between the state and non-state sector. We saw, for example, how dynamic growth in the non-state sector in Guangdong province and Guangzhou city eroded the 'iron rice-bowl' in state enterprises at a time when the policy was foundering elsewhere. This is but one, fairly radical, reflection of an emerging dualism in the Chinese economy between a basically unreconstructed state sector (particularly the older and larger firms) and a more dynamic and competitive semi or non-state sector which is both the product of the economic reforms and the potential basis for their future progress. To the extent that the balance of economic power between these two sectors shifts in favour of the latter, then the balance of power shifts inexorably in favour of the proponents of economic reform. This sectoral dualism also has important implications for two other balances of power, between centre and localities and between more advanced/open provinces and more backward/closed provinces. To the extent that the first sector largely accrues to the central government and the second sector to the localities, the power of the latter is strengthened in relation to the centre; to the extent that the latter sector is concentrated in the more advanced and open coastal provinces, such as Jiangsu, Zhejiang, Fujian and Guangdong, then their hand is strengthened not only in relations with the centre but also with less fortunate provinces. The future of the industrial reforms depends heavily on movements in these basic economic and political balances and it is the thesis of this chapter, and indeed this book, that the underlying movement is in the direction of further market-oriented reform, regardless of the political complexion of the regime in Beijing.

5

Economic Reform and Ideological Decay: The Decline of Ideocracy

'You can't teach an old dogma new tricks.'—Dorothy Parker

The overriding political rationale for economic reform was the desire to rebuild the power and authority of the Communist regime. This could be achieved in part by improvements in popular welfare arising from a successful programme of economic reform. But a major shift in political ideas and institutions was also needed, not only because these had fallen into disrepute and disrepair over the previous decade, but also because they had to be brought into line with the radically different economic system which was the ultimate objective of economic reforms. In trying to re-establish their political hegemony, the CCP leadership faced two major tasks: first, to redefine the official *political Ideology* in such a way that it became an effective force for legitimating the CCP regime in the context of the 'socialist commodity economy'; and, second, to re-establish the *Party* as a coherent and credible political nucleus of the nation in the new economic environment. I shall be discussing these two aspects of political change in this and the next chapters.

In the event, the decade of economic reform proved disastrous for both these objectives. This conclusion is not the mere result of empirical hindsight. It was evident from the outset that, even if market reforms were economically successful (as indeed they were), they carried within them certain political dangers and, without a

147

high degree of political will, skill, and vision as yet unwitnessed in the communist world, these dangers might well inflict fatal wounds on the state socialist body politic. Another historical Catch 22 for a communist leadership, it would seem – damned if they don't reform, damned if they do. Let us tackle the question of Ideology first.

The distinctive importance of the official political ideology in state socialist or communist regimes has received a lot of scholarly attention (for the Soviet case, Meyer 1966). The central point is that communist systems, more than other regimes (except other forms of 'totalist' polities such as fascism or religious hierocracy), are ideocratic: they rely on an explicit and systematised Ideology which functions to legitimise the regime, justify the Party's monopoly on power and guide the actions of the political élite. This classic role of Ideology reached a high point of development in Maoist China (Schurmann 1968).

In terms of political behaviour, Ideology ideally operates at three levels: at the cognitive level, it acts as a language (or, as some would prefer, 'discourse'), which defines the central concepts of politics and principles of political action and provides a selective map of the world which charts the believer's way through the reefs and shoals of real-world politics. At the level of values, it provides a set of basic beliefs about what is good or bad, right or wrong. At the pragmatic or instrumental level, it provides a set of principles to guide the action of political leaders and the operation of political institutions. Looking at it a different way, moreover, ideology has two analytical levels, as Franz Schurmann pointed out:[1] a deeper and relatively fixed 'theoretical' substratum (of basic beliefs, values and concepts) and a more contingent and flexible layer of 'operational' ideas and practices which govern the day-to-day world of politics and policy-making.

Chinese political discourse defines political action in terms of different relationships between these two levels: 'redness' or 'dogmatism' are (negative and positive) descriptions of people whose practical behaviour is governed directly by their basic beliefs; conversely, 'opportunism' or 'pragmatism' are (negative and positive) descriptions of people who maintain a flexible relationship between the two. In the post-Mao era, there has been an implicit notion that there is an optimal 'balance' between these two levels which avoids both the Scylla of extremism and the

Charybdis of unbelief. Reformers have attacked the Maoist Ideology of the Cultural Revolution era as dogmatic: they argue that it attempted to impose a distorted view of the world and a set of moral/political values which were socially disruptive and economically damaging; operationally, it was a disastrous guide to politics and economics alike because it encouraged mechanistic applications of theory without regard to their practical feasibility or effects. As the campaign against 'whateverism' in the late 1970s demonstrated, the reform leadership has sought to tip the balance between the theoretical and practical aspects of Ideology in favour of 'pragmatism', thereby allowing themselves room for manoeuvre on the policy front.

Ideological orthodoxy is not confined to the political élite; there is also a massive attempt to spread the main values of the Ideology not merely to Party members but also to the population as a whole (through control of the mass media and educational system). The logic of Leninism presupposes a clear difference between the impact of Ideology on the political élite and the general population, in terms of the degree of internalisation and strength of commitment. This distinction is reflected in the inherent paternalism of élite-mass relations in state-socialist systems. Over the long term, as the 'transition to socialism' proceeds, the ultimate aim would be to incorporate the mass of the population into the ideological world of the political élite. In the meantime, the hope is that there will be a mutually beneficial interaction between élite and mass: on the one side, the political élite is better able to lead because the Ideology provides it with intellectual clarity and moral authority which in turn affects the 'masses' through good example and effective leadership; on the other side, the 'masses' are more willing to accept leadership to the extent that they have been socialised into or otherwise accepted reigning values and they perceive the leadership to be living up to their ideological pretensions. There is an ideally virtuous cycle of élite-mass relations here but, if the relationship gets out of kilter through élite incompetence and corruption on the one side and mass cynicism on the other, a vicious cycle is generated. The fact that the Cultural Revolution had already set this vicious cycle in motion was very much in the minds of the post-Mao leadership and the economic reforms can be seen in their light of their attempt to reverse it.

n decade, official attempts to re-establish the
ology can be divided into two broad phases: an
demolition of the Ideology of the Cultural
and a later process of ideological reconstruction and
adaptation. Party reformers were tackling three basic tasks here: the first was to repudiate the perceived ideological distortions and dogmatic excesses of the Maoist era; second, to revive a perceived 'healthy' ideological heritage from the pre-Maoist era of political 'normality'; third, to adapt the existing ideological framework to the new economic environment of market socialism. Let me outline the argument of this chapter in brief. In tackling the first task, the reformers succeeded in reducing the ideological influence of remnant Maoists, but in doing so they also weakened the political credibility of ideological orthodoxy in general and Marxism–Leninism–Mao Zedong Thought in particular. To the extent that the second task was achieved, it resurrected a traditional kind of Stalinist political thought which had less and less relevance to changing socio-economic realities in China. The third task, which was hampered by conflict among the leadership, led to an increasingly diffuse and diluted framework of ideas which lacked cogency and vision. The net result was ideological decay, a loss of political faith and direction, not merely among the general population, but also among the political élite in the Communist Party.

Ideological Demolition and the Legacy of Mao

In the immediate aftermath of the death of Mao and the arrest of the Gang of Four, the emerging reform leadership under Deng undertook to repudiate the ideological heritage of Maoism to clear the ground for a reformulation of the official Ideology which would legitimise the new leadership and prepare the way for their reform programme. In the late 1970s, this was not merely a repudiation of the radical Maoism of the Cultural Revolution, but also part of the conflict with remaining 'developmental Maoist' leaders symbolised by Party Chairman, Hua Guofeng, which continued until the resignation of Hua as Party Chairman at the CCP's Sixth Plenum (XI) in June 1981. As we saw in Chapter 1, in the period before the crucial Third Plenum (XI) of December 1978, the Hua leadership continued to use certain key Maoist ideological formulae and to continue certain Maoist political practices (notably the rather pathetic attempt to establish a leadership cult round the decidedly uncharismatic Hua) and strategic policy notions (notably Mao's notion of economic development as being accelerated by political campaigns and mass mobilisation). Though 'Mao Zedong Thought' was still championed, however, Hua and his associates were at pains to redefine it in more moderate, flexible terms – the revolutionary Mao of the 1960s and 1970s was downplayed and his more 'sensible' 1956 speech 'On the Ten Major Relationships' now became the key document defining an overall framework of economic policy.

The ideological critique of Maoism emerged gradually at the end of the 1970s. We can detect three strands therein. First, there is a desire to desanctify and secularise Ideology to some degree, in order to correct a situation in which Ideology had become a set of immutable precepts (a kind of 'Marxist superstition'), strictly binding on all, which emanated from an infallible source, the Supreme Leader, and brooked neither opposition nor qualification. This form of dogmatism, it was thought, set the context for the political extremism of the Cultural Revolution, stultified thinking about practical policy and contributed to social and economic stagnation. This sacral style found continued expression in Hua Guofeng's and other residual Maoist leaders' notion of the 'two whatevers'[2] and was the target of a key theoretical attack in May 1978, written by Professor Hu Fuming of the Philosophy Department of Nanjing University, entitled 'Practice is the Sole Criterion for Testing Truth'.[3] This echoed and systematised Deng Xiaoping's call at the Eleventh Party Congress the preceding year for a revival of the Party's style of 'seeking truth from facts', arguing against a dogmatic and deductive approach to analysing concrete problems and advocating greater flexibility in the application of ideological principles to specific issues. This new approach, championed by Deng's supporters among the CCP leadership (and reinforced by Deng's intervention on its behalf at an all-army political work conference in 1978) opened up greater political space for the new leaders to change concrete policies, encourage diversity of thought more generally and, ultimately, to revise key tenets of the Maoist creed. The principles of 'seeking truth from facts' and 'practice as the sole criterion of truth' were buttressed theoretically by selective references to Mao's own emphasis on the importance of 'social practice' and statements by Marx himself in 'Theses on Feuerbach'.[4] This process of 'de-dogmatisation' brought with it a more flexible approach to ideological diversity, in both the Party and society at large; it allowed criticism of intolerance and imposed uniformity and encouraged some degree of open disagreement and 'airing of views', in contrast to Maoist political mobilisation techniques of 'investigation, criticism and struggle'.[5]

The second strand of ideological demolition was the attempt to limit the penetration of Ideology into the everyday lives of the population, fostering a process of depoliticisation or political 'demobilisation'. During the Cultural Revolution decade, under the slogan 'politics in command' (*zhengzhi guashuai*), Ideology had penetrated into every nook and cranny of urban society (the rural sector was less profoundly affected, except intermittently during certain key campaigns). This penetration took the form of pervasive 'ideological and political education' (through small study-groups in workplaces and residential areas, or political study-classes in schools) and comprehensive political control over all means of mass communication. 'Politics in command' embodied an attempt to ensure that the thought and behaviour of ordinary people was ideologically 'correct'. Intellectuals and professionals were under particularly heavy pressure to be 'both red and expert', which meant that their specialised knowledge was to be permeated by and subordinated to the 'proletarian line' of the day. The aim of Deng and his reform allies was to reduce the range of politicisation, expand the space for private life and allow greater autonomy for intellectuals and experts. In practice, this meant less attention to organised political education; less emphasis on political criteria in recruiting and assessing people for specialised training or professional jobs; a decline in the visible manifestations of political Ideology (removal of posters and statues and reducing the political content of the mass media); and, overall, an effort to encourage greater intellectual and cultural freedom under the slogan of 'let a hundred flowers contend'. As we shall see, however, there was considerable disagreement among the new leadership about how far this depoliticisation should be allowed to go.

Thirdly, the post-Mao leadership sought to deny or revise certain tenets of radical Maoism which they felt had pushed China in the wrong direction and precipitated the excesses of the Cultural Revolution. Particularly important was the attack on the radical

Maoist definition of socialist development as a continuation of 'class struggle' under 'the dictatorship of the proletariat'. In their view, this ideological notion had damaged the Party itself by organising vindictive and unjustifiable campaigns against key leaders (including Deng Xiaoping himself). It had also created a general atmosphere of conflict and antagonism (directed, for example, at remnants of the former 'exploiting classes' and their families, or that 'stinking ninth category', the intelligentsia) which had poisoned relations between people and between the Party and the people. Moreover, the notions of 'class struggle as the key link' and 'politics in command' hampered economic development by subordinating economic policy to the requirements of a vacuous and unproductive political struggle.[6]

The reformers tried to reverse these emphases, arguing that 'class struggle', while still visible in society, had already lost most of its political importance. In terms of Marxist ideological categories, this meant that, though 'contradictions' still existed in society, they were largely 'non-antagonistic' ones 'among the people', not 'antagonistic' ones between enemies. The central strategic task for the future was economic development (or 'raising the level of productive forces'), to be reached through the 'four modernisations' and higher levels of efficiency achievable through structural reforms in the system of economic management. While it was admitted that economic development should be subject to political direction, politics could not be allowed 'to brush aside or supersede economics'. Economics was a separate sphere operating according to 'objective laws' and was thus resistant to political manipulation. Politics could only 'command' economics in the much narrower sense that it is political leaders who define the strategic goals of economic development and the policy framework which regulates economic activity. The Maoist conception of economic development as a politicised process of mass mobilisation was thus repudiated. Models which formerly embodied Maoist virtues in the economy, most notably the Daqing (*Tach'ing*) oilfield in industry and the Dazhai (*Tachai*) production brigade in agriculture were ignored or repudiated. The role of specialised expertise was to be given its full due as a central element in the modernisation process, which meant political rehabilitation for the cultural, scientific and technical intelligentsia who had been targets of the Maoist onslaught against 'new bourgeois elements'.

Central elements of Maoist economic theory were also repudiated. Radical antipathy to the market, expressed in terms of Maoist hostility to the operation of the 'law of value' under socialism, was rejected, along with its policy implications such as opposition to 'economic mechanisms' seen as 'bourgeois', such as price policy, interest rates and wage incentives. For example, wage differentials was seen as economically essential and radical attempts to restrict them (as in the last two years of the Cultural Revolution when Zhang Chunqiao and Yao Wenyuan, two of the Gang of Four, had led a campaign to attack the inequalities of 'bourgeois right') were dismissed as irrational 'egalitarianism'. Indeed, in the era of economic reform, 'egalitarianism' was to become a term of political abuse and a consistent target of commentaries on economic policy. Maoist notions of economic 'self-reliance' were also attacked: at local levels, they were held responsible for fostering an introverted cellular economy within communes, counties or provinces, and at the national level because they denied China access to much needed foreign technology and finance and to the benefits of the international division of labour and of comparative advantage in international markets.

This process of ideological repudiation and demolition was politically essential to strengthen the political hand of the reform leadership, but it was also politically costly. While cynicism and apathy were already well advanced among the population by the late 1970s (particularly the youth), the propaganda of the preceding two decades had not been without effect. Members of the élite – political, administrative and managerial – particularly those socialised and recruited during the Cultural Revolution decade, were now being informed that most of what they had been told by the then Party leadership (including the formerly infallible Mao himself), and much of what they still believed, was at best wrong-headed and at worst heinous. Members of the general population (except the intelligentsia who were clear beneficiaries of this new ideological atmosphere) had good cause to wonder why they had been treated like cultivated mushrooms for so long (kept in the dark and covered in (ideological) excrement). At the same time, however, ideas such as 'self-reliance' and 'egalitarianism' had set down broader roots among the population, often because they echoed previous beliefs (such as an egalitarianism with roots in the poor peasantry) or rationalised current interests (of manual as opposed to professional workers). In consequence, efforts to discredit them were not greeted with general approval.

The post-Mao leadership tried to limit the potential political damage of this ideological volte-face by identifying scapegoats (the Gang of Four and Mao's would-be assassin, Marshall Lin Biao). This enabled people to avoid personal responsibility for previous 'mistakes', because, it was acknowledged officially, they had been 'hoodwinked' by a small clique of political careerists who had used the names of Marx, Lenin and Mao for their own sinister purposes. China thus became a nation of political 'victims' with precious few perpetrators. At the same time, however, this convenient demonology dramatised the ways in which official Ideology had been used for over a decade as a tool for political deception and repression, by an allegedly 'correct' leadership at the head of a 'proletarian' party. Why should this not happen again in another form? In their efforts to reject the 'abnormalities' of the past, the reformers had implicitly revealed much of the 'normal' substance of ideological and political control in a traditional state socialist system, thereby undermining themselves as well as their enemies.

The political contradictions inherent in this effort at ideological demolition were also evident in the problem of how to assess the role of Chairman Mao himself, the architect of the previous two 'disastrous' decades. After all, Mao was also the acknowledged leader of the communist revolution in China, hailed for so long as the person who had converted the foreign ideologies of Marx and Lenin (no doubt, alien and incomprehensible figures to most Chinese) into a powerful Chinese political creed. How could the new leadership redefine Mao's heritage without undermining their own legitimacy and avoiding a repetition of Mao's mistakes (for example, by erecting a comparable leadership cult around Deng Xiaoping)? They grasped this nettle at the Sixth Plenum (XI) of the CCP Central Committee in late June 1981, convened at a time when the reform leadership's position had been consolidated, remnant Maoist leaders at the top level had been displaced and the Gang of Four (along with former associates of Lin Biao) had been publicly tried and sentenced (for an account of the trial, see Gardner 1982: pp. 178–83). The Plenum passed a 'Resolution on Certain Questions in the History of our Party since the Founding of the PRC'. This document, which had been through successive drafts since 1980, criticised the late Mao (from 1958 onwards) for his arbitrary leadership style, ideological errors and poor choice of both allies and enemies and, in particular, for his role as initiator and leader of the Cultural Revolution which, the Resolution stated, conformed 'neither to Marxism–Leninism nor to Chinese realities'.[7] While the cause of Mao's mistakes were not clarified precisely, they were partly mitigated by reference to China's historical heritage of 'feudal autocracy', the difficult domestic and international circumstances of the 1960s and the influence of scheming associates on an aging leader . Unspoken was the commonly held belief that Mao's judgement had been seriously impaired by senility and disease in his later years, making him prey to delusions and subordinates.

However, these criticisms were more than counterbalanced by an appraisal of Mao's merits 'as a great proletarian revolutionary' who had played a crucial role in liberating China and establishing the system of political and economic institutions which had survived the ravages of the Cultural Revolution. 'Mao Zedong Thought' was hailed as 'a valuable spiritual asset of our Party', as an expression of the integration of Marxist–Leninist theory with the realities of the Chinese Revolution, which had evolved in the experience of pre-revolutionary struggle before 1949, and of socialist construction up to 1957 (and no further). This attempt to bowdlerise Mao led to rather uncomfortable intellectual contortions; witness the following statement from a leading theorist of political reform, Su Shaozhi (Chang 1988: p. 16):

I think Mao Zedong Thought must be distinguished from the thought of Mao himself. Mao Zedong Thought is a theoretical system that is the crystallisation of the contributions of our entire party, not only Mao himself. Since Mao made such a big contribution, we call it Mao Zedong Thought. Mao Zedong Thought as a correct theoretical system can include only the correct thought. Some of Mao's own thought is correct and some in error, but the wrong part cannot be included in Mao Zedong Thought.

It was in this highly unconvincingly deodorised form that Mao's ideological heritage was confirmed as a central plank of the composite official Ideology of the new era – Marxism–Leninism and Mao Zedong Thought.

The ambiguity and less-than-wholeheartedness of the Sixth Plenum document reflected the serious political dilemma facing the new leadership. They could not completely reject the heritage of Mao since to do so would be to reject much of the political rationale of the Chinese Revolution itself – its creation, the People's Republic of China, and its supreme institution, the Chinese Communist Party. Moreover, the Resolution's balanced verdict on Mao reflected disagreement within the leadership (and the Party at large) about his political merits and contribution to China, disagreements which were mirrored among the general population where Mao's name was still respected, particularly among sections of the peasantry who identified him with their liberation from the landlords. The Resolution thus represents a political compromise and, as such, its impact was blunted from the outset. Mao Zedong Thought emerged as a contrived and incoherent set of ideas cobbled together for political convenience, which did not reflect the past adequately and was to become an increasing impediment to coming to terms with the future. However malleable Mao might be, it was well nigh impossible to portray him as a market-oriented economic reformer.

Ideological Reconstruction and Adaptation

The leadership's strategy for reconstructing the official Ideology was ambiguous. This partly reflected their internal disagreements; it also reflected the contradiction at the heart of 'market Stalinism', namely the desire to bring about radical changes in economic theory and practice, while adhering to a basically unchanged conception of the theory and practice of politics. While the political doctrine which emerged in the early 1980s did differ considerably from its Maoist predecessor, it was not new. Rather it reflected by and large an attempt to refurbish the political theory of the mid-1950s which derived from a Stalinist creed inherited from the Soviet Union. This was embodied in the 'Four Basic Principles' enunciated by Deng Xiaoping as defining the basic elements of a socialist polity (Marxism–Leninism and Mao Zedong Thought, the socialist road, the dictatorship of the proletariat and the leadership of the Communist Party), which maintained the concept of a ruling ideological orthodoxy as the guiding principle for China's socialist state.

This formulation did not go unchallenged, from both inside and outside the Party; it was also questioned by Deng Xiaoping in a cardinal speech to the CCP Politburo in August 1980 in which he sanctioned certain limited areas for permissible political reform (*albeit* within the framework of the Four Basic Principles).[8] The central point here is that, despite the limited scope for reform of political institutions licensed by Deng and despite challenges from within the leadership (notably by Hu Yaobang in 1986 and Zhao Ziyang in 1988–9), the official ideological position on the nature of a socialist political system has remained basically unchanged into the 1990s. Indeed, the reform era saw a reversion to the mid-1950s, a period which Deng and other leaders of the older generation regarded with nostalgia.

However, while the central tenets of political theory remained, there was an attempt to bring Ideology's economic theory into line with a new era of market socialism. In an 'ideocratic' polity of the Chinese state socialist kind, practical policies must be clothed in a suitable ideological raiment; radical changes in policy require changes in theory, which may in turn provoke accusations of 'revisionism', or, in the 1980s, 'bourgeois liberalisation', from more conservative political opponents.

We have already discussed these efforts at conceptual deStalinisation in economic theory in Chapter 1. The most salient elements were, first, ideological ratification of the role of the 'law of value', i.e. markets, in the spheres of finance, labour and commodities, both domestically and internationally, which also enlarged the scope for market-oriented material incentives both in wages and incomes more generally (thus the post-collective peasantry were urged to 'get rich' and resulting inequality was officially accepted, nay welcomed, as developmentally beneficial). Second was the official rethinking on questions of ownership which allowed greater scope for private enterprise and challenged the traditional conceptions of 'state' and 'collective' ownership. This ideological revision was justified in terms of the overriding priority of 'developing the productive forces'. In other words, a wide range of ownership forms were permissible if they resulted in higher levels of economic productivity – 'what is good for the development of the productive forces is good for socialism'.[9]

While such willingness to innovate conceptually might appear sensible, the results were often unrecognisable as anything that could be described, even charitably, as 'Marxism' (let alone 'Marxism–Leninism' and still less 'Mao Zedong Thought') and therefore with any claim to 'scientific' rigour or plausibility. The intrusion of reality into theory diluted the latter into sometimes bizarre theoretical concoctions whose inadequacies were only concealed by their increasing irrelevance. Let us take one example, the attempt to change the Ideology to accommodate changes in the labour system. As we have seen, the reformers wished to raise labour productivity in the state sector by encouraging greater labour mobility and granting greater freedom to both employer and employee in decisions about employment – in other words, moving towards a labour market. In order to justify this ideologically, however, they had to come to terms with the fact that, in the Marxist canon, acceptance of a 'market in labour power' requires a recognition that labour power is a commodity. Since this equation is a defining characteristic of a distinctively capitalist mode of production, it would seem incompatible with the labour system of an avowedly socialist economy. Sensitive to possible charges of 'bourgeois' tendencies, reformers have had to decide how far to go in the process of theoretical revision: from the minimum, some kind of cosmetic tinkering through various kinds of linguistic fudging, to an outright attempt to revise fundamental principles. As the reform process deepened and the more radical reformers gained confidence in the mid-1980s under the aegis of Zhao Ziyang and Hu Yaobang, the ideological frontiers have been pushed back and previously heretical ideas have received a public airing.

But labour reform has been a contentious issue and disagreements over policy have mirrored, or been mirrored by, disagreements at the ideological level. Ideology has provided the conceptual matrix within which, and the language with which, policy debates have been conducted. The range of views reflected in the public debate has in fact been remarkably wide. Answers to the crucial question 'Is labour power a commodity under socialist conditions?' have ranged from an emphatic 'no' to an equally emphatic 'yes', with a spectrum of shades of opinion in between. The traditional ideological position, which underpinned the previous reality of administrative allocation of the state labour force, held that labour power is not and cannot become a commodity (i.e. there can be no labour market) in a socialist economy worth the name. This idea still has support among both analysts and officials on the grounds, for example, that 'public ownership is practised and the labourers jointly possess the means of production. We cannot say that labourers are selling labour power to themselves'.[10]

This argument can, and indeed is, used to oppose deregulation of the labour system. In response, some reform economists try to avoid the ideological problem by retaining the basic precept that labour power is not a commodity under socialism, and separating that issue from that of whether or not 'labour markets' can exist. These analysts prefer to use more anodyne terms such as 'labour services market', 'labour resources market', or just plain 'job market'. In contrast, other reform economists wish to take the dilemma by the horns and change the theory to fit the new policies. They argue that it is necessary to recognise that labour is also a commodity within the wider framework of a 'socialist commodity economy'. They criticise the traditional view of labour as naive, arguing to the contrary:[11]

> In socialist society, although the means of production are under public ownership, they are not combined directly with labour power in a simple manner. This combination is achieved through recruiting and hiring, with one side paying the wages and the other hiring out its labour power ... Although labourers are the elements that constitute an enterprise, an individual labourer cannot be equated with this body. The seller and buyer of the labour power are two different legal persons.

For this author, Zhuang Hongxiang, the fact that labour power remains a commodity in a 'socialist' economy is determined by 'objective economic law'. Other reform economists, such as Zhao Guoliang and Dong Fureng,[12] take a different theoretical tack, arguing that the answer to the question of whether or not labour power is a commodity depends on the nature of the labour system actually in operation. In the previous situation in which the state labour force was allocated by state labour bureaux and the freedom of individual employers and employees was severely constrained, there was in fact no labour market and labour power could not be construed as a commodity. However, if reforms were introduced to give more power to employers to hire and fire and to workers to choose jobs, then labour power would in fact become a commodity. The key issue, they argue, is to use the reforms to *transform* labour power into a commodity, a course of action which rests on a recognition that this is not only desirable but also unavoidable in the context of the transition to a 'socialist commodity economy'. Here, these radical reformers are, implicitly or explicitly, arguing against the views of their more moderate colleagues who prefer to fudge the ideological issue. At the same time, however, they are aware that they themselves may be vulnerable to charges from Party conservatives that they are advocating 'bourgeois restoration' or the like. They are therefore at pains to point out that, although there will be labour markets in the post-reform economy and this labour power would become a commodity, this would have a different significance under socialism than under capitalism:[13]

> In capitalist production relations, the system of wage labour reflects the relationship between the exploiting class of capitalists and the exploited class of workers. However, in a socialist economy the system of wage labour reflects the relationship of equality and mutual benefit. The fundamental difference lies in to whom the surplus products belong and whose interests they serve.

Leaving aside the intellectual plausibility of this argument, the statement gives us some notion of the political treacherousness of innovations in economic theory and the pervasive role of Ideology in the process of reforming policy. The Ideology is not inelastic; it contains some potential for theoretical revision and provides a common language for debate between different viewpoints. Yet it serves to constrain innovation and limit debate; given its canonical status (not to mention its instrumental role as a tool to defend the embedded interests of the political status quo), the Ideology has an inherent tendency to polarise debate, to turn analytical and policy disagreements into questions of unambiguous right and wrong, permissible and taboo, and convert the participants in the debate into believers and heretics. Thus intellectual argument becomes a potentially dangerous political game, a fact which cannot but restrict the ability to think about and implement reforms. To the extent that Ideology acts to restrict necessary adjustments to new realities and priorities, it undermines its own credibility and the authority of its creators. Yet the reverse is also true. If policy leads ideology by the nose, becoming a contrived and convenient after-thought or cosmetic rationalisation, it also loses force and credibility. Even if agreement is reached between contending policy positions, the result, if converted into ideological pronouncements, is likely to be an implausible hotchpotch of incompatible elements. Thus, whether Ideology impedes or adjusts, it goes into decay either way.

As the tide of economic reform rolled forward in the mid 1980s, emboldened by its initial successes, and as 'the market' increasingly came to be seen as the 'open sesame' to prosperity, the new policies began to stretch the Marxist–Leninist–Mao Zedong Thought canon out of shape. Ideology increasingly lost its role as a comprehensive view of the world and a programme for the future and came to function more as a mode of adjustment to current realities and relatively short-term policy objectives. Nowhere was this more apparent than in the much vaunted 'theory' of 'the initial stage of socialism' which was unveiled by Zhao Ziyang as the ideological explanation of the reform era at the Thirteenth Party Congress in October 1987.[14] Zhao argued that traditional Marxist concepts about the transition to socialism should be abandoned; it should be recognised that China, as an underdeveloped country in which the commodity economy was weak, was merely in 'the initial stage of socialism' in which the sole priority in the economic sphere should be modernisation of the means of production. During this period, a wide range of economic forms and policies were admissible as long as they fostered economic growth. While this document was clearly a serious attempt to harmonise ideology with the real world of policy, it failed on several counts: it did not succeed in its goal of being a 'blueprint' for a reformed future since the conception of the future was vague and contradictory; it was hardly a projection of any kind of 'socialist' future since the whole question of socialism in the economic sphere was postponed for a century; in the meantime, anything was possible so long as the leadership thought it advisable and it could thus be dubbed 'socialist'. Not surprisingly, some Chinese called this theory a 'hundred treasure bag' (*bai bao dai*), in other words a ragbag into which anything can be stuffed. It loses the predictive, inspirational and utopian element of communist ideology and appears as merely a rationalisation of the policies of the current Party leadership. As Maurice Meisner points out (1989: p. 356), this theory 'serves the function of severing any meaningful relationship between the practice of the present and the socialist goals of the future'. The distinctive features of Ideology – its ability to motivate and guide the political élite, its claim to provide a framework for a long-term strategy leading towards a credible future, its aim to establish a coherent and credible set of moral principles to provide a new social identity for the members of a 'socialist' society – seem to have atrophied. In the political world of Chinese reformism, Ideology has increasingly become a residual.

To many of China's economic reformers, this is hardly lamentable since they regard ideology as a fetter on creative thought and policy. In fact, one can see the very idea and process of market-oriented economic reform as a dagger aimed at the heart of communist ideocracy. Yet this recognition of the incompatibility between ideological orthodoxy and the political demands of economic reform illustrates yet again the fundamental contradiction at the heart of the 'market socialist' project – economic change versus political rigidity. One resolution of this contradiction, which would keep alive the utopian and teleological character of traditional state socialism, would be a conceptual breakthrough towards a new vision of a 'socialist' future which succeeds in accommodating markets with socialist values and institutions, of the kind towards which Gorbachev was groping in the Soviet Union until the coup of August 1991. The theory of 'the initial stage of socialism' falls far short of this mark and, in the light of the collapse of reform experiments in the Soviet Union and Eastern Europe, it has yet to be proven that such a radical transformation of ideas is in fact possible. If it were, it would require that ideocracy be preserved, albeit in a much weaker form. This poses a choice for the reformers – if they reject the very notion of ideocracy, they also reject any notion of economic reform as a guided process within a political context which is still recognisably 'socialist'. It is hard then to avoid an Eastern European scenario, where demands for a market economy and political democracy combine to bring the destruction of the previous regime and the complete rejection of its legitimating Ideology. In such a scenario, the 'market socialist' project of reforming socialism from within has no future.

If the economic reformers face serious dilemmas, the conservatives within the Party face even worse ones. They have realised that ideological decay is a concomitant of economic reform. In their eyes this operates at all levels: at the leadership level in the increasing incompatibility between economic policy and ideological precepts; at the institutional level in the decline of political and moral

standards within the Party; and at the mass level in the spread of
'unhealthy tendencies' and non/anti-socialist sentiments and a
general decline in public morality. Their response has been to
mount periodic campaigns – negatively against 'bourgeois liberalisation' and 'spiritual pollution' and positively to strengthen a
'socialist spiritual civilisation'- which tend to coincide with con-
traction stages in successive reform policy cycles.[15] These political
movements, in ways characteristic of the Maoist period, select
targets for criticism, remove objectionable figures (notably Party
leaders or prominent members of the intelligentsia) and raise the
overall political 'temperature' in society by increasing requirements
for 'ideological and political education' and saturating the media
with ideological themes.

These elements are visible in the 'anti-bourgeois liberalisation
campaigns' at various points in the evolution of the reform
programme. The first was in early 1981 when there was a backlash
against what were seen as the unhealthy ideological effects of the
first wave of economic reform in 1979–80 (including an increase in
'juvenile delinquency'), the Democracy Movement in 1979 and the
very limited steps towards political reform in 1980 (notably the
marginally more open local election campaigns in late 1980). The
Polish events of 1980 had also alarmed the leadership. During this
period, the movement to criticise 'bourgeois liberalisation' was
apparently pushed by the PLA (Dittmer 1982: pp. 41–2) and took
a number of familiar forms: media reports nostalgic about the
austere conditions of revolutionary life in Yan'an; a campaign to
emulate the Maoist hero, Lei Feng; criticism of 'harmful' works of
art (notably the story *'Bitter Love'* by Bai Hua which allegedly gave
readers a bad impression of socialism and the CCP). The movement, which called upon the population to aspire to a socialist
'spiritual civilisation' (*jingshen wenming*) as well as material well-
being, was kept within bounds by Deng Xiaoping who was engaged
in one of his characteristic balancing acts between different factions
and tendencies within the leadership. It continued into 1982, but
was gradually wound down as the power of the new reformist Party
chairman, Hu Yaobang, was consolidated.

In late 1983, however, a similar backlash was launched by
speeches by Deng and Chen Yun at a Party Central Committee
plenum in October, in the form of a concern over the 'spiritual
pollution' (*jingshen wuran*) accompanying the economic reforms,

particularly in the wake of the increased interaction with the outside world resulting from the Open Policy. Targets of this campaign were far-ranging: from prominent Party figures, such as Zhou Yang, who in early 1983 had been using Marxist concepts to analyse 'alienation' in socialist society and develop a version of Marxist 'humanism',[16] to instances of 'corrupt' or 'degenerate' practices, particularly those allegedly imported from the West, such as rock music, clothing fashions, pornographic books and the like. This campaign was extinguished fairly quickly as the economic reforms, particularly in agriculture, were demonstrating their effectiveness and reformist leaders took the opportunity to sweep the reform process forward. The next upsurge was not until early 1985 when the charge of 'bourgeois liberalisation' was again levelled against Party members and the mass media – again the campaign was linked to the potentially baleful influence of the foreign presence encouraged by the Open Policy (Party ideological specialist, Deng Liqun, called on Chinese patriots to 'oppose the trend of worshipping foreign things and fawning on foreigners'[17]). This movement too was dampened down, in particular through the intervention of Deng Xiaoping in defence of the Open Policy (for a detailed account of this campaign, see Sullivan 1988). Although Party conservatives were successful in getting the issue of ideological, cultural and moral degeneration onto the agenda of the Party Sixth Plenum (XII) held in September 1986, the resulting Resolution, which sought to lay down guidelines about socialist culture and ethics, was an inconsistent hodgepodge which compounded rather than mitigated the problem, reflecting as it did the deep disagreements among the top Party leadership.[18]

The next, and by far the biggest, backlash came in early 1987 in response to moves towards political liberalisation in late 1986 encouraged by reform leaders, notably Hu Yaobang and Zhao Ziyang, and student demonstrations for 'democracy and freedom' at the end of 1986 and beginning of 1987. A large-scale movement against 'bourgeois liberalisation' was launched in January 1987, accompanied by the dramatic resignation of Hu Yaobang as Party General-Secretary on 16 January. High profile targets were selected, notably the astro-physicist Fang Lizhi, who was accused of advocating wholesale Westernisation and fomenting student demonstrations. Newspapers or journals were censored or forced to close and criticism was directed at literary and art circles where, it was maintained, 'the ideological trend of bourgeois liberalisation ran wild' (for a detailed account of this campaign, see Rosen 1988). Again, it was Deng, throwing his weight behind Zhao Ziyang, who brought the movement to heel, concerned over the balance of power within the leadership and the potential damage which the campaign could inflict on the economic reform programme.

The largest backlash was to come in the aftermath of the May–June events and the Beijing Massacre of 4 June 1989. The central elements of the new movement against 'bourgeois liberalisation' were similar to the earlier ones: a reiteration of the importance of ideological and political education (for example, more political study sessions in schools and colleges, military training for incoming university students and training in Marxism for CCP members); the need to inculcate socialist morality and 'spiritual civilisation'; attacks on key opposition figures (such as Chen Yizi, Yan Jiaqi, Wan Runnan, Su Shaozhi and their political sponsor, Zhao Ziyang); criticism of 'contamination' from abroad; a return to previous ideological themes and methods (for example, a resurrection of the Maoist idea that 'class struggle exists in the ideological sphere' and yet another reappearance of the old Maoist role-model, Lei Feng); and a general slow-down in the process of economic reform. The difference this time was that the backlash was far more violent than its predecessor and the ideological balance swung much further back, bringing more lasting curbs on intellectual, cultural and political life and the hounding of dissidents, both at home and abroad. It seems that the former fragile consensus between contending ideological positions and political leaders, which had been preserved up till the end of 1988 with the aid of Deng Xiaoping's role as balancer and mediator, had broken down irretrievably.

Ideology in Decay

By the dawn of the 1990s, China was a radically different place from what it had been a decade earlier and the effort of conservative leaders to reimpose some kind of ideological consensus smacked of desperation. The resort to force on 4 June 1989 and afterwards itself dramatised the bankruptcy of Ideology as a force for creating and maintaining the political authority of a regime which was increasingly held together by force and self-interest. The conservatives' diagnosis, however, was that things were getting out of hand because ideological education and political controls had been relaxed, or because ideological and political work had been neglected or botched. The conservatives are right in the sense that there had been a marked trend towards depoliticisation during the 1980s – anyone walking through the streets of a Chinese city in the mid-1980s might have been hard put to find a political poster, but might easily come across large hoardings advertising Japanese consumer goods. The desanctification of ideology in the 1980s had allowed people to become indifferent to politics and concentrate on private/material things. In the logic of the economic reform, this was not only allowable but desirable because it removed political fetters on productivity and provided incentives for personal initiative. People were urged to consume, to become rich, to open their minds to foreign ideas, to develop themselves as 'entrepreneurs' by seizing business opportunities, to compete with each other and regard inequality as a social good rather than evil (in spite of ideological hedging about the need for 'common prosperity' and 'comradely relations'). The calls for people to 'liberate thought', particularly in the context of greater openness to the outside world, led to a proliferation of new (or revived old) values and the recognition of uncomfortable facts which clashed with ideological claims. For example, information about the continued dynamism of advanced capitalism and the impressive developmental performance of Taiwan and South Korea made the ritual claim about the alleged 'superiority of socialism' ring very hollow.[19] The political consequences of these trends were not merely widespread indifference, but also confusion or cynicism; where political passions were aroused it was likely to be for some 'foreign' creed such as 'democracy', 'freedom' or 'human rights' or a nostalgic yearning for the simpler egalitarian values of a previous Maoist era, visible, for example, in the resurgence of the Mao cult as a popular fad in 1992.[20] There has been a growing gulf between official ideology on the one hand and socio-economic realities on the other; the reformers have tried to bridge it by revising ideology; the conservatives by revising reality. Either way, the hegemonic role of Ideology was doomed.

The effort to rebuild the hegemonic position of Ideology to help reconstitute the authority of China's communist regime has thus failed dismally. This failure was the result of certain inherent contradictions in the reform project, which were exacerbated but not fundamentally determined by disagreement within the reform leadership. The new conceptual terrain of market economics and the increasing social space which it opened up undermined the legitimating validity of the official Ideology – Marxism, Leninism and Mao Zedong – in cognitive terms, as a plausible map of the world, present and future, as a basis for a credible and coherent set of moral/social values, or as an operational guide to practical problem-solving and policy-making. Ideology had lost its claim to be the sole basis of authority in society, the ultimate political arbiter, the source of political and developmental truth.

The Ideology was failing at both mass and élite levels. It failed at the mass level as a force to resocialise society and unify it in support of the Party. In the eyes of a more aware and sceptical population, particularly in the cities, the period of economic reform differed little from its predecessor, in the sense that Ideology had been patently 'instrumentalised' yet again, used in the battle within the leadership or the clash between social interests, and serving as an increasingly threadbare rationalisation for authoritarian one-party rule. In the late 1980s, the Chinese government was dealing with a population who were increasingly devoid of any ideological illusions and increasingly aware of the gap between the ideological pretensions and the actual behaviour of the regime. In the absence of a credible Ideology, the regime was increasingly judged in terms of its ability to deliver economic growth and higher living standards. But this seriously weakens the Party's base of legitimacy; it is vulnerable to the kind of economic problems which arose in the late 1980s and gave rise to political discontent. However, in the absence of a deeper source of legitimacy, even continuing economic success could not restore the Party's authority. Popular living standards may have gone up but so had expectations, thus raising the baseline for discontent – as the Chinese phrase has it, the population were 'picking up the bowl to eat meat and putting it down to complain'. As such, the Ideology was a casualty of that wider process of 'political decay' identified by Huntington (1968: p. 86) as resulting from a contradiction between political authority on the one side and an accelerating process of social mobilisation and political participation on the other.

Ideology had also lost much of its efficacy and an intellectually cogent, practically useful and personally compelling doctrine for the political élite in the Communist Party. The institutional capacity and effectiveness of the Party declined in tandem. Thanks to economic reform, the Party's role was shrinking and much of its activity was increasingly defined as at best irrelevant and at worst obstructive to China's future wellbeing. We shall explore this process of institutional decay in the next chapter.

6

The Party's Over? Economic Reform and Institutional Decay

At the beginning of the reform era, the Communist Party, the central core of the Chinese political system, was itself in crisis. It could look back over two decades of bitter political strife not merely among the central leadership but between individuals and groups at each level of the Party organisation, down to the grassroots. The institution bore the scars of this heritage in terms of continuing personal and factional animosities and a general lack of political self-confidence and identity. Party leaders saw the economic reforms as a way to recoup political credibility both for themselves and for the Party as an institution. However, the difficult process of implementing the new economic strategy and the potential long-term dangers it posed to the fundamentals of state socialism presented the Party with a major challenge which, at the dawn of the reform era, it was ill-prepared to tackle. Alongside the reforms, therefore, there was a parallel attempt to rebuild the Party and reshape it for its new role.

The political conflicts of the Cultural Revolution decade had left it riven with internal hostilities and trellised by protective networks of personal, patron–client relations (*guanxiwang*) and departmental or local 'independent kingdoms'. It had lost a good deal of its prestige among the population as a coherent, authoritative and effective political force. The post-Mao leadership faced two formidable political tasks, on the success of which depended the very future of Chinese state socialism. First, there was the need for institutional *rehabilitation*, of re-establishing the Party as a stable, legitimate and developmentally credible political organisation capable of, and entitled to, act as the nation's sole nucleus of political power, in the eyes of both its own members and the general population. Second, there was an equal important need for institutional *reform* to adapt the Party to the requirements of achieving and maintaining a 'socialist commodity economy'. This required sweeping changes in its social composition, range of action and operational behaviour. In this section, I shall examine the ways in which CCP leaders have attempted to achieve these two objectives and assess their success or failure over the decade of reform. Though the issues raised here are complex, I shall simplify things by concentrating on the relationship between institutional change and economic reform rather than pursuing broader issues of reforming the political system, and on officially sponsored attempts at institutional reform rather than more radical alternatives which have not been put into practice.

Efforts at Institutional Rehabilitation

We can discuss the process of attempted institutional rehabilitation under two headings: first, the effort to restore stability, discipline, order and 'normality' in the Party after nearly twenty years of turbulence and, second, the desire to 'rectify workstyle' in order to improve the *modus operandi* of the Party as an institution and of its individual members and cadres. These headings coincide with the two basic approaches actually adopted by the reform leadership: first, a bureaucratic approach which emphasised the reimposition of regular procedures governed by precise rules and, second, a person-centred approach which stressed the need for political and ideological training and education of Party members and cadres. The former is a familiar aspect of Western administrative systems; the latter contains elements which are both distinctively communist and distinctively Chinese.

Regularisation and 'Normalisation'

This process can be looked at both from the point of view of both individual Party members and the Party as a whole. For the former, the 'struggle between the two lines' in the 1960s and 1970s had brought political disorientation and insecurity. They had responded by building networks of fellow Party members which not only protected them against threats from factional enemies within the Party, but also insulated them from their mass constituencies outside the Party. From the point of view of the organisation as a whole, there was a need to break through these factionalist networks to reimpose overall Party discipline, but also to provide members with a more stable and predictable environment free from the political 'anarchy' of the past. This involved the attempt to 'bring order out of the chaos' in Party life, a new 'normality' which looked nostalgically back to an organisational golden age before the onset of Maoism and its never-ending series of political movements.

In part, this depended on the re-establishment of a unified leadership at the Party's helm and the emergence of a clear political line to define the overall goals and main functions of the Party. This did begin to happen in the early 1980s as a new reform consensus emerged among the central Party leadership after the removal of remaining Maoist leaders from high office. In part, the restoration of 'normality' involved an attempt to 'reinstitutionalise' the Party by introducing a systematic set of procedures to regulate organisational life, to establish the dominance of institutional over personal power. Deng Xiaoping put it as follows:[1]

> It is true that the errors we made in the past were partly attributable to the way of thinking and style of work of some leaders. But they were even more attributable to the problems in our organisational and working systems. If these systems are sound, they can place restraint on the actions of bad people; if they are unsound, they may hamper the efforts of good people . . .

In political terms, this involved an effort 'to institutionalise and legalise inner-Party democracy',[2] to restore the norms of Leninist 'democratic centralism' and 'collective leadership' which, it was held, had been undermined by the Cultural Revolution and which had brought a trend towards the over-concentration of power in the hands of higher cadres at each level who tended to operate on a 'what I say goes' basis. Deng Xiaoping analysed the problem as follows:[3]

> Another cause of our bureaucracy is that for a long time we have had no strict administrative rules and regulations and no system

of personal responsibility from top to bottom in the leading bodies of our Party and government organisations...

The new leadership responded by attempting to clarify the operational principles of 'democratic centralism' and the rights and duties of individual Party members within it. For example, it was stressed that all Party members were equal, that leadership posts within the Party should be filled by due democratic procedures, that Party meetings should be conducted according to established procedures and that the role of Party committee secretaries (particularly the First Secretary) should be clearly defined, in order to prevent the personal abuse of power and to restore the principle of 'collective leadership' by the Party committee at each level.[4]

These operational norms were to be established by means of incessant exhortation and in-house training (for example, through a resuscitated system of Party schools which provided regular longer-term courses and short-term rotational courses for Party cadres).[5] However, since these traditional methods for regulating organisational life had proven ineffective in the past, two additional methods were used to strengthen their impact. First, a plethora of new rules, regulations and guidelines were introduced to regulate all aspects of Party life, down to its minutiae. At the broadest level, these included a set of 'Certain Guiding Principles for Inner-party Political Life', published in 1980, and the Party Constitutions adopted by the Twelfth and Thirteenth Party Congresses in 1982 and 1987.[6] There was an attempt to provide rules to regulate specific areas of Party activity: for example, regulations on the living arrangements, pay and work conditions of senior cadres; on methods to combat 'bureaucratism' through the use of deadlines; on ways of maintaining 'close ties with the masses'; and on foreign visits by Party officials and members.[7] For example, CCP Central Committee regulations on the perks of senior cadres at the Centre stipulated that each was to be allowed one car instead of two; personal requests for film-shows were forbidden (cadres should buy tickets in the normal way); all gifts received while abroad should be handed over upon return; they were not allowed to use state transport to travel for pleasure and no extra holidays could be granted except to the elderly or ill.[8] In its 'Ten Rules for Maintaining Close Ties with the Masses', for example, the Liaoning provincial party committee stipulated that media reports on Party officials should be reduced; there should be no 'flowery language' in reporting their speeches and that there should be strict limits on public expenditures on entertainment.[9] This kind of response to problems of 'bureaucratism' was itself highly bureaucratic – every organisational malady was treated with a stiff dose of regulations. While the above sets of regulations were targeted at specific problems, there was a broader effort to improve the 'organisational life' of the Party as a whole by setting up a general framework of bureaucratic regulation. This was particularly evident in personnel management or 'organisational work', under the Organisation Department of the Central Committee Secretariat. One of the main tasks of the post-Mao era was seen as 'systematisation' (*zhiduhua*) of the recruitment, training, appointment evaluation, and promotion of cadres. Deng Xiaoping stressed the need for this in 1980 when he complained that the Party currently had 'no regular methods for recruiting, rewarding and punishing cadres for their retirement, resignation or removal'.[10]

> Whether they do their work well or poorly, they have 'iron rice-bowls'. They can be employed but not dismissed, promoted but not demoted.

Personnel policy can be seen as a fundamental bulwark of the Leninist state since the choice of officials, in both the Party and state machines, is a crucial source and expression of the Party's political dominance – it is a replica of the Soviet Union's nomenklatura system. New thinking on this key question (Chinese leaders cite Stalin's dictum that 'cadres decide everything') was concentrated in a new version of a manual of Questions and Answers on Party Organisation Work, published in 1983 (Manion 1984 and 1985). This manual lays down detailed procedures for screening and selecting officials; regular assessment of their performance, particularly in the context of a new 'post responsibility system'; appointment, promotion, transfer, removal and retirement.

These are classic means of bureaucratisation in the sense described by Max Weber, i.e. to establish a framework of institutionalised rules and procedures to regulate organisation life (Gerth and Mills 1958: pp. 196–7). As a response to the legacy of disorder left by the Cultural Revolution, this was understandable and would seem to be necessary. As a cure for 'bureaucratism', however, it looks like administering poison to cure a highly toxic patient. Yet we must remind ourselves of the organisational measures were designed to counter – the fact that the internal life of the Party had degenerated into a complex system of clientelistic networks which operated in *ad hoc*, particularistic and uncontrollable ways. The Chinese term 'bureaucratism', *guanliao zhuyi*, often translated as 'bureaucracy', is broader than our own common use of the term 'bureaucracy' because it includes not merely the rigidities and formalism which we associate with complex public organisations, but also a wide range of non-institutionalised behaviour, stemming from the 'deviant' behaviour of individuals and cliques. Witness Deng Xiaoping's own definition of the term:[11]

[Bureaucratism's] harmful manifestations include the following: standing high above the masses; abusing power; divorcing oneself from reality and the masses; spending a lot of time and effort to put up an impressive front; indulging in empty talk; sticking to a rigid way of thinking; being hidebound by convention; over-staffing administrative organs; being dilatory, inefficient and irresponsible; failing to keep one's word; circulating documents endlessly without solving problems; shifting responsibility to others; and even assuming the airs of a mandarin, reprimanding other people at every turn, vindictively attacking others, suppressing democracy, deceiving superiors and subordinates, being arbitrary and despotic, practising favouritism, offering bribes, participating in corrupt practices in violation of the law, and so on.

It is particularly at the informal behavioural world of Party official and members – the world of élitism, personal privileges, talk not action, vaingloriousness, trading favours, covering up mistakes, bending or ignoring procedures for personal or group gain – that the new attempt at institutionalisation was directed. To this extent, in the words of Max Weber, it was a means to secure 'a discharge of business according to calculable rules and "without regard for persons"' (Gerth and Mills 1958: p. 215). Unlike Weber's model bureaucracy, however, the prime 'business' of the Party was politics, thus the personal character of the individual Party member or official – political and ethical not merely professional – was deemed critical to the functioning of the organisation as a whole. Let us examine this question next.

The Restoration of a 'Correct Workstyle'

The central attention paid to the 'workstyle' (*zuofeng*) of Party members and officials is a longstanding element of CCP political doctrine as the classic study on leadership by John Lewis (1963) demonstrated. In earlier years it was identified with the 'mass line', a set of behavioural norms which were designed to create a 'correct relationship' both between Party members and the 'masses' and between leaders and members within the Party. In the eyes of the post-Mao leadership, the 'workstyle' of the Party as a corporate body and of its individual cadres and members had declined alarmingly over the previous two decades. This alarm is particularly visible in statements by leaders of the Central Discipline Inspection Commission (CDIC), which was established under the chairmanship of Chen Yun after the Party's Third Plenum (XI) of December 1978, and was charged with the job of 'rectifying' and cleaning up the Party. In Chen's view, workstyle was 'a matter of life and death' for the Party.[12] Huang Kecheng, the Permanent Secretary of CDIC, identified a long list of 'unhealthy tendencies' and argued that the main problem was 'the decline in revolutionary will, not lack of ability'.[13] The 'unhealthy tendencies' included ideological 'deviations' such as 'leftism', 'ultra-leftism' or 'bourgeois decadence'; privilege seeking and nepotism (particularly the pervasive practice of officials procuring jobs and privileges for their own children); corruption (such as embezzlement, bribe-taking and smuggling); authoritarian and dictatorial behaviour, 'acting like officials' in suppressing different opinions and democratic participation inside and outside the Party; careerism (taking the inside track to personal advancement through Party membership); and various kinds of bureaucratic behaviour (shelving difficult problems, buck-passing, foot-dragging, and words without actions). Moreover, the Party was out of touch with the people. As Huang Kecheng pointed out, 'the masses are very different from twenty years ago' – they have a 'power of observation and a greatly improved ideological level'; they watched the Party more closely, had greater expectations and were more inclined to be critical. For example, 'in the 1950s we could send cars to bring our children home from primary boarding schools at weekends and no-one complained; now we can't even send an orderly without hearing criticism'.[14]

The CDIC's answer was to restore a 'healthy' workstyle, the definition of which drew heavily on revolutionary nostalgia. There were calls to 'inherit and carry forward the Yan'an workstyle' of the pre-revolutionary era of revolutionary struggle, epitomised by Mao's theory of the 'mass line' and the spirit of 'serving the people'. There was an attempt to re-establish the old model of the Party cadre and members as people who were dedicated to revolutionary ideals, frugal, selfless, democratic and self-critical.[15] The methods proposed to achieve this transformation were the familiar modes of institutional self-improvement which had been in use for the past forty years: in the short term, a *'rectification'* movement and over the longer term a stress on providing intensive ideological/political *education*. The latter emphasis on the need to create a politically 'correct' and ethically superior élite is a reflection of a combination of a Leninist insistence on the superiority of the 'vanguard' party and a neo-Confucian stress on the need for a political élite of morally superior individuals moulded by education in a supreme orthodoxy. Likewise, the Party 'rectification' campaign, which was announced in 1982 and began in 1983, was redolent of the Anti-Rightist Movement managed by no less than Deng Xiaoping himself in 1957.[16] The campaign strategy was laid out in a document ratified by the Party Committee's Second Plenum (XII) in October 1983 which specified four major goals: ideological unity, rectification of workstyle, strengthening of discipline and the purification of Party organisations. Deng himself made an important speech in October arguing the case for Party rectification.[17] The campaign involved an intensive study of selected documents and a process of 'criticism and self-criticism' and was under the titular leadership of Party Secretary-General Hu Yaobang (as chairman of a specially established Central Commission for Guiding Party Rectification) and Bo Yibo who, as deputy-chairman, managed the campaign on a day-to-day basis. The campaign lasted over three years (a summary report was published in mid-1987 by Bo Yibo) and covered Party organisations from the centre down to the grass-roots.

There was clearly a good deal of opposition to this rectification, particularly from its main political targets – those who joined the Party and/or became cadres during the Cultural Revolution decade (estimated at about 18 million). The work teams sent out to implement the campaign met a good deal of resistance, as Party groups, both formal and informal, closed ranks to repel boarders; there were also allegations that many members of the work teams themselves did not have their heart in the job.[18] Bo Yibo himself admitted slow progress in its middle stages[19] and in mid-1986 a veteran member of the Central Advisory Committee lamented that there had been 'no turn for the better'.[20] Although Bo Yibo claimed in his summary report in mid-1987 that 200 000 people had been expelled from the Party during the campaign, this was a small fraction of the 46 million party members at the time and of the 18 million recruited during the Cultural Revolution.[21] Moreover, other estimates of the direct results of the campaign put the number of expulsions much lower (as low as 34 000). Moreover, purges tended to be at lower levels in the Party hierarchy and were overwhelmingly ordinary Party members, not cadres (Rosen 1989: pp. 21–2). Again, the informal 'networks' were in operation diverting the political dagger and protecting people of influence and their protégés. This lack of success is hardly surprising, moreover, given the fact that the operational head of the campaign was Bo Yibo, usually identified as a conservative figure, while the titular head was a leading reformer, Hu Yaobang. Thus the political impetus behind the campaign was ambiguous from the outset. There was evidence that Bo Yibo disagreed with Hu's handling of the campaign (Dickson 1990: p. 184). In its latter stages its aim swung away from the original target, the 'Leftists' of the Cultural Revolution, towards 'bourgeois liberalism'. Indeed, its very last stage became entangled with the purge of its own chairman, Hu Yaobang and the Anti-Bourgeois Liberalisation movement of early 1987.

Though the effect of the Rectification Campaign seems to have been relatively superficial, it was not the only mechanism employed by the central leadership in the 1980s to rehabilitate the Party's political image and improve its performance. After the 1978 Third Plenum (XI), a significant role was accorded to the Central Discipline Inspection Commission (and its subordinate agencies at lower levels which were subject to the 'dual leadership' of the central CDIC and the local Party committee). This was to function as an 'external' watch-dog, exercising 'impartial supervision' over the Party and was charged with both the basic tasks of rebuilding the Party as an institution and improving the 'workstyle' of its members. This organisation was a new version of a pre-existing institution, the Central Control Commission, which was established in 1955 and had operated up to, and immediately after, the Cultural Revolution.[22] It was the CDIC which drew up 'Some Principles for Guiding Inner-party Political Life' in 1979. Its remit was very broad; in the words of its then Permanent Secretary, Huang Kecheng, it was 'to ensure that the Party's ideological and political lines and organisational principles are implemented', to investigate and correct 'violations of law and discipline', to 'supervise bureaucratism' and counter 'special privileges and violations of financial and economic discipline'. Its disciplinary role involved cracking down on 'factionalism, anarchism, and public compliance but private opposition'.[23] In operational terms, it was responsible for drafting suitable rules and regulations, conducting education on their significance and enforcing them through specific investigations and sanctions. CDIC organs were also active as grievance machinery, for complaints from both outside and inside the Party. In the early years, moreover, it was also charged with rehabilitating Party officials and members disgraced during the Cultural Revolution and rooting out remnant radical leftists in positions of influence.

In the first three years of its operation, under the leadership triad of three veterans – Chen Yun, Huang Kecheng and Deng Yingchao – the CDIC pursued these goals energetically. In overall terms, they become not merely a guardian of 'pure Party spirit' and 'correct Party style', but also a force to ensure that the new strategic economic policies were adhered to. They were particularly assiduous in rooting out cases of corruption or 'economic crimes' as they were labelled officially (smuggling, tax evasion, illegal dealings in foreign exchange, reselling controlled goods at a profit, bribery, embezzlement, 'backdoor' deals and the like). This role became particularly significant as the economic reforms began to bite during 1982–5 and the incidence of 'economic crimes' multiplied in tandem.[24] Leaders of the CDIC were alarmed at these trends and supported the formal rectification campaign launched in 1983. By 1985, Chen Yun was arguing that the new role for the CDIC which coincided with the concerns of conservative leaders, namely that it should act to counter the ill-effects of economic reform on the Party: the decline of ideological commitment resulting from a 'neglect of building spiritual civilisation' and the damaging inroads of 'decadent capitalist ideology and conduct'.[25]

The CDIC was certainly not a cipher during the 1980s. Between 1982 and 1988, its organs put over one million cases on file for investigation and disciplined about 880 000 Party members for disciplinary offences (roughly 2 per cent of total membership). Of these, the main offences were as follows: 24 per cent were 'economic crimes', 12.4 per cent illicit sexual activities, 12.2 per cent 'violations of family planning policy' (presumably having too many children), 5 per cent gambling, 4.8 per cent 'abuse of power for personal gain', and 3.9 per cent 'serious bureaucratism and dereliction of duty'.[26] In spite of this record, however, the overall impact of the CDIC was superficial and it was its failure to make serious inroads in rooting out 'unhealthy practices' in the Party (notably corruption and nepotism) which contributed to the hostility to the Party visible in the popular protests of April–June 1989. The percentage of Party members affected was very low (only 2 per cent) and 'disciplining' did not usually involve any serious punishment such as expulsion from the Party or imprisonment. CDIC interventions made a very small impact on problems which were increasingly systemic to the Party as an institution (note, for example, the small percentage of people disciplined for 'abuse of power for personal gain'). There was a feeling, moreover, that it was the little fish that were being caught in the net while the big fish, with a few exceptions, got away.

How can we explain this failure? Three reasons suggest themselves. First, there was strong resistance from threatened individuals, their allies and protectors, who used 'hard and soft tactics' to cover their tracks, falsify evidence and retaliate against informers in order to undermine investigations launched by CDIC personnel. There was also retaliation against the latter. For example, in some areas of Shanxi province, where senior cadres were under investigation ('personages having strong backers and real power'), as soon as the CDIC investigators had left the scene, the senior cadres visited their CDIC 'superiors to lodge a complaint against their personnel and try to establish a relationship'; in some cases, they allegedly sent threatening and falsely incriminating letters.[27] In one county, Wenxi, where Party cadres and members had been involved in illegal land transactions, the case was only brought into the open when an individual cadre of the county DIC wrote to a central leader in Beijing – in this case, not only had the county CCP committee been unwilling to act but the county DIC had gone along with their inaction.[28] In a similar case in Jinjiang prefecture, Fujian province, local enterprises had allegedly been producing counterfeit drugs and marketing them throughout the country by means of bribes; the matter had been ignored by both the prefectural Party Committee and the DIC and was not investigated until the *central* DIC intervened (responding to a press exposé).[29] It seemed that in many, if not most, cases, the DIC at each level simply lacked the authority to take on their Party Committees. Faced with a host of pervasive problems to tackle and such powerful organisational opposition, the CDIC's task was difficult indeed.

Second, the CDIC itself, rather than acting as an external check on the Party, became itself enmeshed in factional conflict among the top leadership. It has tended to be an institutional power base for relatively conservative leaders. In the earlier years, it was under Chen Yun who gradually turned it away from its original concentration on Cultural Revolution remnants into a weapon against 'bourgeois liberalisation' within the Party. By the end of the decade (now under the leadership of Qiao Shi), it had become a weapon for ferreting out and punishing Party members involved in the demonstrations of April–June 1989.[30]

Third, both the above two sources of weakness reflect a deeper factor – the failure of the Party leadership to endow the CDIC with enough power and autonomy to play a watch-dog role of 'impartial supervision'. The CDIC was the Party's traditional answer to the question of how to make new rules, regulations and rectifications effective when their targets are the very people who are supposed to carry them out. This is a version of the age-old political dilemma of *quis custodiet ipsos custodes?* – who will guard the guardians themselves? At least one political reformer within the Party, Liao Gailong, proposed that the CDIC should be one part of a tripartite 'separation of powers' between supreme Party organs (the other two being the Central Committee and the Central Advisory Committee) which would each be responsible to the CCP's National Congress, would have their own specific functions and would act as a check on each other.[31] This proposal was deemed too radical by Deng himself and the major conservative leaders; in consequence, the CDIC never succeeded in freeing itself from organisational 'capture' by the Party machine and subordination to the vagaries of political conflict within the leadership.

Summarising this section, it is clear that the methods which the Party used to rehabilitate its institutional self-confidence and internal discipline were far from effective. To the extent that there had ever been a 'golden age' of the Party (before the onset of Maoism), it was not possible to recapture it. The methods used were old ones – ideological education, political rectification, organisational supervision and bureaucratic regularisation – and they seemed increasingly irrelevant at a time when the Party was not only trying to free itself from the ravages of the Cultural Revolution, but recharge itself to operate with new strategic goals (economic development) and a new economic environment (a 'socialist commodity economy'). Clearly, the Party needed not so much to rehabilitate itself along old lines but to reform its *modus operandi* to meet the challenge of economic reform. In turn, the social and economic changes of the 1980s were to have a profound effect on the Party. It is to these issues that we now turn.

Efforts at Institutional Reform

At the beginning of the reform era, the new leadership was sensitive to the need to change the Party to meet its new historical tasks. Deng Xiaoping himself set the framework of the reform in a cardinal speech 'On the Reform of the System of Party and State Leadership' on 18 August 1980 (to which I have already alluded) and a series of speeches on political reform when that issue came to the forefront of the Party agenda in the second half of 1986. I shall be concentrating here on reforms conducted *within* the limits laid down by Deng since these have conditioned actual policies on Party reform. I shall first clarify the official rationale for reforming the Party; second, identify the main elements of the reform programme; third, attempt to assess their impact on the Party; fourth, identify reasons for success or failure and, finally, conclude by tracing some implications for the future of the CCP as a viable political institution.

The Rationale for, and Content of, Party Reforms

The main purposes of reforming the Party, in the eyes of Deng Xiaoping, were to prepare it for the tasks of guiding economic development and to improve 'socialist democratisation'. Both were premised on the continuance of one-party leadership by the CCP, the most important of Deng's 'four basic principles'. In the short and medium term, economic development has taken precedence over democratisation. Deng has in the event only been willing to promote the latter to the extent that it serves the former, in spite of attempts by more radical reformers to promote political reform *for its own sake* in 1986 and early 1989.

To the extent that the Party's role becomes one of stimulating economic growth rather than organising social, economic and political transformation as in the past, it loses its function as a pervasive director and mobiliser and takes on more of a managerial role, operating in more selective, flexible and indirect ways. In making this switch, Deng not only supported the measures for rectification and rationalisation discussed above, but also stressed the need for reform in three major areas. First, he targeted the over-concentration of power, which referred not merely to concentration of power at the Party centre, but, at the centre and each level below, the concentration of power away from the membership towards the Party committee, within the committee towards its secretaries and among the secretaries towards the first secretary.[32] This led to arbitrary decision-making which ill accorded with 'the extremely difficult and complicated task of socialist construction'. The answer to this was a greater decentralisation of power within the Party and the encouragement of collective as opposed to individual leadership at each level of Party organisation.

The second area of reform was the rejuvenation and professio-nalisation of the Party, to be achieved by promoting young and middle-aged members to positions of responsibility in the Party apparatus and raising the general educational level and professional expertise of Party members, partly by retraining and partly by recruiting more members from among the intelligentsia.[33] Intern-ally, this meant a planned and accelerated promotion of younger, better educated cadres; externally, this meant a change in the target of party recruitment, away from the 'red' but uneducated worker-peasant classes towards the more educated, more skilled or more entrepreneurial (though these experts were still expected to become 'red' also if they wanted to join the Party).

A third major problem was the lack of a clear division of responsibilities between the Party and the government. In the first instance, this applies to relations with government bureaucracies but the same principle could be applied to those between the Party committee and professional managers in state enterprises. This required steps towards a clarification of the precise functions of different institutions and their separation in the real world. In Deng's mind, this would strengthen rather than weaken Party leadership because in the past the Party had grossly over-extended its area of direct intervention, becoming less effective in the process.[34]

Before asking how effective were any of these reforms, it is worth noting what is missing from Deng's programme of Party reform. There is no insistence on, and proposed measures for, an institutionalisation of intra-Party democracy. Moreover, in spite of some mention of the need for 'mass supervision' over the Party and the need for Party members and officials to be bound by the law and the state Constitution,[35] there is little stress on the need to institutionalise a system of external checks on the Party, either by other state institutions (such the people's congresses) or by the 'masses'. In the main, these were outside Deng's purview and their advocacy depended on more radical elements inside and outside the Party, particularly during the debates on political reform in late 1986 and early 1989. In this latter period, other reformist leaders such as Hu Yaobang and Zhao Ziyang were prepared to go further, but in the event lost out in the factional struggle.

The Effects of Official Party Reforms

Internal reforms in structure and procedures. There have been various efforts during the 1980s to counter the problem of over-concentration of power within the Party through structural reforms. At the centre, there was an attempt to diversify institutional sources of power by establishing the CDIC and   the Central Advisory Commission (CAC, of which more below) and by setting up the Secretariat as a counterweight to the Politburo. However, the latter measure was reversed at the Thirteenth Party Congress in 1987 and the CAD and CDIC, to the extent that they did acquire any political autonomy, became bastions of conservative opposition to further structural reforms within the Party.[36] There was also a fair amount of talk about the need for decentralisation (by delegating power from higher to lower levels of the Party apparatus) and intra-Party democracy (by reducing the power of Party committees *vis-à-vis* members and leading groups *vis-à-vis* their committees, and by working out a more explicit and democratic system of Party elections, for example by having more candidates than posts). These reforms were particularly visible in Zhao Ziyang's report to the Thirteenth Party Congress in October 1987.[37] But little progress was made in any of these areas, let alone in adopting more radical proposals such as those suggested by Liao Gailong in 1981, or the spate of ideas which emerged during the debate over political reform in 1986 and 1988–9, such as the idea of allowing open competition and a legal opposition faction within the Party.[38] There was no significant progress towards institutionalising democratic procedures (for example, by adopting an intra-Party electoral law), or guaranteeing the right of dissent.

Though this failure can be attributed to several causes, particularly important was the fact that efforts to 'normalise' and re-establish discipline within the Party in the early and mid-1980s had also been largely unsuccessful. In this context, it was simply not possible to introduce sweeping structural reform within the Party. On the issue of decentralisation of power within the apparatus, for example, the problem was that there was already too much informal decentralisation which blocked any attempt by reform leaders to impose some form of 'principled decentralisation'. Moreover, attempts to institute democratic procedures and curb the power of powerful individuals at each level were blocked by those very people and there was little the centre could do, even if it wanted to. But the centre itself became increasingly split on the issue of political reform after 1986 so any reform impetus (such as that launched by Zhao Ziyang at the Thirteenth Party Congress in 1987) was weakened. After the 4 June Incident, it disappeared completely.

Changes in the social composition and character of the Party. Three aspects of this issue are important here: first, the question of rejuvenation; second, changing the social origins of Party recruits and, third, raising the educational and professional level of Party officials and members. Together with the insistence on 'redness', these were the goals of what was termed the 'four transformations' (*si hua*) by a meeting of CCP's Central Organisation Department in May 1980 (Manion 1984: 7); i.e. Party cadres (and Party members generally) were to be 'revolutionised, rejuvenated, intellectualised and professionalised' (*geminghua, nianqinghua, zhishihua, zhuanyehua*).

The age problem was very worrying since there was a venerable stratum of revolutionary veterans (in their seventies and older) in positions of authority throughout the Party who were unsuitable for work in the new environment; on the other side, in the early 1980s, only 3.3 per cent of Party members were 25 years old or younger (compared to 26.6 per cent in 1950). From 1980, there was a serious effort to usher older Party (and government) cadres, who had joined the Party before the revolution, into a dignified retirement. The transition was eased by pensions, other welfare benefits and by according them a residual work role as 'advisers', both in ordinary units such as factories and villages and as ancillary workers within the Party. At the central level, a lead was set by the establishment of the Central Advisory Commission (CAC) at the Twelfth Party Congress in September 1982 under the chairmanship of Deng Xiaoping (with counterparts at the provincial level). In the words of Hu Yaobang in his report to that congress, these were 'to give our many veteran comrades rich in political experience a role as consultants in the service of the Party's cause'.[39] According to the new Party Constitution adopted then, the CAC was to act 'as political assistant and consultant to the Central Committee'; its chairman was supposed to be a member of the Politburo Standing Committee and its vice-chairmen could attend plenary sessions of the Politburo.[40] Thus, though the CAC was originally intended only as a temporary, transitional body to ease out the revolutionary veterans, it was certainly not toothless. At the Thirteenth Party Congress in 1987, the right of its chairman to sit on the Politburo Standing Committee was rescinded, ostensibly as a move to encourage younger aspirants, but not unconnected with the desire of Deng himself and the reformist wing of the leadership to knock the new CAC Chairman, Chen Yun, off this influential perch.[41]

To replace the older Party cadres being retired, steps were taken to establish a regular system of 'reserve cadres' for both Party and state who would be in place at each level as potential successors –

this was sometimes called building the 'third echelon'.[42] By 1987, this was apparently in place with over 1000 reserve cadres at provincial and ministerial level (with an age range of 40–45), 20 000 at prefectural and bureau level and 140 000 at county and section levels.[43] Some of the 'third echelon' cadres were selected on the basis of their youth and education and rose quickly on the strength of these qualifications, even if they lacked experience or managerial ability. This sparked criticism and opposition from their seniors who regarded them as a modern equivalent of the 'helicopter people' who had risen quickly during the Cultural Revolution.[44] On the other hand, many people entered the 'third echelon' through sponsorship by senior officials, particularly the children of senior Party cadres. This was so widespread that it led to talk of a 'princes' party' (*taizidang*).[45] Thus, though the programme to elevate younger people to responsible posts was proving effective, it is unclear whether it was succeeding in its objective of promoting the most talented and competent. However, some progress was made in reducing the average age of the Party membership in general – this was reduced to 43 by the end of 1987, largely thanks to a rapid recruitment drive which concentrated on people under 35 (between the Third Plenum in December 1978 and the end of 1987, nearly 13 million new members were recruited of whom two-thirds were under 35 (Rosen 1989: pp. 5–6). However, this trend was halted after the 4 June Incident when the older revolutionary generation stepped in, reinforcing the political staying-power of their own echelon and raising doubts about the political rectitude of many of the recent younger recruits; moreover, many of the latter either left the Party or lapsed into passivity. It is more unlikely, moreover, that talented and educated young people would want to join the Party in its current state, thus putting the post-Mao leadership's strategy for rejuvenating the institution in jeopardy. For example, when the graduating students of top-notch Qinghua University in Beijing were interviewed about their future in 1986, 73.8 per cent wanted to go abroad for further study, while only 5.5 per cent wanted to join the Party and become an official (Rosen 1989: p. 10). While this sample is hardly representative (since Qinghua is an élite institution), it does indicate that even in 1986 the CCP was being shunned by the most talented among Chinese youth; after the 4 June Incident, this situation has probably deteriorated further.

Looking at the decade as a whole, however, the attempt to lower the average age of Party members and bring in younger people has had an important impact on the political character of the Party. At the leadership level, the passing years brought a gradual shift in the balance of power between the older generation of revolutionaries in their seventies and eighties and a younger, more modern and reform-minded stratum in their fifties and sixties. These trends opened up a political gap between the generations. Deng Xiaoping has alluded to this, seeing himself (until June 1989 at least) as a mediator or bridge between them. In 1987, for example, in reply to a question from a foreign guest ('Do you mean that old people are "left-leaning" while young people are "right-leaning"?'), he replied 'You could say that'.[46] During the Tiananmen events of 1989, however, he threw his weight behind the older generation.

As of the early 1990s, the Party contained four broad 'political generations' (for discussion of this notion, see Yahuda 1979). This idea reflects the fact that the political formation of Party leaders and members takes place in certain distinctive periods and this experience continues to influence their attitudes to politics thereafter. First are the remnants of the old revolutionaries shaped during the wars against Japan and the Guomindang in the 1930s and 1940s; second are those in their fifties or early sixties by the beginning of the reform era who joined the revolution shortly before or after its success and who were shaped by the Soviet-style experience of 'socialist transformation and construction' in the 1950s and were shocked by the experience of the Great Leap Forward and Cultural Revolution; third, a Cultural Revolution generation shaped politically by the turbulent events of 1966–76; and, fourth, a reform era generation, represented in the Beijing Spring of 1989 whose political views reflected both the promise and the problems of the reforms and who had little or no direct experience of the Maoist era. Broadly speaking, there is a rough coincidence between political age and attitude to the reforms. To the extent that the older generations gradually disappear, the political ground is cleared for a more radical approach, including both economic and political reform. Since this actuarial process is inexorable, the re-entry of the first generation to direct power after the events of June 1989 may in retrospect only appear to be a transient political phenomenon.

Another change in Party recruitment was to stress educational background and specialised training as a key criterion for Party membership and cadre positions, in line with the Party's new role as an agent of economic modernisation. As late as the end of 1983, only 1.9 per cent of Chinese college students were members of the Party and in 1984 only 4 per cent of Party members had received some form of higher education.[47] Thus, during the recruitment drive beginning in 1983, the emphasis was on admitting people with senior-middle school education and above. The results of this shift in recruitment strategy were significant, as Table 6.1 demonstrates.

Table 6.1 *Educational Level of Party Members (%)*

	1978	1984	1986	End of 1987	End of 1988**
Senior-Middle School and Above	12.8	17.8	26.4*	28.5	30.4
Junior-Middle	–	30.0	–	29.0	–
Primary School	–	42.2	–	34.8	–
Illiterate	–	10.1	–	7.7	7.27**

Source: Rosen 1989, Table 3; *NCNA* (English), 29th September 1987; **NCNA* (English), 19 September 1989.

There is a steady increase in the proportion of Party members with senior-middle school education and above and a corresponding decrease in those with only primary or no education. There was also improvement in key target groups, such as university students: for example, Party membership among students in Beijing rose from 8.25 per cent to 11.5 per cent between 1984 and 1986 (Rosen 1989: Table 4).

Mention of target groups introduces the broader question of the social composition of CCP membership, i.e. the nature of those social groups which the Party deems particularly suitable for membership and who are thus targeted as priorities for admission. In the Maoist period, this would have been referred to as the 'class line' in recruitment. There has been a major shift in the

Party's 'class line' during the reform era, but, like virtually every other serious political and organisational issue, it has been a subject of dispute within the leadership and in the Party as a whole. In the context of modernisation and economic reform, the 'intelligentsia' (i.e. those with some form of higher education) were a prime target. During the Cultural Revolution they had been castigated as the 'stinking ninth' (*chou jiu*) category of political undesirables and tarred with a 'bourgeois' brush. But in the reform era Party spokespeople were at pains to stress that they were part of the 'working class' and thus very suitable for admission into the Party. This led to a general stress on attracting the intelligentsia and specific campaigns were launched to attract certain groups such as students, teachers, scientists and specialists within enterprises. This meant that there was less emphasis on those strata which had been favoured during the Maoist period, viz. ordinary workers and the 'poor and lower middle peasants'. The new recruitment strategy concentrated on particular sections within these classes: skilled workers and the richer and more economically dynamic sections of the peasantry (including members of 'specialised households', those 'who have taken the lead in becoming rich' either through agriculture or by moving into local industry, trade or transportation) (for a discussion of the new 'class line' in the rural areas, see Kelliher 1991). By late 1987, for example, about 20 per cent of rural Party members were working outside agriculture.[48] Overall, however, the proportion of peasant members in the Party dropped from 45.5 per cent in 1981 to 39.5 per cent in 1987 while the proportion of intellectuals probably increased (there are no clear figures available on this) and worker recruitment stayed fairly constant (there was a marginal drop from 18.8 per cent to 17.1 per cent between 1981 and 1987).[49] Note here that the new emphasis was not merely on the most educated or skilled, but also on the economically most successful. This is consistent with the new notion of 'socialism' as the 'development of the productive forces'; from this perspective, these people were potentially the most 'socialist'. In the context of market reforms, this often meant entrepreneurs who had shot to prosperity by exploiting some niche in the market or manipulating official connections to their advantage. During the mid-1980s in particular, when the reformist impetus was at its strongest, these groups were lionised in the press. At the Thirteenth Party Congress in 1987, for example, a good deal of publicity was given to Guan

Guangmei, a Party delegate from Benxi in the North-Eastern province of Liaoning, who had joined the Party in 1983 and had become a successful businesswomen by leasing eight state-owned shops. Though Guan was obviously supported by reformist leaders, the issue sparked off a heated debate in the media about the political significance of such entrepreneurs.[50] Another comparable case was that of Liu Xigui, a farmer from Shenyang in Liaoning province, who had become a millionaire through a private transport business. His application to join the Party had been refused but he had received hundreds of letters of support from Party members throughout the province; others on the other hand said that 'his wealth is the result of exploitation'. The provincial Party committee was unable to decide what to do about him, leaving it to Liu's local district Party branch which was also split on the issue and unable to make a decision.[51]

This kind of dissension about recruitment criteria is a common feature of the 1980s. Party members and officials recruited earlier often did not share the official enthusiasm for the intelligentsia and the *nouveaux riches*, partly on ideological grounds and partly no doubt because they represented a potential threat to their own position within the Party. In spite of pressures from the centre, many local and basic-level branches dragged their feet on implementing the new standards of recruitment (in one case, for example, an applicant was allegedly rejected because he wore a Western suit!).[52] In the countryside, there was local resentment against the 'new rich peasants', who were preferentially recruited in large numbers in some areas (for example, Yanggu county in Shandong province reported in 1984 that 40 per cent of its new Party recruits were 'advanced elements of specialised and key households').[53] Some rural cadres grumbled: 'In the past, the Communist Party loved the poor, now they love the rich... In the past, entrance to the Party depended on a person's class background; now you see if a person is in a specialised or 10 000 yuan household. In the past, you looked at class consciousness; now you look at the ability to become rich' (Rosen 1989: p. 8). In the aftermath of the Beijing massacre, the new leadership themselves reflected this resentment when they ruled that 'ex-ploiters' could not be admitted to the Party and those who were already there should spend their post-tax profits on production and public welfare and not on private needs – some of them were even to be investigated and expelled.[54] The new emphasis in Party recruitment was on industrial workers, particularly those in larger state-owned concerns. Jiang Zemin, the new Party General-Secretary, complained that 'in recent years, we have failed to pay sufficient attention to recruiting Party members from among workers at the basic level'.[55] At the same time, some of the younger intellectuals who had joined the Party in the mid–late 1980s were leaving the Party. The new approach to recruitment by the post-Tiananmen leadership is likely to prove difficult to implement given their lack of political credibility and, to the extent that it is successful, will prove self-defeating since the Party will be shutting its door to those strata of the population – professional or entrepreneurial – which are crucial to its drive for modernisation and a market economy. This indeterminacy in the 'class line' in recruitment is one more expression of the broader political contradiction which has pervaded efforts at Party reform more generally during the 1980s.

Efforts to separate the functions of Party and government. The issue of relations between the Party on the one side and government/state agencies on the other is but one part of a complex set of issues concerning the CCP's 'external relations' with other political, social and economic institutions. These include relations between Party committees and professional management in state-owned enterprises; between the Party and its 'transmission belts', the 'mass organisations' such as trade unions, the Women's Federation, the Young Communist League and official student associations; between the Party and other political institutions, notably the system of people's representative congresses, the 'democratic parties', the Chinese People's Political Consultative Congress, and the legal system; between the Party and the organisational expression of different social groups (notably the various 'associations' of entrepreneurs and professionals which have sprung up in the 1980s). Some of these issues (such as the role of the Party within enterprises, the function of trade unions and the issue of policy towards new kinds of social organisation) are dealt with elsewhere in this book. Others which concern   the nature of the political system more generally are, strictly speaking, more appropriate to a book on political reform proper as opposed to one concerned primarily with the politics of economic reform. They will be dealt with in future work. Here I shall concentrate on the attempt to change the Party's political role by separating its organisation and functions from those of state institutions.

This issue was raised relatively early, by Deng himself in August 1980 and by an authoritative 'commentator's' article in the *People's Daily* in December that year. The general rationale was clear from the outset: that in China, to an even greater extent than in other state socialist polities, the Party penetrated other political spheres, including the state administrative apparatus; that this 'unified leadership' by the Party was a relic of the pre-revolutionary era and the struggle to improve centralised control in the 1950s, but was inappropriate to a new era; that the Party's new role in promoting modernisation did *not* mean that it should directly involve itself in technical and economic work; administration should be left to professional administrators and experts and the Party should withdraw from multi-faceted intervention into state institutions at all levels to concern itself with ideological education, policy-making and overall political supervision and co-ordination of the bureaucracy. The system of 'interlocking directorates', whereby officials 'wore two hats', as both Party and government officials, should be discouraged. Administrative activity should have its own realm of operational autonomy with its own chain of command governed by general and administrative law. The strengthening of state power, the administration and the judiciary (the mass organisations were included as well) did not contradict the strengthening of the Party's power – a leaner, more selective Party would be more effective.[56]

Though certain experiments in separating Party from government took place in the early 1980s, the practice of the Party's 'unified leadership' remained dominant.[57] The issue did not come squarely into the political agenda until 1986, again at Deng's initiative, and it was one of the major planks of the political reform programme launched by Zhao Ziyang at the Thirteenth Party Congress in 1987. Zhao defined the Party's role as follows:[58]

The Party exercises political leadership, which means that it formulates political principles, points the political direction and makes major policy decisions and recommends cadres for the key posts in organs of state power. The principal method by which it exercises leadership in state affairs is as follows: through legal procedures what the Party advocates becomes the will of the state, and the people are mobilised by the Party organisations and the good example of Party members to implement the Party's line, principles and policies.

This proposal to redefine the Party's role is relatively modest since it stays within the framework of leadership by a single party and retains the power of appointing state officials (the nomenklatura system). Nor was it motivated by any attempt to institute a formal 'separation of powers' between the legislative, executive and judicial functions along Western lines – Zhao ruled this out of court as a 'bourgeois' heresy.

Zhao's formulation of the issue also contains more than a little wishful thinking about the putative benefits of the reforms. For example:

When there is no distinction between Party and government, the Party has to bear the burden of administrative work and may easily become one opposite of a contradiction or even the focal point of many contradictions; only when the two are separated is it possible for the Party to handle contradictions with ease, assume overall control of a situation and co-ordinate the work in all fields.

The first half of this statement is sensible; the latter half seems over-optimistic, at least as long as the Party remains the sole significant political force in Chinese society. It raises many questions about what all this would mean in practice. However, it was Zhao's intention to launch a series of experiments to ascertain what exact forms this separation between Party and government would take in different institutional contexts and at different levels and this process did indeed get off the ground in 1988. Most important were the attempts, first, to abolish the 'party groups' (*dangzu*) in specific administrative bodies. These were composed of the Party members working in each agency who acted as the real nucleus of power within the agency (as in other state institutions such as universities or factories); second, to phase out all Party departments at each level whose work overlapped with those of state departments at each level; third, to stop the previous practice whereby a Party Committee at a given level would designate one of its secretaries or a member of its standing committee to take charge of the work of government at that level;[59] and, fourth, to transfer *a part* of the power to appoint government officials to government agencies, particularly at lower levels of the bureaucracy.

Progress was slow, however, and largely confined to experimental areas and institutions. This is partly the result of the practical difficulties of separating the complex system of intermeshing institutions which had built up over decades; partly because of resistance on the part of Party officials who thought such a separation unnecessary. More worrying from a reform point of view is the vagueness of the Party's new role. In practical terms, the Party retained large powers of direct intervention, but how could one distinguish 'legitimate' from 'illegitimate' intervention. If the Party organisation at a given level withdrew from government work and the latter was conducted badly, who would be responsible? Moreover, if the Party withdrew more decisively from state institutions (and other institutions throughout society), then what role did it have left and how could it exercise its function of 'political leadership'? If it lost all this power, why would anyone want to join or make a career in the Party in future?

With a continued reformist impetus from the top of the Party, perhaps many of these problems could have been worked out gradually by trial and error. However, the coming to power of the Party conservatives after the 4 June Incident brought a backlash against the policy of separating Party and government. The new General Secretary, Jiang Zemin, for example, argued that central state agencies should have *stronger* Party organisations because they had succumbed to 'bourgeois liberalism'. Li Peng added that it was not enough for officials in state organs to be merely professionals – they should be 'revolutionaries' who did their jobs 'with the support of Party organisations'.[60] The same principle was affirmed for lower levels of the bureaucracy and state-owned institutions and enterprises and Zhao Ziyang was accused of weakening Party leadership by diluting it and relegating the Party to the role of an 'assistant'.[61] Corresponding practical measures were taken to restore the *status quo ante*. But these reversions ran against the logic of a position sanctioned by Deng Xiaoping himself, i.e. that the tradition of comprehensive and direct involvement of the Party in all aspects of political, social and economic life was not only detrimental to economic modernisation and reform but also damaging to the Party itself. While the reformers offered the Party a future which was uncertain, the conservatives offered a past that might prove fatal.

Conclusion: The Struggle between the Two Parties

It can be argued that the Party ended the 1980s in worse shape than when it began, that a process of institutional decay, already well-advanced, had grown worse: the Party was more divided, less disciplined, more demoralised, less prestigious, more alienated from society and less capable of implementing its policies. In many conventional accounts, much of this is attributed to the damage caused by leadership dissension and conflict and it is true that different sections of the leadership held different visions of the character and role of the Party. The conservatives still hankered after a party of professional revolutionaries inspired by the political enthusiasms of yester-year and exercising direct and comprehensive control over society at large. The reformers were groping towards a more circumscribed notion of the Party which was more secular in its beliefs, more professional and technocratic in its outlook, playing a more indirect managerial and co-ordinative role in society and sharing power to some limited extent with other groups and institutions.

But these differences among the leadership over issues of Party reform are symptomatic of the deeper processes at work when state socialist systems seek to reform themselves. At the historical level, this transition crosses two historical eras, each of which finds expression in the outlook, organisation and operation of the Party; it contains elements of both eras, yet this very diversity obstructs the transition and creates an institution at war with itself. This basic contradiction finds expression in the coexistence of old and new ideologies, operational styles, institutional arrangements and types of people. In the human aspect, it creates politically explosive discord between an embittered older generation and a frustrated younger generation. Change and reform is thus a deeply-rooted political struggle which weakens the organisation internally and paralyses its ability to implement thoroughgoing reforms, even if they are only confined to the economic sphere. The Party becomes a 'halfway house' in which new tenants have arrived to move in but the old tenants refuse to move out. To rephrase the Maoist slogan of 'the struggle between two lines within the Party', the reform era has created a 'struggle between two Parties within the Party'. History would appear to favour the Party of reform and modernisation, but the possible trajectory of the Party's future political evolution is far from clear – I shall return to this question in the last chapter.

The pressures for change or continuity in the Party are not of course generated purely from within the Party itself. Part of its historical dilemma rests on the fact that, both as a heritage of the Cultural Revolution era and as a result of the partial success of the economic reform programme, the context within which it operates has also gone through major changes: in the political culture of the population, the nature of social structure and popular mores and the operational logic of the economic system. It is to the linkages between economic reform and broader socio-political changes in Chinese society that we turn in our next chapter.

7

The Social Impact of Economic Reform: The Rise of Civil Society?

It is the thesis of this chapter that the economic reforms have brought about major changes in the structure and dynamics of Chinese society and that these changes have important political consequences. My aim here is briefly to trace the main dimensions of social change and trace their political implications, focusing on two aspects of this process. The first concerns the impact of economic reform on different components of Chinese society. We have already seen in Chapter 1 that Chinese society before the reforms contained pervasive tensions and discontents which provided a kind of social mandate for economic reform in the late 1970s. In turn, to the extent that reforms have affected specific social groups in different ways and have led to changes in existing social groups and the rise of new ones, a new constellation of social interests has been created. Since social groups have experienced the reforms in different ways and have benefited/lost from them to varying degrees, they have created a new political environment which affects the basic credibility of the regime and influences the policy process (as we have seen already in the cases of industrial and agricultural policy). The evolving pattern of social interests thus has an important impact on the course and content of the reforms.

The second aspect concerns the impact of economic reforms on the relationship between state and society. Since they have brought about, albeit unevenly, a *redistribution of economic power* – away from the state and its ancillary agencies and towards individuals, households, firms and groups – they have also brought about a shift in the balance of power between state and society. This dispersion of social power has opened up the potential (Marxists might call it the 'material basis') for a new social sphere which provides a realm of (greater or lesser) social autonomy *vis-à-vis* the state. To the extent that this new social space is occupied by new types of organisation which are organised spontaneously and enjoy a degree of autonomy from the state, then we can discern the shoots of an incipient 'civil society' which has crucial implications for China's long-term political future.

The main focus of this chapter, therefore, will be on the political implications of changes in social structure and organisation. I shall begin with a brief description of Chinese social structure and organisation before the reform era to provide the background necessary to assess changes after 1978.

Chinese Social Structure and Organisation in the Pre-Reform Era

In spite of impressive progress towards the establishment of a comprehensive industrial capacity and certain egregious technological achievements (most notably in nuclear armaments), the structure of Chinese society on the eve of reform was similar in many ways to an archetypical less-developed country in what used to be called the Third World. An overwhelming proportion of the population lived in the countryside (in 1978 the rural population was 82.1 per cent of the total) (*ZGSHTJZL* 1990: p. 23) and a large majority of the labour force worked in agriculture or related activities (71 per cent in 1978) (*ZGSHTJZL* 1990: p. 49). A vast majority of the working population were engaged in manual as opposed to 'mental' labour (the proportions were 93.3 and 6.7 per cent respectively in 1981) (*ZGSHTJZL* 1990: p. 50). Overlaying these gross occupational divides was a system of organising production relations, based on ownership, which was characteristic of state socialist regimes in general. Since the private sector was negligible, the main distinction was between the state and collective sectors with the vast majority of the labour force working in the rural or urban collective sectors. In 1978, these proportions were 76.3 and 5.1 per cent respectively, compared with 18.6 per cent working in state concerns (*ZGSHTJZL* 1990: p. 48). This institutional divide, which largely overlapped with and reinforced the urban–rural distinction, reinforced sectoral differences because levels of income and conditions of work were in general superior in state enterprises. This dual system of social differentiation was the matrix of a society which was unequal in terms of economic sector, geographical area (notably the rural–urban divide), economic institutions and occupation. In spite of Maoist efforts to compress social differentials, this was a society stratified in terms of income, status and power (for more detail on the stratification of pre-reform society, see Parish and Whyte 1978 and Whyte and Parish 1984).

In spite of these strong elements of social differentiation and inequality, however, Chinese social structure could be described as relatively homogeneous in the following senses. First, there was a systematic attempt by the regime to contain society within a limited number of categories; indeed the 'official' social structure contained only three components viz. two classes (workers and peasants) and one stratum (the intelligentsia).[1] Second, the rise of other strata and classes that one might find in other comparable societies (notably self-employed workers and private entrepreneurs) was prevented or inhibited. Third, there was an attempt to homogenise the members of each social category, by imposing uniform conditions of work on them and limiting the emergence of internal differentials (for example, through egalitarian policies on wages in industry and workpoints in agriculture).

Underlying and extending beyond the distinctive system of ownership institutions in the economy, there was a basic feature of social organisation which is also characteristic of state socialist societies, the phenomenon of 'verticality'. This means that the prime principle of social organisation was 'vertical' in the sense that each individual and social group was incorporated into a hierarchically organised system of some kind as opposed to belonging to social institutions organised horizontally by their members. At the macro level, this was based on the pervasive system of centralised bureaucratic 'systems' (*xitong*) organised on the 'branch' (*tiao*) principle; at the micro level this was based on the all-important work 'unit' (*danwei*), be it state enterprise or rural collective, which encompassed the individual's lives in a much more comprehensive way than work units in non-socialist and non-Chinese settings. This system of 'verticality' led to what has been called economic 'cellularisation' and social 'encapsulation', the latter meaning that individuals and groups were cloistered within their 'systems' and units and separated from comparable systems and units at the same level. The key relationships which affected their lives were primarily vertical within their unit or system rather than horizontal with counterparts .in comparable enterprises or occupations (for the notions of 'cellularisation' and 'encapsulation', see Shue 1989 and Vogel 1989: ch. 12).

This social encapsulation was reinforced, from the early 1960s onwards, by a remarkable stability of the working population, a lack of mobility in geographical, inter-sectoral and intra-sectoral terms. In the state sector, employees tended to stay in the same enterprise for life and their children often inherited jobs there to boot; in the rural sector, peasants were restricted in their movements by a system of household registration (*hukou*) which made it very difficult, for example, to go to the cities or other provinces to find work. To the extent that there was large-scale migration during the Cultural Revolution decade, for example, it was sponsored and organised by the state (for example, the campaigns to send Shanghai youth to Xinjiang or urban youth to the countryside).

There were countervailing forms of social organisation which worked against this pervasive verticality and encapsulation. Official institutions, such as the Party itself and all organisations with a co-ordinating, committee-type function were designed to cut across vertical divisions (Schurmann 1968: p. 89). However, these official 'horizontal' organisations were themselves caught up and fragmented by the divisions they tried to transcend. Where this 'horizontal' (*kuai*) principle of Party and governmental organisation coincided with powerful local interests at the provincial, urban or county levels (the phenomenon of 'localism', *difangzhuyi* and 'independent kingdoms', *duli wangguo*), it was considerably more successful in transcending the fragmentation caused by the branch organisations emanating from Beijing. Another pervasive countervailing principle of social organisation were the networks (both vertical and horizontal) based on personal relationships (*guanxi*) which operated in terms of both symmetrical reciprocity (horizontally, between equals, for example between colleagues in the same or different work units or localities) and asymmetrical reciprocity (vertically, between unequals, for example between an ordinary worker and a cadre in a work unit) (for discussions of *guanxi*, see Walder 1986; Oi 1987: ch. 7 and Gold 1985).

Chinese social organisation in the immediate pre-reform era was thus based on a dual system of countervailing principles: an official institutional matrix based primarily (but not exclusively) in vertical terms and an unofficial (and often illegitimate or illegal) system of social relationships based primarily (but not exclusively given the prevalence of vertical *guanxi*) on horizontal ties. The society which resulted was highly 'encapsulated' and immobile. To the extent that the basic tenets underlying economic reform posed a fundamental challenge to this mode of social organisation and to the extent that substantial changes did take place in China's economic system in the 1980s, one would expect there to have also been substantial changes in the structure, organisation and dynamics of Chinese society in this period. It is to an investigation of this hypothesis that we now turn.

The Impact of Economic Reform on Chinese Society

There are certain central elements of the economic reforms which would, if realised, bring about major changes in Chinese society. They set out explicitly to foster economic diversification, in terms of the system of ownership and the general pattern of economic activity; they tolerated, nay encouraged, an increase in material inequality to stimulate economic effort; they encouraged greater mobility (occupational, sectoral and geographical); and they called for a proliferation of horizontal relations between economic actors in the context of the spread of market relations.

The Social Impact of Reform: General Trends

In the event, the social impact of the reform programme has been extensive and deep.[2] There have been shifts in the distribution of the labour force across three basic economic divides: agriculture/industry, state/non-state ownership and urban/rural. Compared with 71 and 15.4 per cent working in agriculture and industry in 1978, the proportion had changed to 60 and 17.1 per cent by 1990 (*SSB* 1991: p. 77). Part of the workers moving out of agriculture had gone into the burgeoning rural industrial sector and part into commerce and services (the latter, tertiary, sector expanded from

11.7 to 18.6 per cent over the same period) (*SSB* 1991: p. 80). There was also an important shift in the ratio of people working in state and non-state enterprises. In the urban/state sector, the proportion of the labour force in state and non-state enterprises changed from 78.4 and 21.6 per cent respectively in 1978 to 70.2 and 29.8 per cent respectively in 1990, the latter figure including nearly seven million 'individual labourers' who had been negligible before (*SSB* 1991: p. 78). In the countryside, the percentage of the labour force in agriculture dropped from 89.7 to 79.4 per cent during the same period, a large proportion of the surplus being absorbed into collective enterprises run by townships and villages (*SSB* 1991: p. 94). Within agriculture, moreover, as we have seen, there was a *de facto* privatisation of agricultural production which conferred far greater economic power on the peasant household, weakened rural collectives and loosened the link between the rural community and the state. Overall, to the extent that the balance of economic power and the proportions of the labour force had shifted between the state and non-state sectors in favour of the latter, the direct power of the state over the everyday lives of citizens had lessened in consequence.

These shifts are part of a broader process of rapid social differentiation. Chinese society has become more *complex*, in terms of both structure and attitudes. Existing groups have become internally more complex as a consequence of diversification in economic sectors, forms of ownership and levels of income. New groups and strata have also emerged: in the countryside, 'new rich peasant' households which have made money quickly in recent years through specialised agricultural production or diversification into local industry, trade and services; in the cities, private business-people generally, and a small number of successful entrepreneurs in particular, who have amassed small fortunes through personal initiative, specialised skills or good connections, and, harder to discern, a growing number of entrepreneurial managers in state enterprises well attuned to the spreading logic of market competition.

Empirical studies differ on whether this increasing social differentiation has created greater inequality to Chinese society. While a majority of analyses, impressionistic or systematic, tend to admit that material inequalities have increased to a limited degree this trend is counter-balanced by two other consequences of the reforms.

First, there has been an overall increase in incomes and living standards which has benefited an overwhelmingly large percentage of the population, even though this may be by different amounts (for example, see the data on the rural population in Table 7.1). Second, in one important dimension – rural/urban – the trend was the other way, towards a decline in the relative income disparities of the rural and urban population as rural incomes climbed more rapidly than their urban counterparts; beginning in 1985, the rural/urban differential began to increase again (Table 7.2).

Table 7.1   *The Composition of the (Annual) Average Per Capital Net Incomes of Rural Households According to Group of Households (percentages)*

Household groups divided by net income	1978	1980	1981	1985	1986	1987	1988
less than 100 yuan	33.3	9.8	4.7	1.0	1.1	0.9	0.5
100–500 yuan	31.7	24.7	14.9	3.4	3.2	2.4	1.5
150–200 yuan	17.6	27.1	23.0	7.9	7.0	5.0	3.3
200–300 yuan	15.0	25.3	34.8	25.6	21.8	17.5	13.5
300–400 yuan	2.4	8.6	14.4	24.0	21.7	21.3	17.5
400–500 yuan	2.4	2.9	5.0	15.8	16.5	17.2	16.7
over 500 yuan	2.4	1.6	3.2	22.3	28.7	35.7	47.0

Source: ZGSHTJZL 1990, p. 68.

From a social and political perspective, however, such objective economic indices may be of less relevance than the facts that many Chinese *perceive* that the reforms have brought greater inequalities and that these perceptions have given rise to social hostilities and conflict. In China, this is known as the 'red-eye disease' (*hongyanbing*), in other words social envy. This is partly a reflection of the continuing influence of the pre-reform ideological atmosphere of 'egalitarianism' which radical Maoists had found to be politically useful in launching ordinary workers and peasants against 'class enemies' among the intelligentsia and officialdom. While these perceptions reflect real material differences, they tend to be exacerbated when an inequality arises rapidly, when it is proximate (for example, members of one's own (extended) family, neighbours, the next village, school-friends or local officials), and

Table 7.2   *Average Annual Income of Residents and Workers (in yuan)*

Year	Residents' incomes			Labourers' income			Rural/urban ratio-rural as 1	
	Total	Urban	Rural	Total	Urban	Rural	Residents' income	Labourers' income
1964	120	222	97	–	–	–	2.29	–
1981	265	476	213	524	753	445	2.23	1.69
1982	311	509	260	595	784	530	1.96	1.48
1983	357	549	299	619	825	548	1.84	1.51
1984	435	633	343	699	951	616	1.85	1.54
1985	510	730	385	781	1071	641	1.90	1.67
1986	602	877	407	816	1271	660	2.15	1.92
1987	692	975	445	893	1407	712	2.19	1.98
1988	843	1146	525	1024	1566	831	2.18	1.88

Source: ZGSHTJZL 1990, p. 67

when it takes highly visible forms (such as ostentatious displays of wealth at festivals or marriages, the construction of fine houses or the acquisition of expensive consumer durables). Behind the envy lurks the notion that the rapidly rich and the suddenly successful cannot become so unless they have resorted to shady or immoral means (and there have been enough sharp business practices and corrupt officials around to reinforce such a view). This phenomenon appears to have become worse as the reforms ran into trouble after 1986 – as inflation started eating into urban incomes (see Table 7.3) and farmers found themselves facing a growing price 'scissors' whereby state procurement prices were not rising while input prices were soaring. In addition to the 'red-eye disease', one can identify another psychological phenomenon which one could call 'ratcheting discontent', whereby even people who have benefited substantially from the reforms are dissatisfied with temporary reverses because their level of expectation has risen in the meantime. This puts reform policy-makers on a treadmill. To the extent that their own popularity and the credibility of the political system they represent depends on their ability to deliver ever higher amounts of welfare, even temporary reverses, often prompted by the dictates of sound economic policy (such as the austerity

programme beginning in 1988), bring popular discontent which is
translated by opposition activists into a challenge to the regime
itself (as in early 1989).

Table 7.3   *Price Indexes 1978–91 (preceding year = 100)*

Year	Overall retail price index	Overall staff and workers' cost of living index
1978	100.7	100.7
1979	102.0	101.9
1980	106.0	107.5
1981	102.4	102.5
1982	101.9	102.0
1983	101.5	102.0
1984	102.8	102.7
1985	108.8	111.9
1986	106.0	107.0
1987	107.3	108.8
1988	118.5	120.7
1989	117.8	116.3
1990	102.1	101.3
1991*	102.9	103.4

Note: These official figures probably substantially understate the real rate
of inflation, so they should only be seen as indicators of broad trends.
Sources: SSB 1991, p. 198; **NCNA* 28 February 1992.

Chinese society has also become more fluid and dynamic. There
has been a rapid increase in horizontal mobility within the
countryside, between countryside and cities and between regions.
According to official statistics, the ratio of rural and urban
population has changed steadily from 1978, when the urban share
was 17.9 per cent to 1990 when it was estimated to be 26.4 per cent
(*SSB* 1991: p. 61). This trend reflects both migration to the cities to
seek work and, more importantly, migration to small rural towns
which have been encouraged as growth poles and centres of local
industry. Greater occupational and geographical mobility has in
turn brought a widespread process of 'delocalisation' as the state-
defined, vertically integrated boundaries of previously encapsulated
communities have broken down or become more porous. A larger

proportion of household members in the countryside retain their residence but now work outside their immediate community. Moreover, in both rural and urban areas, there are increasing numbers of itinerant workers, skilled and unskilled, who are operating away from their home area on a contract or casual basis.

Increasing mobility has undermined the previous verticality of Chinese social organisation, a process intensified by the spread of market relations between individuals, households and firms. Both capital and labour are more mobile before and horizontal ties have proliferated between economic actors whose relations had previously been mediated, at least formally, by one or other of the vertical systems. For example, rural households and individuals have joined together to form 'economic associations'; manifold forms of joint venture have emerged, often on an inter-regional basis; rural enterprises have linked up with large urban companies on a sub-contracting basis; the 'open policy' has led to a complex array of co-operative arrangements with foreign firms. And yet, as of the early 1990s, the organisation of Chinese society is structurally ambiguous. While there has been a rapid emergence of 'horizontal' relations, the vertical principle of hierarchical control by the vast 'branch' institutions is still in place, though its impact is increasingly uneven (for example, it has more control in the cities than in the countryside, and in the north and interior provinces than in the more marketised coastal provinces). To the extent that these two principles of social organisation represent the old and the new, a social expression of the relationship between 'planning' and the 'market' in economics, they are at war with each other and the contradiction between them represents the current deadlock in the overall reform process.

The Impact of Reform on Different Social Groups

While the social impact of the reforms has been remarkable, it has also been uneven. How have the reforms affected different groups/strata/classes in Chinese society? Can we identify any clear losers or winners; if so, what have they won or lost and what are their attitudes to the reforms in consequence? This inquiry will provide a background for our next set of questions about the possibility for the emergence of a new form of social organisation akin to 'civil society'.

Let us begin with the largest group; the peasantry, which still constitute by far the largest group in the population. In general, the agricultural population was one of the clearest beneficiaries of the reforms, at least until the mid-1980s, as disposable incomes rose more rapidly than in the cities (between 1978 and 1984, their average per capita real incomes rose by nearly 20 per cent per year) and peasant households and individuals were granted greater freedom to determine their own output and working methods in agriculture and to move into other areas or occupations (the increase in rural incomes was substantially the result of non-agricultural activity, such as 'sidelines' and local industry).

Clearly there is a 'rural interest' which has benefited, and would continue to benefit, from improvements in procurement prices, subsidies for agricultural inputs, a larger flow of industrial consumer goods at reasonable prices and greater freedom of economic action and social mobility. At the same time, however, it is increasingly difficult to define the 'rural interest' or describe 'the peasantry' since the rural population has become increasingly differentiated: within agriculture (with greater specialisation in output), and between agriculture and non-agriculture (industry, commerce, transportation and services). Particularly striking was the rapid increase in rural small-scale enterprises which employed nearly one quarter of the rural labour force by the late 1980s. There is evidence, moreover, of a trend towards greater rural income inequality: spatial differentials, between better and worse situated regions (about 70 million peasants, mostly in the poorer Western and interior provinces, are still estimated to be in dire poverty) and socio-economic differentials within each locality, between entrepreneurial 'new rich peasants' who have made the most of the reforms on the one side, and households poorly endowed with labour or expertise on the other (Conroy 1985; Kelliher 1991).

While the rural interest did well in the first phase of the reforms, as we saw in Chapter 3 the picture began to change in the mid-1980s as problems escalated: shortage of agricultural investment and a deterioration in previously acquired rural capital assets (such as irrigation works); shortages of, and price increases in, basic agricultural inputs such as fuel, plastic sheeting, pesticides and fertiliser and a reluctance on the part of the state to increase purchasing prices because of political pressure to keep down food prices in the cities and the desire to rein in the burgeoning financial burden of consumer subsidies; a decline in the ability of state purchasing agencies to pay cash on the nail; and increasing full or semi-unemployment as more unviable rural small-scale industries have been forced to close because of shrinking markets, supply shortages and credit constraints in the context of the austerity programme of the late 1980s. The level of rural discontent reached alarming levels by 1988–9; however, the peasantry were not involved in the mass protests of May–June 1989 and the Deng regime was thus free to move against urban unrest. However, the rural situation contains the seeds of political upheaval and the CCP needs to maintain its power base there as a bulwark against urban discontent, a fact which is reflected in efforts by the Li Peng government after June 4 to put more resources into agriculture and encourage the growth of rural enterprises.

Turning to the cities, there is evidence of a general 'urban interest' in the form of increasing dissatisfaction among *urbanites* generally, and particularly those on fixed incomes, who feel that they have been losing out to the peasantry. They point to visible evidence of prosperous peasants doing unprecedented things (even little things like taking a 'soft-seat' couchette in long-distance trains) and feel that they are bearing part of the burden for rural prosperity through escalating food prices. Though urban incomes have risen more slowly than rural, however, there has been substantial improvement (for example, the average real per capita of 'workers and cadres' rose by 23 per cent between 1981 and 1985). However, these material gains have not been evenly distributed so we need to look more closely at specific categories within the urban population, beginning with *urban workers*. State manual workers benefited from a substantial increase in real wages in the early/mid-1980s and, in relative terms at least, have been able to defend themselves against inflation in the late 1980s by maintaining pressures for bonuses on enterprise managers. At the same time, however, state workers had been a relatively privileged segment of the labour force before the reforms and, as we saw in Chapter 4, certain aspects of the reforms threatened their status. In particular, labour reforms have threatened their job security and the advent of a bankruptcy law for state enterprises conjures up a spectre of large-scale unemployment; they have resented a real or perceived tendency for some of the workers in the previously 'second-class' collective and private sectors to be doing a lot better than themselves; and have been very concerned about the erosive effects of inflation on their incomes).[3] In consequence, their attitude towards the reforms programme as a whole has been ambivalent. Workers in the non-state collective and private sectors have increased as a percentage of the urban labour force (to about 30 per cent). At least until 1988, workers in the non-state sectors were doing well out of the general burgeoning of the urban economy and the fact that an efficient tax system was not yet in place to cream off a percentage of their profits. However, they were subject to arbitrary levies by local administrative agencies and were treated as second-class economic citizens in the sense that they often found it difficult to compete with state enterprises in gaining access to scarce raw materials or energy (these bottlenecks had to be opened through *guanxi*). Moreover, in many cases they lacked the welfare benefits and job security of their counterparts in the state sector and in consequence were more vulnerable in times of economic down-turn such as in 1988–90. In net terms, however, workers in these non-state sectors have a interest in a continuation and deepening of reforms since this will provide greater freedom from what they perceive as the bureaucratic stranglehold of officialdom and enable them to compete on a more equal basis with their counterparts in the pampered state sector.

Economic fluctuations and pressures on enterprises to shed surplus labour have created a stratum of urban unemployed or semi-employed. Though official unemployment figures ('number of persons awaiting jobs') indicate that the annual urban unemployment rate had dropped from a high of 5.3 per cent in 1978 to an average of about 2 per cent annually between 1984 and 1989 (SSB 1990: p. 123), these figures underestimate the real figures and the economic retrenchment of 1988–90 probably increased these substantially. Moreover, there is a large casually or semi-employed 'floating population' in the cities (including what Marxists might call 'lumpen elements'), mostly recent immigrants from the countryside who are working on term contracts (for example, as domestic servants or construction workers), eking out a minimal living from intermittent casual work or hawking, or engaged in a variety of illegal or criminal activities. In times of economic retrenchment, many of such workers on short-term contracts for state firms (particularly in construction) may be among the first to be laid off (with minimal or no social benefits). Rough estimates put this stratum at about 10 million people by the end of the decade (with 1.15 million in Beijing alone), in addition to a statistically admitted urban labour force of about 150 million.[4] The situation was reaching crisis proportions by early 1989 when there was a huge influx of peasants into the big cities in search of work.[5] Since this 'floating population' is so large, it is hard to identify any set of consistent attitudes to the reforms. However, since their very presence in the cities is a consequence of reform; since their ability to remain there depends on the loosening of administrative controls which the reforms have achieved; and since they appear to regard even this marginal urban existence as superior to any hypothetical alternative in their rural home-areas, they would seem to be a clear beneficiary of existing reforms and a supporter of further reform. Given the fact, however, that their marginal and often illicit existence brings them into relatively frequent contact with the urban authorities, they are a stratum with strong political grudges and potentially explosive political proclivities.

The differential positions of these sub-strata of urban workers conditioned their responses to the events of May–June 1989. State workers went along with student protests, yet did not provide widespread support; though there was a move towards autonomous worker organisations in a number of large cities, it had limited effect in terms of the percentage of workers recruited and its political impact on the urban movement. Workers in the non-state sectors, on the other hand, angered by government efforts to levy part of their incomes and worried about the growth of inflation and the retrenchment policies of late 1988, provided more active support to the students. Self-employed workers (such as taxi or trishaw drivers, couriers, haulage contractors and the like) were particularly involved in aiding the student movement in Beijing and elsewhere. But perhaps the most volatile, and intensively engaged, urban group were members of the 'floating population', notably unemployed and casual labourers. In Nanjing, for example, a group of unemployed youths was arrested in June 1989, reportedly carrying banners inscribed 'We want democracy, we want freedom, we want wives' and 'We want bread, we want coffee, we want Marlboro and Long Kent' (Ostergaard 1989). This stratum also provided a fertile soil for petty criminals and even these played e in the urban protests of 1989. In Beijing, for example, p reportedly marched under a banner which announced that they were 'petty thieves of Beijing City' who had pledged 'In support of the students, no theft for three days'! (Friedman 1989: p. 3). It is also likely that this motley stratum was responsible for much of the popular violence which met the invading PLA in Beijing on 4 June.

It seems that the economic reforms have had an ambiguous impact on China's state *enterprise managers*. On the one hand, they have gained a limited amount of freedom of manoeuvre in relation to their bureaucratic superiors as a result of the partial success of industrial reforms intended to 'enlarge the autonomy of enterprises'. With the spread of the notion of 'scientific management' and training in Western/Japanese management methods, there have been attempts to exert more systematic and 'scientific' control over their workforces (Warner 1985), though progress has been slow and uneven. New incentive systems and greater control over enterprise funds has enabled them to increase their own incomes substantially through subsidies and bonuses. On the other hand, they still operate within strong constraints. They are still heavily dependent on their bureaucratic superiors and must work out formal and informal ways of accommodating them and gaining their support (Huang 1990 and Walder 1989a). They are still dependent on the co-operation of their own workforces which, bolstered by virtual tenure and by the continuing nature of the state enterprise as a mini-welfare state, have successfully pressed for bonuses and welfare benefits to match or exceed productivity gains (Walder 1989a). They are still hedged in by enterprise Party secretaries/committees who have been reluctant to grant greater autonomy to professional managers and continue to exercise their right to 'supervise' their activities (Chamberlain 1987).

This ambiguous position reflects the fact that the managers of China's state enterprises are a stratum in transition. In general, existing managers have been willing to accept only partial reforms, because they have been able to establish mutually beneficial relations with their administrative supervisors which are comfortable enough not to want to press reforms much faster and further (Huang 1990). While a new breed of younger, more market-minded professional manager is being trained in new management schools and departments, they are fresh on the scene and have not yet been able to stamp their authority on the enterprise. Though the balance of power between the newer and older managers was gradually shifting, particularly from the mid-1980s on, the slowing of industrial reforms in 1989 slowed down this process, leaving the existing cadre of enterprise managers as an influential but socio-politically ambiguous stratum, acting both as a brake on, and stimulus to, deeper-going reform.

Turning to Party/state *officials*, they were clearly the stratum with potentially the most to lose from a successful economic reform programme since the latter would undermine the previous nomenklatura system. Unsurprisingly, there is ample evidence that, in general, they have sought to blunt or slow the reforms in both cities and countryside or turn them to their own advantage, both as individuals and as agents of particular institutions (for industry, see Shirk 1985; for agriculture, Zweig 1983). By a defensive strategy which combines both bureaucratic self-preservation with active entrepreneurship, officials have been very successful in preserving their positions and privileges. They have also fortified and extended their power by seizing the opportunities for rent-seeking offered by new policies (notably the two-track pricing system) and by forging alliances with other strata (very often informally through *guanxi*), notably with managers of state enterprises and emergent private entrepreneurs. These tactics have also served to protect or improve their living standards since, as they are predominantly on fixed salaries, they do not have access to the regular bonuses available to managers and workers in state factories.

However, one should not over-generalise about the conservatism of Party/state officials. There are important variations across sectors: for example, bureaux of heavy industry are particularly conservative while officials in new state organisations created by the reforms or those whose role has increased as a result of the reforms, such as foreign trade and financial agencies, have a more positive attitude. There are also differences, along the conservative-reformist spectrum, between older, less qualified and 'redder' cadres and a new crop of younger, more professional and technocratic cadres who have moved into the Party and state bureaucracy in the reform era. Their banners were visible at the Tiananmen demonstrations in

May–June 1989), but the balance of institutional power has yet to shift decisively in their favour.

As for the *intelligentsia*, one should also be cautious in generalising, given the hierarchical (higher, middle and lower intellectuals with corresponding differences in educational attainment) and horizontal (cultural v. scientific, Party v. non-Party) distinctions within them. However, one can argue that, certainly compared with other social groups, the intelligentsia tend to have a particularly strong aversion to Party rule and bureaucratic/political interference in their professional lives. The reforms have sought to increase their professional autonomy and improve their position in society: by according them political legitimacy as part of the 'working class'; by downplaying the significance of 'redness' and encouraging a 'hundred flowers to bloom'; by granting them greater influence in the policy-making process; and by attempting to improve their material living standards. In consequence, intellectuals have strongly supported the reforms and the reformist wing within the Party leadership (notably Hu Yaobang and Zhao Ziyang against Deng Xiaoping and Li Peng in 1988–9). They (and we should of course include students here, as the intelligentsia in formation) have not merely acted in pursuit of their own professional or material interests (though this is of course a powerful motivation). Indeed, many intellectuals on fixed salaries had been badly hurt by the inflation of 1987–89 as the reforms raced out of control. While their scientific and technical wing has done reasonably well in getting a better price for their services without attendant political risks, the cultural/educational/mass communications wing has fared worse materially (for example, educational expenditures have not kept pace with national needs, in the eyes of key academic spokespeople) and have been more vulnerable to political encroachment.

But elements of the intelligentsia have also acted as guardians of the nation, representatives of true patriotism, the distilled conscience and rationality of 'the Chinese people'. As such, they make claims comparable to the Party itself and thus have become a potential counter-élite. When this consciousness was embodied in calls for 'democracy' and 'freedom' in 1989, the Party leadership saw a serious challenge and reacted violently. The brutality of this response has radicalised a significant portion of the politically active intelligentsia and created a significant group of alienated and organised 'dissident' intellectuals, comparable to their former Soviet equivalents, operating both abroad and clandestinely within China. However, while politically vocal, this movement involves only a small minority of the intelligentsia. Many of the rest have responded by withdrawing into safe passivity, keeping their heads down; some have sought to leave the country until things improve; some leave their jobs on the state payroll to try their hand at business; others stay in post and manoeuvre to keep the reforms going. Whatever the case, the post-Tiananmen regime cannot depend on their active support and must waste a vast amount of political effort in securing their co-operation and neutralising their opposition.

Last, a completely new stratum has emerged in both cities and countryside over the past decade which can be regarded as a creation of the reforms, *private entrepreneurs*. More than the rest of society, their future depends on the continuation of the reforms, yet they are very vulnerable to fluctuations in economic policy (for example, the post-Tiananmen leadership has imposed tight strictures on private enterprise, while but two years earlier, successful business people were being hailed as pioneers at the Thirteenth Party Congress in October 1987). The number of private enterprises established during the reforms is hard to estimate since there is a variety of types of ownership: private, 'associative', co-operative, joint ventures and so on. Many if not most of the 'associative' and 'co-operative' enterprises are in reality private concerns. By the end of 1986, the number of private enterprises had already reached over 12 million (Gold 1988). But a significant minority of individuals, families or groups have done very well indeed and, as such, have run into problems: on the one side, from the 'red-eye disease' of their fellow citizens and, on the other, from the depredations of local officials. It is not surprising that many of them have sought to buy popular acceptance by becoming local benefactors, doling out support for less fortunate relatives or members of their own communities. Nor is it surprising that they have sought to buy official protection, or at least indifference, through 'connections' and bribes. On the other hand, as we shall see below, they have sought to organise their own associations, particularly as a way of protecting and expressing their collective interests in relations with the state. In the events of May–June 1989, the larger entrepreneurs preferred to keep their heads down politically and, to the extent that they supported the student movement, did so by providing money and material behind the scenes. There was one very significant exception, Wan Runnan, perhaps China's best-known private entrepreneur and head of the sizeable Stone Computer Company in Beijing – he gave open support to the student movement and was driven into exile in Paris. In spite of this overall political restraint, however, private business people did not escape official suspicion, publicly aired after 4 June by the new CCP General Secretary, Jiang Zemin, that they sought to 'create in China a so-called "middle class" to act as their support base through which to subvert our socialist system'.[6]

The effects of the reform on gender relations, and on the social position of *women*, appear to have been ambiguous (for general analyses, see Croll 1983). On the positive side, the reforms have opened up new opportunities for women: in private and small collective enterprises in the urban economy and in sideline production and petty trade in the countryside. The overall enlivening of the economy and the easier availability of consumer goods and services may also have reduced the burden of house-work to some limited extent. On the negative side, the spread of the household economy, particularly in agriculture, may well have strengthened the control of the male household head over family labour power; male peasants are also more likely to get the more lucrative and attractive jobs in the burgeoning rural enterprises. In the cities, the sexual division of labour in the economy meant women being absorbed disproportionately into jobs in the private and collective sectors with lower status, lower pay and less welfare benefits. Moreover, previous official gender criteria regulating the recruitment of workers to state enterprises (some of which tried to impose quotas for women) have increasingly been resisted or ignored. Moreover, in times of retrenchment (for example, 1988 to 1990) women were often the first to be laid off. Women also still endure the 'double burden' and, to the extent that the general intensity of social labour has increased during the reform era, the double burden may also have increased, especially in the countryside.

To summarise, this rapid overview of the social impact of the economic reforms suggests that, though they have benefited some groups more than others, the overall effects (at least until 1988–9) were positive for a very large proportion of the population. In other words, the social impact of the reforms has a 'positive-sum' character – most people have gained something though they may have gained less than someone else. The potentially most threatened groups – state officials and state workers – have been able to defend their positions quite successfully (to the detriment of the reform process). There are, however, certain strata or groups whose interests have either been ignored or brought into jeopardy through the move towards the market: groups unable to take advantage of market opportunities such as the old or the disabled; peasants in labour-poor households, or in badly situated, backward areas who lack the expertise, capital and geographical access necessary to participate advantageously in the market economy; the unemployed and 'floating' populations in both rural or urban areas whose lives are ruled by the uneven operation of the market; and women and children, particularly in the countryside, who are tethered to the household economy.

In spite of this overall positive social impact, however, the level of discontent in Chinese society had escalated to alarming proportions by 1988–9, involving all sectors of society. The sources of discontent are many and vary from group to group: fear of threats to status, power or income; disappointment because the reforms were delivering less than they had promised; disgruntlement arising from the 'red-eye disease'; concern that gains already achieved were in danger of erosion (through inflation and leadership mismanagement); contrarily, impatience at a deceleration of the reforms and anxiety at an acceleration. In this context of this pervasive discontent and these contradictory pressures, the Jiang Zemin – Li Peng leadership faces a well nigh insuperable task in regaining control over the reform process and re-establishing the battered authority of the CCP.

Economic Reforms and the Rise of 'Civil Society'

As we saw earlier, redistribution of control over economic resources, together with an intermittently more liberal social and political climate has created the basis of, and context for, new forms of socio-political participation and organisation, to varying degrees independent of and/or in opposition to the Party/state. To the extent that these actions and institutions are self-organised on a voluntary basis and enjoy a degree of independence from the Party state, they merit the use of the term 'civil society' (for a general discussion of this idea, see Keane 1988). In any long-term or institutionalised sense, 'civil society' of this kind could not exist in the context of the pervasive system of socio-political controls which characterised Chinese Marxist–Leninist state socialism in the pre-reform era.

We can discern three dimensions of this trend towards an incipient civil society. First, there are more or less organised public expressions of social and political discontent which have arisen in opposition to the policies or institutions of the Party/state. These include specifically political actions and organisations, such as the 'big-character posters' and the publication of dissident journals during the Democracy Movement during 1979–80 (for a review, see Goodman 1981) and street demonstrations, notably the student processions of late 1986 and the broader popular movement of May–June 1989. There have also been innumerable social and economic incidents, such as street protests, building occupations, violent attacks on individuals, strikes and work stoppages which have occurred sporadically throughout the decade.

It is not my intention to cover this first category of participation and organisation here. Merely to analyse the social basis and organisational character of the May–June 1989 events in Beijing and elsewhere would require another book and this topic has already received a great deal of scholarly attention (interested readers should consult Saich 1990; Simmie and Nixon 1989; Fathers and Higgins 1989; Walder 1989b and Gold 1990). More-over, while the intensity and scale of these protests is new and the reforms have provided both the issues and the opportunity for them, the particular forms they have taken are not necessarily a product of the post-Mao reforms. Organisations and actions such as these, which were a direct political response to the impact of the Party/state on society, have been a recurring feature of Chinese political life from the mid-1950s onwards, with periodic explosions during the Hundred Flowers Movement in 1956–7 and the Cultural Revolution in 1966–68.

I shall focus here on two other tendencies towards an incipient civil society which have received less attention and have flourished distinctively in the context of economic reform: first, changes in the role and function of existing official 'mass organisations' which have found greater scope for autonomous action in the more liberal atmosphere created by the reforms and, second, the development of a new form of social organisation which is an integral response to the spread of market relations in the economy.

Existing Mass and Mass-Type Organisations

In the previous institutional system, the Party/state reached   down to incorporate social and residential groups in an all-encompassing network of mass organisations. There are two categories we should investigate here: first institutions which organise specific sectors of the population, such as children, women, youth or workers, which are called 'mass organisations' (*qunzhong zuzhi*) and, second, institutions which organise on a residential or community basis, referred to as 'mass-type self-governing organisations' (*qunzhong-xingde zizhi zuzhi*), comprising 'residents committees' (*jumin weiyuanhui*) in the cities and 'villagers' committees' (*cunmin weiyuanhui*) in the countryside. Both types of organisation have been subject to pressures for reform: partly the result of an environment which was changing rapidly under the impact of economic reform and partly, in the period from 1987–9 in particular, the result of targeted efforts at institutional reform.

Official 'mass organisations'. There has been a marked improvement in their institutional status compared to the Cultural Revolution decade, when they fell into disuse or before the Cultural Revolution when they were used primarily as political instruments of the Party (with the exception of a brief period during the Hundred Flowers Movement when they tried unsuccessfully to assert their autonomy). However, in the post-Mao period, the Party has been unwilling for them to assume a degree of autonomy which would take them outside the bounds of Leninist politics in which the role of mass organisations is to serve as 'transmission belts' between the ruling Party and the population. Yet at the same time the Party leadership has realised that, in the increasingly pluralistic environment created by the economic reforms, without some degree of autonomy and attention to the particular interests of their members, they lose credibility with their own constituency and become empty organisations. This lesson was given particular force by the rise of

Solidarity in Poland in the early 1980s.[7] There has been pressure from above, particularly from the more radical reformist wing of the Party and the leaders of mass organisations, to expand their ability to represent the interests of their members and act on their behalf in relation to, and even *in opposition to*, the Party/state. Moreover, to the extent that the economic reforms have caused concern to certain sections of the population (industrial workers and women, for example), there has been pressure from below (implicit and explicit) on the mass organisations to do something about it.

The trade unions are a good example since their members are mostly in the state workforce,[8] and their interests may be jeopardised by the economic reforms, notably by moves towards a labour market (with its threat of involuntary redundancies and unemployment) and efforts to increase the power of enterprise managers. The trade unions had been eclipsed during the Cultural Revolution and any hint of independent trade unionism was dismissed as 'syndicalism' or 'economism'. With the onset of the reforms, their pre-Cultural Revolution status as 'transmission belts' was restored. This at least gave them an organisational identity and a specific role within the enterprise, notably some degree of institutionalised influence in relation to management on issues which affected the material and social welfare of the workforce, such as bonuses, work conditions, housing and welfare benefits.[9] However, in reality the trade union had little say on all significant issues within the enterprise in relation to the management and the Party committee; organisationally, moreover, the Party still continued to dominate trade union work. The official position on the role of trade unions admits that there may be contradictions between workers and management and that, in such situations, the trade union has some responsibility as the organised voice of the workers.[10] In practice, however, disputes tended to be suppressed by the Party committee or, if tackled and resolved either by the Party committee or the management, the trade unions were bypassed. Though untoward Party manipulation of trade unions was officially condemned, there was an inbuilt structural tendency for this to take place given the continuing predominance of the Party in the enterprise. Criticisms abound, for example, of Party manipulation of trade union elections in ways described by one critic as 'feudal patriarchal leadership'.[11]

Thus, the trade union, as a institutional force which makes a significant difference to workers' lives and position in the enterprise, is largely irrelevant. Where trade union leaders do take a stand in opposition either to management or Party committee, they run a serious risk. The situation could well be worse in enterprises which have been leased out to private entrepreneurs.[12] Trade union officials face a double frustration: on the one side, they cannot protect their members *vis-à-vis* management in an increasingly marketised economic environment; on the other side, they face Party interference in exercising the few powers that they do enjoy. It is not surprising, therefore, that some trade union cadres have protested, demanding a greater role not merely in the enterprise but in wider policy forums.[13] They have received (implicit if not explicit) support from reformist Party leaders and members.[14]

Nor is it surprising that the role of trade unions is not taken seriously by their own members. For example in a survey of one million staff and workers conducted by the national union federation (ACFTU) in 1986, 56 per cent said that the status of trade unions in their enterprises had dropped over recent years and 70 per cent felt that the workers' congresses (organised by enterprise trade union branches) had little influence on major matters. The general opinion, according to the survey, was that the position of trade unions in enterprises should be upgraded and it should have the right to elect, assess or dismiss enterprise managers.[15] It is significant that this survey was published at a time (late 1986) when political liberalisation was on the agenda. The ACFTU was in fact pressing at this time for a greater role for trade unions, not only within the enterprise but also at all levels of policy making; it took the opportunity to press the case again in the relatively liberal atmosphere surrounding the 13th Party Congress in late 1987.[16] Trade union leaders meeting in Beijing in December 1987, for example, reportedly went so far as to say that the trade unions did not represent the interests of the workers and are not trusted by them. According to a 'random survey' which they cited, 40 per cent of union members did not regard them as their own organisations and 20 per cent knew nothing about their activities. The leaders argued for trade union reform to establish organisations which were formed voluntarily by workers and represented their interests more effectively, admitting at the same time that thoroughgoing trade union reform would not be possible until overall political reform was set in train.[17] This case was still being put in mid-1988 by no less than the head of the ACFTU, Ni Zhifu.

The Tiananmen events of 1989 postponed significant changes in the role of trade unions, but the issue is serious and needs tackling. The current leadership, however, faces a seemingly intractable dilemma on this question. On the one hand, they are aware of a deterioration (from their viewpoint) in the political and moral character of workers and the weakness of trade unions in doing anything about this. This point was rammed home by the appearance of autonomous trade unions in Beijing and other cities during the mass movement of 1989, along with other expressions of workers discontent such as strikes, go-slows and absenteeism. Yet their reaction to these threats has been to emphasise the role of trade unions as instruments of political control and ideological education and to deny any moves towards greater independence on their part. As a long-term approach to the problem, this would appear to be doomed from the outset.

At the same time, however, in terms of organised worker opposition, the regime escaped relatively lightly in 1989 because, with the possible exception of Beijing, the organised worker protest was not widespread: for example, the Beijing Autonomous Workers' Union may not have had more than 30 or 40 official members. While many workers turned out to applaud the students as they marched by and may have participated in mass demonstrations, their response in terms of forming alternative organisations was weak. This partly reflects the 'cellular encapsulisation' of workers within their own enterprise, the social distance between manual workers and the intelligentsia (including students) and worry about the impact of deeper reforms on their livelihoods.

It was younger workers who tended to be active in May–June 1989, and this is part of a broader political phenomenon, the widespread alienation of youth, particularly the students who claim to be their standard-bearers. The Young Communist League (YCL), the CCP's mass organisation for youth, has clearly lost credibility and membership and was virtually swept aside in the universities in 1989 by a wave of autonomous student organisations across the country. While the YCL had been trying to find a new role, it was more in terms of providing social and cultural benefits for young people rather than as an agency of political socialisation and recruitment. The post-Tiananmen leadership might like to restore the YCL's political role, but this task will be far more difficult than in the case of the trade unions, given the widespread alienation of urban youth and the institutional degeneration of the YCL over the decade.

We could expand our analysis to other mass organisations, such as the Women's Federation which showed signs of becoming a more important social force and of increasing its independence from the Party in the early and mid-1980s (Croll 1983; Croll *et al.* 1985); but there is not enough space here for a proper treatment of the subject. To summarise, however, each of these three cases illustrates the same point: that the reforms have acted to increase pressures on existing mass organisations to change their roles and demonstrate greater independence or risk losing their institutional credibility; that significant changes along these lines cannot be accommodated within a traditional Leninist political framework; that lack of change leads to pressures for alternative, more autonomous mass organisations; and that the Party conservatives cannot countenance significant changes in the latter, thereby intensifying the problem and laying the basis for further and more acute popular discontent and turbulence in future.

'Mass-type self-governing organisations'. While there are two types of such organisations, the 'residents' committees' in the cities and the 'villagers' committees' in the countryside, I shall only discuss the former partly because slightly more is known about them and partly because, from the point of view of the issues discussed in this chapter at least, these two organisations are comparable in basic ways.

Urban residents' committees (RCs) are organised on the basis of locality, they vary in size (in large cities such as Beijing and Tianjin they have an average of 2000 inhabitants) and in structural complexity. They are formally classified as 'non-governmental institutions', organs of direct as opposed to representative democracy, theoretically operating according to three principles – 'self-service, self-management and self-education' (White and Benewick 1986: p. 33). In doctrinal terms, they are supposed to be nascent tutelary institutions, creating a 'democratic spirit' which in the (very) long term will gradually bring about the ultimate abolition of the state. However, over the decades the trend has been decidedly in the opposite direction. First, since for most employed people the main focus of everyday life is on their workplace not their place of residence, they are not likely to become involved in the running of residents' committees, nor in pressing for greater autonomy. Hence, RC cadres are mostly retired people, particularly older women who are a familiar sight on the streets of Chinese cities (maintaining public order, road safety, etc.). Second, they have become agents of urban government – without them the latter would find it much more difficult to implement its policies and thus have a vested interest in keeping them subordinate. This is a process which has intensified with the economic reforms since the activities of local governments have become more complex. Their responsibilities are thus many and varied: economic (running small-scale enterprises to provide jobs for local youth, housewives and pensioners); political (disseminating current propaganda, 'reflecting the opinions of the masses' to higher levels of government and helping the local public security bureau to keep order); legal (organising mediation committees to handle local disputes); and social (providing basic health care, carrying out preventative public health campaigns, and making special provision for vulnerable groups, such as children, the disabled and pensioners). In financial terms, most of their revenue comes from the level of urban government immediately above them. In consequence, they have virtually no independence; they have become the 'hands and feet of local government, an agency for everything and everyone'. Where their responsibilities are complex, moreover, they have become 'bureaucratised' (*jiguanhua*), taking on the organisational characteristics of a government department (Liu 1985: p. 302).

Reformers in China have sought to strengthen and democratise the RC by simplifying and codifying its functions and freeing it from the grasp of local government. Thereby, they hope to re-establish its proclaimed character as a 'mass-type, self-governing' institution. They also propose that its aging cadre force be replaced by younger, better educated cadres drawn from local schools and enterprises (Liu 1985: pp. 303–4). While these ideas may find favour with over-burdened RC cadres, local government officials are reluctant to relax their hold on this convenient organisational instrument. They argue, somewhat disingenuously, that RCs have a 'dual role', as a self-governing organisation and 'an agency of basic-level local government' (Liu 1985: p. 302) – in reality, of course, the latter by far outweighs the former. Given the fact that the political odds are stacked against reforming the RCs, it is hardly surprising that this conception of the 'dual role' was embedded in the new law on RCs presented to the National People's Congress in 1989, which included the requirement that RCs should 'help the government' in a wide range of activities, i.e. essentially legalising the *status quo ante*.[18] Indeed, in the wake of the urban unrest of mid-1989, their role as agents of social control is even more important and any pretensions that they have real autonomy or function as a 'school for socialist democracy' has become even more far-fetched. In sum, it seems that, perversely, the economic reforms have acted to limit the potential independence of RCs; as such they are in no sense harbingers of a new 'civil society'. Any significant moves in this direction must await a broader process of political and institutional reform.

The Embryonic Social Institutions of Market Society

The above two types of organisation are clearly deeply enmeshed in the institutional network of China's Leninist polity – as such, they can only be changed substantially by political reforms. The third set of organisations discussed in this last section are new. They are the organisational consequence of the changing balance of power between state and society and of the spread of market relations in the economy (involving a proliferation of horizontal ties between increasingly autonomous enterprises and a diversification in the ownership system). This process creates both the need and the opportunity for organisation creativity: first, there is need for increasingly separated entities to come together to regulate their own economic environment and engage with the state; second, the changing balance of power between state and society brought about by a very considerable redistribution of economic resources has created the space and the resources necessary to create organisations. As such, this is a transaction of world-historical proportions, comparable to the emergence of bourgeois civil society from the 'pores' of feudalism. Fundamentally, this process reflects a diversification of the sources of social power, organisations based on market-based economic power rising within and in opposition to organisations based on political/administrative power. The British sociologist Michael Mann calls this the process of 'interstitial emergence' which creates 'new relations and institutions that have unanticipated consequences for the old' (Mann 1986: p. 15).

Preliminary investigation suggests that there are three types of association which share these characteristics, listed in order of their ascending socio-political significance at the dawn of the 1990s. It should be emphasised at the outset that none of the organisations listed below are wholly 'autonomous' or represent 'civil society' in any fully-fledged form; rather they represent tendencies in that direction. First are the professional associations which link together specialists from different institutions with common interests and skills, represent a potentially influential principle for organising intellectual capital and constitute an important social resource on which the Party/state depends to achieve its developmental ambitions. One example, taken at random, is the Chinese Association of Boiler and Pressure Vessel Inspection, established in April 1990, 'to promote managerial and technical progress' in this area. This organisation, whose members are all engineers, is described as 'the first nation-wide, non-governmental organisation engaged in inspection' and was claimed to be 'independent of manufacturers, users and the government', maintaining a 'third-party view'.[19] Second are the associations of enterprise managers (from state and non-state enterprises), either across the economy as a whole (as in the case of the Chinese Enterprise Management Association) or in particular sectors, in the form of 'chambers of commerce' or 'guilds'. For one example of the latter among many, a China Chamber of Commerce for Electronic Products was established in Beijing in January 1988, described as an 'unofficial body' which seeks 'to guide, co-ordinate and supervise marketing and to serve as a bridge between enterprises and the government', working under the 'leadership of the Ministry of the Machinery and Electronics Industry';[20] Third, there are associations of private business people and entrepreneurs based on sector or locality. One example, again among many, is the China Non-Government Science and Technology Entrepreneurs Association, which established its sixteenth branch in Shenyang, Liaoning province, in February 1988. The Shenyang branch had sixty members and the national association, set up in May 1987, represents 10 000 non-governmental scientific and technological institutions throughout China. They are mostly engaged in various kinds of consultancy work. The author visited one such private company in 1987, the Shanghai Modern Consultancy Corporation which was a share-based enterprise financed and staffed by specialists from local universities, research institutes and government departments – it claimed to be the first such organisation in China (White and Bowles 1987: pp. 85–6). There are also associations of entrepreneurs in small and medium scale private or 'associative' enterprises, particularly in the more advanced (and reformed) South-Eastern provinces. For example, in the mid-1980s collective, co-operative and private enterprises in Shanghai were organising themselves into trade associations according to sector (ibid.: pp. 83–4). In the cities, there are organisations for small-scale individual or family businesses, such as the Individual Labourers' Association in Nanjing, which the author investigated in 1985 ('individual', *geti*, meant private businesses with no more than seven employees). It was described, by an official of the local government agency charged with supervising it, as a 'mass-type' institution and one of its functions was to 'express the rational opinions and demands of its membership to the government and to help the government departments to do their job' (White 1985: p. 57).

Besides these three types of organisation, there has been a broader flowering of associational life over the past decade: in the countryside the government has urged producers to form their own marketing associations; in some areas, 'specialised households' have set up their own organisations to co-ordinate activities and bargain with the state; in other areas there are 'three types of (peasant) organisation' viz. societies for the study of specialised technology, support-the-poor reserve fund societies and councils for administering weddings and funerals.[21] In early 1987, for example, there were reportedly over 2000 peasant societies in Liaoning province (particularly in the realm of marketing and technical extension), including the headquarters of a rabbit-raising association with 3200 members from all over China.[22] Consumers' associations have also emerged – by early 1988 they could be found in two-thirds of the provinces and one province, Zhejiang, alone had 703. By early 1989 there were reportedly 1088 such associations across the nation.[23] Apart from these economic organisations, there are myriads of new associations for cultural activities, hobbies and sports.

This flowering of associational life, which appeared to accelerate between 1986 and 1989, has even spawned its own 'association', the Chinese Research Association of Mass Organisation (CRAMO) which was founded in August 1989. It was set up with a view not merely to investigating the phenomenon but also to laying the basis for legislation to regulate their activities.[24] This concern about regulation has clearly been given a degree of urgency by the events of May–June 1989 when many 'undesirable' organisations emerged like bamboos after the rain. The emphasis on registration and legislative regulation can be seen as an attempt by the state, through the Ministry of Civil Affairs which is clearly the power behind CRAMO, (operating through its Administrative Office of Mass Organisation) to impose order on a potentially chaotic and slippery social reality.

Though many of these organisations are described as 'non-governmental' or 'semi-governmental', the amount of real autonomy they enjoy varies a great deal. Some are no more than creatures of state organs while others have some freedom of manoeuvre. Either way, they have to have a formal link with a relevant state agency which has the responsibility for supervising their activities (Whiting 1989). There has been an attempt to tighten this system of controls in the aftermath of Tiananmen, partly in response to the fact that some of these organisations took on a political role during the events of early–mid-1989. The post-4 June leadership has been politically sensitive to the political potential of organised private business. For example, in a speech attacking 'bourgeois liberalisation', the CCP Propaganda Department chief, Wang Renzhi, alleged that one dissident (Wen Yuankai) had declared that he was 'interested in promoting the establishment of a Chinese Federation of Private Entrepreneurs. They should have their own political spokesmen. Private entrepreneurs should be allowed to become China's decisive force.'[25]

Organisations of specialists, particularly social scientists, took part in the 1989 movement: for example, the Beijing Economics Study Society for Youth published documents, in co-operation with the State Council's Rural Development Research Centre, the International Research Institute of the China International Trust and Investment Company and the Chinese Institute for Restructuring the Economic System (IRE), allegedly at the instigation of the IRE's head, Chen Yizi.[26] But the political activity of intellectuals was not confined to such formal organisations. In the period before Tiananmen, they used informal and semi-formal means, co-ordinated by networks of personal acquaintance, to concert their forces and press public demands. After the events of 1989, Wang Renzhi, described the phenomenon as follows:[27]

> Advocates of bourgeois liberalisation clustered to become a kind of political force through invisible, or visible and unfixed, or relatively fixed forms, such as certain forums, seminars, salons, societies and social organisations, and so on... These gradually clustered political forces actually became political opposition factions and groups of political dissidents, or, using their own term, 'pressure groups'.

This is an interesting description of the continuing importance of informal *guanxi* ties and the overlapping role of informal and formal modes of association in co-ordinating political action. Underlying the concern about the political potential of both intellectuals and entrepreneurs lies a broader worry about the increased political power of a new 'middle class' created by the economic reforms. For example, Wang Renzhi cited a member of the Chinese Academy of Social Sciences as saying: 'There is no middle class in China. I hope I will be able to see the re-emergence of a few million capitalists and entrepreneurs. It is difficult to turn back the democratic reform in Taiwan because it is backed by a strong economic force comprising hundreds of thousands of capitalists.' He also cited the opposition intellectual Liu Binyan as saying: 'A new social force is rising. It is the middle class. It comprises individual entrepreneurs and managers of collective enterprises. These people have a lot of money in their hands, that is, they are rich and rough. When there is economic strength, there will also be political strength. Some of them are not satisfied with making more money; they demand the right to participate in state administration and to air their views. They also want to have their political representatives.' If the analysis in this chapter about the potentially momentous political significance of the economic reforms is correct, Wang's fears are well-founded.

Conclusion: Towards a Civil Society?

In current circumstance, it is too early to talk about the emergence of 'civil society' as an established fact. Though the tendency is clear, the new forms of social organisation do not enjoy full autonomy and operate in a political environment which does not accord the right to operate as 'interest groups' in the Western sense. At present, the relationship between the Party/state and social organisations can be seen as one between two radically different and potentially contradictory social principles: one based on voluntary association rendered both possible and desirable by the spread of market forces and the shift in the balance of power between state and society; the other based on a hierarchical imperative of monocratic political domination and control. There are possibilities for 'peaceful coexistence' between these two and there are possibilities for conflict.

At present, this tension is reflected in the variety of existing relations between state and social organisations. Some of the latter are merely creations and puppets of particular state agencies, others are subject to stringent and intrusive state supervision. Clearly, 'autonomy' should be viewed as a question of a position on a continuum. Even if the regulation of social organisations is put more on a formal, legal basis, moreover, the proposed law will give state civil affairs departments the right to 'register and administer' mass organisations to determine their organisational structure and, if dissatisfied, to abolish them.

Looking to the future, the 'conflict' and 'co-operation' aspects of the relationships between state and social organisation suggest two possible scenarios. On the 'conflict' side, one can argue that the proliferation of such organisations will lead inexorably towards an undermining of the Leninist state and provide the social under-pinnings for political democratisation. Some Chinese theorists admit this possibility, arguing that it is 'the relative independence and development of these "intermediate strata" which will bring changes to the socialist political structure' (Yang 1987). As a longer-term scenario, this argument has much to recommend it and one can expect increasing tension between the two sides in the meantime. However, some Chinese analysts suggests an alternative scenario, involving 'co-operation' between the state and social organisations in some form of 'socialist corporatism' whereby the state formally recognises certain social associations and grants them a degree of autonomy and influence, *as part of a new system of socio-economic regulation* – in effect, as an expression of the new form of 'indirect' planning and regulation which the economic reformers envisage as the proper future role of the developmental state. This idea has been elaborated by the noted economist, Xue Muqiao, who argues that 'non-governmental self-management organisations (such as trade associations and guilds) can be a valuable link in the relationship between the state and enterprises (Xue 1988) – in his words, these intermediaries can help state agencies 'to smoothly exercise indirect control over enterprises'. Horizontally, they help to prevent the potential anarchy of the market and co-ordinate activities on new technology, marketing and strategic direction; vertically 'they serve as a bridge between the state and enterprises'. Xue cites the United States and Japan as countries where such organisations have played an important role; he could also have pointed to their important role in the development of East Asian NICs such as South Korea and Taiwan. Indeed, such a three-tiered arrangement could be a basic element in a new form of socialist political economy of a type more directly comparable to South Korea and Taiwan, as envisaged in the theory of 'new authoritarianism' which was canvassed in early 1989 (Petracca and Mong 1990).

In the present political climate in China such eventualities are probably less likely than when Xue wrote. To the extent that the economic reforms have been slowed down after Tiananmen, the pace of associational proliferation may also slow. Yet the rise of these new types of social organisation is seemingly inexorable and, to the extent that economic reform regains its momentum, will continue to develop, albeit under the watchful eye of the state. It is clear that state managers do regard these organisations as a useful conduit, evidenced by state interest in establishing them where they do not already exist. In spite of this danger of incorporation by the state, however, they do represent a fledgling form of organisational life which is radically different from the traditional 'vertical' Leninist type; as such, tendencies towards conflict of interest and battles over autonomy will be inherent in the relationship.

As to the future of social organisations, *both* Xue and Yang may be right – associations may take on a greater role as intermediaries in a process of 'indirect regulation', yet this assumes that the state has the power to manipulate their activities. In the more rapidly reforming provinces and cities in the south-east, this may become an increasingly difficult task. To the extent that such organisations and their members thus 'get out of control', they will provide powerful political resources for future political reformers. It is to the future of political reform that we turn in our concluding chapter.

8

From Market Socialism to Social Market?

Our analysis has sought to show the clash between the economic and political logic of the reforms and provide an explanation of the paradoxical outcome of the reform era, a combination of economic success and political failure. To the extent that the economic reforms were the spearhead of an attempt to resuscitate the political fortunes of Chinese state socialism, they were a dismal failure. In the context of the early 1990s, the question of political reform clearly needs to be tackled, not only because this is a precondition for deepening the process of economic reform, but also because the present political system has suffered a serious decline in its authority and the national leadership has increasingly lost its power to define policy and control events. To think sensibly about political reform, we not only need to look forward towards possible future scenarios but also look back at the political changes brought about by the era of economic reform which define the political parameters for what is both desirable and possible in the foreseeable future. So let us look back first and then forward.

The Political Impact of Economic Reform: What has Changed?

In our Introduction, we laid out a rough framework for analysing the political dimensions of economic reform and also advanced three hypotheses concerning its political effects. Let us organise our discussion here along those lines and draw on the conclusions accumulated throughout the book to answer two basic questions: what has been the political impact of economic reform and what implications does this have for the future of both economic and political reform?

At the level of political leadership, the reform decade saw an escalating conflict within the CCP leadership, partly based on differences in political generations and partly on contending ideological and policy positions. Any semblance of consensus was destroyed by the Tiananmen events, the reformist wing was eclipsed and more conservative elements sought desperately to re-establish an obsolete political rectitude in an environment which they increasingly were neither able to control nor understand. The result was a disastrous decline in the authority of the CCP leadership and a fundamental deadlock in reform policy, reflecting basic constraints posed by the previous Ideology and polity.

At the level of institutions, the national authority and integrity of the hegemonic political institution, the Communist Party, rather than recovering from the ravages of the Cultural Revolution, continued to decay. On the other hand, state administrative institutions were able to retain much of their power: partly because of the increasing crisis among the central political leadership and a resulting dispersion of power throughout the administrative system; partly because the economic reforms had not gone far enough seriously to undermine their power to direct the economy; partly because they were able to exploit the new opportunities offered by the economic reforms to redefine their own roles or to amass resources in their own interest; and partly because the reforms brought into being a new wave of state institutions with regulatory powers specifically tailored to the requirements of an emerging 'socialist commodity economy'. In addition, there was a shift of power within the politico-administrative system from the centre to the provinces and lower levels of government which increasingly converted the political relationship between centre and region into one of bargaining, conflict and stand-off. As the authority of central politics waned, the prevalence and power of 'local policies' waxed.

At the level of social groups, there was a trend towards a society which was socially more complex and political more assertive. There was a gradual shift in the balance of power between state and society which opened up space for new forms of political participation, social organisation and economic institution and led to increasingly open discontent and friction between the Party/state and society. At the same time, however, it is important to recognise that these problems are more acute in the cities and that the network of Party/state control in the countryside remains more solidly intact and effective. Yet this continuing control is under increasing pressure as the rural economy becomes more complex and rural interests become more diverse and articulate.

In addition to these three levels of domestic politics, one should reiterate the importance of changes in the international dimension. On the economic side, the Open Policy has led to increasing integration between the Chinese and foreign economies which has made the former more dependent on external economic conditions (and conditionality). In the aftermath of Tiananmen, for example, the leadership was subjected to economic sanctions by major Western powers and foreign governments, notably the United States, who were aware of the political leverage they could exert in Beijing through their policies on trade and investment. For example, on the occasion of the visit to Beijing by the United States Secretary of State, James Baker, in November 1991, a former US ambassador to Beijing, James Lilley, remarked: 'This Chinese government may take 20 years to go down the drain. We have enormous clout in Peking. And Jim Baker knows how to wield the scalpel.'[1] While this is a somewhat crude exaggeration and such attempts to exert pressure can be a double-edged sword (because they provoke a nationalist reaction), the point remains that, to the extent that China has become more open economically, it has also become more vulnerable politically. This vulnerability has been intensified by the demise of state socialism in Eastern Europe and the cataclysmic events in the Soviet Union in August 1991, which left China virtually isolated as the last remaining bastion of unreconstructed Stalinist-style socialism, increasingly marooned in a global system in which the balance of power had shifted decisively in favour of the anti-communist camp.

To borrow the language of economics, we can see shifts in certain basic macro-political balances of power in Chinese society: most important are the shifts in power between centre and localities; between regions developing more rapidly and more backward regions; between a weakening Party and a still strong network of administrative institutions; between a relatively sluggish state and a dynamic non-state economic sector; between state economic agencies and state enterprises; between the Party/state and social groups and organisations; and between the domestic Chinese state and its international politico-economic environment. It is within the context of these new macro-political balances that the future of economic and political reform should be viewed.

The above trends provide support for the three hypotheses about the political impact of the economic reforms put forward at the beginning of this study. First, as we saw in our analysis of agricultural and industrial policy, diversification of the social and institutional picture has made the policy process more complex politically and the problems of defining and implementing reform policy that much more difficult. At the level of the reform programme as a whole, the problems of macro-management have escalated alarmingly, to an extent that would pose serious challenges to any leadership, however single-minded and skilled it might be. Second, the decline in the authority of the Communist Party and the dispersion of power, away from the Party/state in general and away from the centre in particular, has increased the amount of 'shadow pluralism' in the Chinese political process, but these new political forces have been granted virtually no formal recognition by the Party leadership. Third, the growing contradiction between the pre-existing political institutions and rules of the game on the one hand, and the pressures of emergent social and political pluralism on the other have indeed created tensions and led to ever more sweeping demands for reform in the political as well as the economic system. Restating this in terms of Samuel Huntington's early notion of political development, we see a contradiction between vastly increased political pressures stemming from economic change and social mobilisation on the one side and political decay of the ruling institutions on the other hand (Huntington 1968: ch. 1). This situation is unsustainable in the medium or longer term. Tiananmen showed that the problem could not be solved (except temporarily and superficially) by seeking to suppress the new political pressures from below; in fact, it has made things worse by increasing tensions between state and society and driving alternative solutions underground. The alternative is to seek some form of reconstitution of the polity which will redefine the rules of the political game, reshape the key political institutions and create a new relationship between them and the political forces emanating from an increasingly civil society. Clearly the pressures for political change are ineluctable, but in which direction?

The Nature and Feasibility of Political Reform: Whither Next?

The aim of political reform would be twofold: first, to pave the way for more radical economic reforms and, second, to reconstitute the Chinese polity on a new basis. These two processes are intertwined since more radical economic reform would have important implications for the role and power of the Party/state (for example, through privatisation of state enterprises, or a radical reduction of the state's role as economic manager). What are the essential components of such a reform? Again, I shall approach the question in terms of the three levels of political actor I have used from the beginning. At the leadership level, there is a need for a new set of leaders in the CCP who will be able to break through the 'ideological constraint' by taking a more progressive attitude to economic reform, will look forward rather than backward politically and will be able to establish a greater degree of unity and firmness of purpose. The post-Tiananmen leadership contains its own gradations: for example, there are (relatively) progressive reformists such as Politburo members Yang Rudai, Li Ruihuan and Zhu Rongji and there are a dimly perceivable group of reformist leaders 'in waiting', some of them (such as Hu Qili) attached to the former coterie of Zhao Ziyang. At the level of institutions, the required changes are multi-faceted. First, there would need to be a fundamental reappraisal of the role of the Communist Party – its internal organisation and its relationship with other political, social and economic institutions. Second, the relationship between central and local governments would have to be renegotiated and put on a more formal basis which recognises their specific roles in a new division of labour and reflects the realities of local power. In the long run, this process may well lead to some form of constitutional federalism. Third, the administrative institutions of the state would need thorough reform: partly through severe personnel cutbacks as the previous apparatus of economic management is dismantled as part of more radical economic reforms; partly through the creation or adaptation of governmental organisations to meet the new and demanding requirements of a market economy; and partly through an internal administrative reform to depoliticise the bureaucracy and put it on a more professional footing. At the level of social groups, there is a need to accommodate their increasing social and political assertiveness by expanding civil liberties, granting them more access to the political and policy processes through the strengthening of representative institutions (notably the people's representative congresses) and recognising the legitimate role of organisations in 'civil society'.

The underlying dynamics of this transition can be summed up in two words: democracy and the market. There are many reasons why these are both desirable and ineluctable in the Chinese context, but, as with any panaceas, they give rise to illusions which need to be scrutinised and, where necessary, punctured. Let us take the first panacea, the market or the 'free market'. The case for moving towards an economy in which the fundamental principle of economic co-ordination is based on markets is a strong one and is accepted by most reform politicians and experts in China, with the exception of the more reactionary members of the post-Tiananmen leadership who still wish to retain the dominance of some kind of directive central planning. However, this consensus raises a host of questions about the developmental impact of markets and the relationship between the market and the state. In terms of human welfare, even when markets work well, they do not necessarily tackle some of the basic developmental problems of a poor society (Sen 1981). When they malfunction, the human consequences in a poor society may be serious indeed. In terms of economic development, moreover, the experience of the most successful industrialisers – the East Asian capitalist NICs – demonstrates clearly that, though the role of markets (particularly international markets) was crucial in their success, the latter could not have been achieved without systematic and pervasive intervention to govern the market in ways calculated to maximise its potential benefits for the national economy (White 1988 and Wade 1991). There are thus powerful doubts to be raised about the developmental efficacy of the market (and *a fortiori* the 'free market'). This raises the question which has been at the centre of the economic reforms: the relationship between state and market. Even if the market becomes predominant through radical reform and even if it takes a capitalist form, which is very probable, there is a continuing need for a new form of developmental state to tackle the social and economic problems identified above. In the short term, moreover, the role of the state is even more crucial because of the need to break through the 'hard policy constraint' and manage the process of transition from a planned to a market economy. This is a process, as we have seen, which is fraught with instability and tensions arising from the opposition of vested interests, threats to economic security, inflation and growing inequality. A strong state is needed to provide the political order and direction necessary to underpin this transition and regulate an emergent market economy and civil society in a huge and increasingly complex country.

This is certainly not an argument for the political *status quo*. The re-constitution of the state in its developmental capacity – its ability to regulate and steer the economic system and tackle basic problems of poverty, insecurity and distribution – depends heavily on its political re-constitution – tackling the problems of leadership, authority, control, institutional capacity and state-society relations which we have identified. Without this, the Chinese state cannot hope to acquire the political strength necessary to break out of the deadlock of the post-Tiananmen era. The answer, put forward by all participants in the debate about China's political future is democracy and democratisation. Again, though the case for democratisation in the Chinese context is a strong one, it tends to produce well-intentioned wishful thinking and raises a host of practical questions which need to be thought through systematically.

Democratisation, Development and Economic Reform: Some General Issues

Let us first tackle the general argument (of which contemporary China is now seen as a clear example) that democracy is in some fundamental way conducive to developmental success and economic efficiency. This recipe is currently being prescribed by major Western governments and international financial agencies as a new cure for the ills of developing countries and is being forced upon them as part of aid conditionality. There are strong developmental arguments that certain democratic processes, such as scope for popular participation and socio-political pluralism (such as a free press, for example) can have a beneficial effect in tackling developmental problems; Dreze and Sen have made this case, for example, in relation to the ability of states to identify and tackle famines (Dreze and Sen 1989: ch. 13). However, in the current climate of debate, to which China is no exception, the argument for democratisation tends to take the following form. First, the particular form of democracy advocated is a liberal democratic multi-party system, characterised by an open competitive political process, periodic free elections and legally guaranteed civil free-doms;[2] second, the transition should be a rapid one and there is a virtue in this since only an abrupt break with the past can weaken the conservative forces of the previous political and institutional *status quo*.

Is 'democratisation' in this sense an essential precondition for solving the developmental problems of developing countries in general and China in particular? In comparative historical terms, one might argue that liberal democracy, in its full-fledged form, is primarily a characteristic of the advanced industrialised societies and is as much a product of socio-economic modernisation as its cause. In the classic case of the United Kingdom, political democratisation, in terms of the development of diverse political organisations and the expansion of legalised political participation and representation, emerged very gradually; it lagged behind the pace of economic change and the growth of a capitalist mode of production, and had to be secured through often bloody popular struggles. 'Late modernisers' such as France, Germany and Japan, experienced long periods of authoritarian rule, and owed much of their developmental success to that fact. As for the successful 'late modernisers', notably the 'four little tigers' of East Asia (South Korea, Taiwan, Hong Kong and Singapore), industrialisation has in all cases been organised by, and presided over, by authoritarian governments of various forms.[3] There are some counter-examples, but they are few and far between. The obvious case is India which has maintained reasonably democratic institutions during most of its post-colonial history. However, Indian developmental performance is not in the same league as the East Asian success stories, the Indian political model has been accompanied by enormous social costs in terms of poverty, corruption, exploitation and insecurity, and India's democratic institutions are looking decidedly fragile at the onset of the 1990s.

It would seem to be sensible to relate the nature of political systems to stages of development. Multi-party liberal democratic systems may well be a prized characteristic of advanced, industrialised societies, but how feasible are they in societies undergoing the traumas of early and mid development? Confusion on this issue is increased by the unexamined penchant, current among Western advocates of rapid democratisation and many Chinese democrats, to single out the political system of the United States as the appropriate case for comparison and aspiration. Given the fact that the United States is unusual among Western nations in being a 'lucky country' able to start out with a relative political *tabula rasa* in the late eighteenth century, such a yardstick can lead to unrealistic political analysis. Ignoring for the moment the fact that democracy in the United States has many inherent deficiencies and thus represents a fundamentally flawed utopia, it can play an important role, along with other systems such as the United Kingdom or Sweden, in defining ultimate political aspirations. But a consideration of China's political options in the here and now would benefit more from a systematic consideration of China's counterparts among previous or contemporary 'developing countries', particularly its close counterparts in East Asia.

As we argued earlier, moreover, the issue of democratisation in China is further complicated by the fact that China in the 1990s faces a double challenge. The developmental task of organising economic modernisation and improving welfare in a large, complex and poor society and the systemic task of changing the previous state socialist system of directive planning into some form of market economy. The experience of Eastern Europe and the Soviet Union suggests that the systemic task, 'economic deStalinisation', is economically destabilising and politically disruptive. This is not only because of political difficulties deriving from the opposition of conservative forces and popular impatience, but also because of the economic difficulties in moving from a centralised command economy to a decentralised market economy. Markets are disruptive entities in the real (as opposed to the academic) world of economics; even more so in post-socialist contexts where the population is accustomed to the provision of certain non-market benefits (such as economic security and basic welfare services) which it would be loath to lose. As one participant in the Soviet reform debates of the mid-1980s remarked, the Soviet people would like the same range of consumer goods as in the West but at subsidised prices. Economic deStalinisation would seem to require a firm hand; while in the long term the introduction of market relations may provide the socio-economic basis for democratisation in real as opposed to formal terms, in the short and medium term the introduction of the market would seem to involve some degree of strong, probably authoritarian control.

On several counts, therefore, there seems to be prima-facie historical and comparative evidence to support the case that, in the Chinese context with its specific conditions and challenges, any rapid move towards and comprehensive process of democratisation (particularly in the form of the immediate introduction of a multi-party system) would be highly problematic. If we stay at this general and abstract level, however, the argument is unconvincing. We should look more closely at current Chinese realities to test its validity. Moreover, the notion of 'democratisation' is itself a vague one and needs to be 'unpacked' for more detailed scrutiny.

The Feasibility of Democratisation in China

Analysis of the relationship between economic progress and political reform in China should be grounded in an understanding of the formidable developmental tasks facing the country: to organise and maintain a 'regime of accumulation' capable of guiding a process of economic modernisation; to generate and redistribute resources to contain regional and class-based inequalities and alleviate widespread poverty; to restrain population growth, provide productive jobs for a vast and expanding workforce and to achieve a rapid rise in overall levels of material welfare. The developmental task often requires the state to make strategic decisions which must be imposed in the teeth of popular inertia or resistance from relatively privileged or emergingly powerful social forces. Judging from the experience of the East Asian NICs in particular, there would seem to be a need for a strong and 'autonomous' developmental state to do the job.[4] Rapid democratisation in such a context, particularly a sudden move towards multi-party competition, might weaken the developmental state by making it prone to empty political demagoguery or the schisms of 'civil society', or vulnerable to powerful (particularly urban and foreign) special interests.

But this kind of scenario needs to be grounded in a more systematic analysis of the factors which are commonly identified as obstacles to democratisation in general and a rapid transition to a multi-party system in particular. We can group these factors into four categories: historical, cultural, material and social. The first two, the historical and the cultural, are well known (for example, see Huntington 1991: pp. 301–2) and I shall be brief here. First, there is an argument that, unlike some communist-led countries in Eastern Europe, China has no historical experience of functioning democracy and this imposes a major constraint on the possibility of any kind of real as opposed to formal democratisation in current circumstances. This argument has validity, as we can see from countries such as Hungary where the transition to multi-party democracy has been facilitated by the ability of post-socialist politicians to draw on the democratic traditions and organisations of the pre-war era. However, the argument has a static quality to it; because x has not been the case in the past, x cannot be the case now. Moreover, Chinese society has changed in certain important ways since 1949 as a result of successful industrialisation and the urbanisation which has accompanied it. These trends, which include the emergence of an embryonic 'middle class' which many political analysts identify as a crucial underpinning for democracy, could support the argument that there are now the incipient social preconditions for democratisation. A similar evaluation could be made of cultural arguments, particular to the effect that Chinese political culture is not conducive to democracy because it has a deeply rooted tradition of authoritarianism and conditioned popular obedience to authority. While one can question the empirical accuracy of the argument (for example, it is hard to see the popular upsurge of the Cultural Revolution as an expression of conditioned political obedience, Mao cult notwithstanding), it is also subject to the criticism of being too static. During the reform era in particular, when the floodgates to ideas from abroad have been opened, there has been considerable change in socio-political attitudes and aspirations, most particularly in the cities and in the coastal provinces. These changes have not only increased public pressure for democratisation in Chinese society, but are also evidence of its potential feasibility.

There are economic arguments against democratisation which would seem to have considerable force. Quite apart from the developmental and systemic tasks analysed earlier, it can be argued that a democracy worth the name, involving not merely a set of procedures but also widespread popular participation and awareness and a high degree of representation of divergent social interests, is difficult in a society in which the vast majority of the population are engaged in a remorseless struggle for material existence and lack the time, energy, knowledge and skills to be involved as active political participants (in the national arena at least). Kitching (1983: pp. 49–50) puts the case strongly when he argues that 'it is impossible to construct meaningfully democratic societies...in materially poor societies', because of the need for people in poor societies 'to bend both physical and intellectual efforts either to mere survival or to the attainment of a minimal degree of security and upward mobility in a sea of poverty'.[5] Of course, Kitching is talking of a 'meaningful' version of democracy, presumably involving high degrees of public awareness and participation. Indeed, he argues that in a poor country 'the bulk of the population...play a marginal or largely passive role in their politics' (1983: pp. 48–9). If we apply this kind of argument to China, it has some relevance. A rapid move to a procedural democracy in the liberal democratic sense might well have two consequences: that the political process would be dominated by a relatively small number of powerful élites, including elements of the previous élite, urban groups, emergent new élites (notably private business people) and foreigners. The bulk of the population, including urban marginals and the vast rural population, would in all probability be disenfranchised, in reality if not in form. However, this is an argument against a flip-flop to liberal democratic forms, not an argument against the need for and feasibility of democratisation. As Kitching himself remarks, 'peasants and other people are capable, as the example of China shows most clearly, of exercising an effective and continuous oversight of local issues, issues immediately within their experience and essential to their interest' (1983: p. 51) This suggests that local-level democracy is not only beneficial to the rural population but is also feasible in the short term. Thus, though we may admit that the economic impediments to a fuller-fledged form of democracy are powerful and that the imposition of a liberal democratic framework in a poor country would result in severe biases in the distribution of power, participation and representation, yet this does not preclude the possibility of certain forms of democratisation in the short term, processes which become more 'meaningful' as socio-economic development proceeds.

Finally, what are the social factors which constrain or facilitate the transition to democracy? We can discuss this under two headings: consensus (or the lack of it) and the presence (or lack) of a civil society to underpin democratic institutions. As we have seen in our analysis of the economic reforms, Chinese society has become a more complex and conflictual entity and, in the latter half of the 1980s, showed clear signs of becoming virtually ungovernable, even by an apparatus as pervasive as the Chinese Communist Party. Power has become more dispersed – to bureaucratic institutions and local governments – and the centre's writ has declined. Inter-regional disparities have widened, a process of economically based class differentiation has begun to emerge, particularly in the countryside, the rural–urban divide is still a vivid socio-economic reality and there is potentially destructive antagonism between the 'wooden soldiers of the (Stalinist) status quo' and new social and political forces emerging under the impact of economic reform. Though these fissiparous tendencies are in no way comparable to those in the Soviet Union or Yugoslavia where national antagonisms have shattered the body politic, they are powerful enough to impose severe strains on any set of political arrangements, particularly one which is designed to express rather than control social conflicts, such as a multi-party system. In such a context, moreover, it may be difficult, in the short run at least, to achieve a consensus on a new set of institutional arrangements, liberal democratic or otherwise. There is a deeper level of concern here, which goes beyond the issue of procedural rules of the political game and provision of new political institutions, notably parties. The Leninist system which still survives not only organised the political system; it was also the main source of social and economic integration. If it collapsed overnight, for example, the task of political reconstitution might (at a superficial level at least) be the easiest: for example, a new constitution could be drafted and political parties could be encouraged to emerge as they have in Eastern Europe in vast quantities. But what would be the institutions which would reintegrate society, which would prevent a potentially destabilising and costly social anomie? As we showed in Chapter 7, there is already a powerful impetus towards the formation of new types of social organisation characteristic of an emergent 'civil society' but this process is as yet relatively embryonic. Moreover, despite the current enthusiasm for 'civil society' among Western analysts, we need to be more clear about its composition in post-socialist contexts. For example, as the recent experience of Eastern Europe suggests, a breakdown of the institutions of the state-socialist order sparks a revival of pre-revolutionary social attitudes and organisations, some of which are inimical to democracy and social progress. To make matters worse, some of the most powerful 'civil society' organisations which had emerged within the bosom of state socialism were illegal or semi-legal. There is a powerful economic 'mafia' in the Soviet Union, for example, and in the Chinese case there are powerful underground organisations (such as the secret societies currently based in Hong Kong but increasingly extending their operations to Southern China) which might take noxious advantage of any breakdown of political and social order. In sum, therefore, there would seem to be powerful social factors which prompt us to caution in recommending a sudden dissolution of the current political order and a lurch towards some form of multi-party system.

This call for caution is all the more necessary when we consider the systemic task which China now faces – that of steering the transition from Stalinist central planning to some form of market economy, whether 'market socialist' or, as seems more likely a post-socialist capitalist economy along Eastern European lines. As the experience of the 1980s demonstrated clearly, the stresses and strains engendered by the process of economic deStalinisation were enormous, stemming from the opposition of 'loser' groups, obstruction by vested interests, popular tensions and malaise generated by economic instability, insecurity and frustration and a gradual loss of political control by the central leadership. If this transition is going to be pushed through, there seems to be a strong argument that a firm hand is necessary to steer the nation through the stormy waters of transition.

However, these kinds of arguments about the 'dangers of democracy' can lead into a blind alley, i.e. they can be used to justify any kind of 'authoritarian' regime so long as it claims to be engaged in development or economic liberalisation. There is also the fallacy of equating a 'firm hand' and a 'strong government' with some form of authoritarianism. But perhaps the key source of the 'strength' of a regime is its claim to legitimate power and the popular consent and co-operation that this entails. As we have seen in this book, the reform era has seen a continued, indeed accelerating erosion of the legitimacy of Chinese state socialism, its core institution, the Chinese Communist Party and the Party's current leadership. As the Beijing Massacre demonstrated, here was a regime increasingly dependent on force not consent.

Reconstitution of the political order is sorely needed. In the short term, this is necessary to break the 'systemic constraint' on economic reform posed by the unreformed nature of the Leninist polity – its Ideology, its institutions and the vested interests embedded in them.[6] In the longer term, political reconstitution is necessary to accommodate the changing economic, social and political character of Chinese society – the growth of markets, the pluralisation of interests, the growth of civil society and the changes in socio-political attitudes and beliefs. Political reconstitution requires a transition – from Marxist–Leninist state socialism to some form of democratic polity. But what form can this transition take? Does the Eastern European and Soviet scenario of political paralysis and collapse await China? Is it the case that state socialist systems in general, and the Chinese variant in particular, are fundamentally unable to reform themselves politically; that their only feasible future is a rapid, more or less chaotic and potentially violent transition towards some form of multi-party polity?

The Nature of the Political Transition to Democracy

Are there any *political alternatives to this 'collapse scenario'*? Is there a form of political transition which can achieve the ultimate aims of political and economic transformation while avoiding the human costs arising from political instability and social anomie? We should begin an answer to these questions by looking more closely at terms like 'authoritarianism' and 'democracy'. The Chinese regime, like other Leninist–Stalinist polities, is a particularly dense and pervasive form of authoritarianism in that it aims at, and to a considerable extent achieves, a 'totalistic' control over state, society and economy.[7] In this respect it is unlike those authoritarianisms common in the developing world where the intended and achieved scope of political mobilisation and socio-economic control is more limited. For example, the authoritarianisms of the 'four little tigers' vary widely. The Taiwanese regime has been the closest to the Chinese, being led by a hegemonic party with Leninist antecedents and with a high degree of social and political control, at least until the mid-1980s. But even here, the economy was 'free' in the sense that private entrepreneurs and managers were able to pursue profit relatively unencumbered by an interventionist state (though the same freedom did not extend to workers who were prevented from organising their own unions and using strikes or protests to advance their own interests). Compared to the Chinese mainland, moreover, there was arguably more intellectual and cultural freedom, even though both these spheres were subject to political manipulation and control. There was also greater space for 'civil society', the formation of relatively auton-omous social organisations and for competitive politics, albeit in non-party form and largely at the local level.[8] Though there is little doubt that the Taiwanese regime was, until the mid-1980s at least, a coercive and oppressive one, not without its own 'totalistic' aspects, there is a qualitative difference when compared with the Chinese mainland. This difference allows us to classify such regimes into two basic ideal types, the authoritarian and the totalist, distinguished by the extent of their intended and achieved scope of control, mobilisation and ideological/social/economic/political engineering.

This familiar distinction allows us to pose the question of China's shorter-term future political evolution in a different way. Not in terms of a hypothetical transition from Stalinism to democracy but a dual transition: first, from a totalist to an authoritarian form of state socialism and, second, from the latter to a liberal-democratic polity presiding over a basically private-enterprise economy. The first stage, were it to be possible, would meet the political requirements of those interested in radical economic reform because it would be compatible with the introduction of a market economy. In this first stage, the Chinese Communist Party would retain a dominant (though diminished) position, rather like its counterpart the Guomindang (Kuomintang) in Taiwan or the Lee Kuan Yew regime in Singapore.[9] This is not such an unthinkable prospect since a large number of China's reformers, particularly within the country, are willing to admit, even after Tiananmen, that it may be advisable for the Communist Party to retain its hegemonic role in the near and middle future, since there is no credible political alternative at this stage and there is a real prospect of anarchy, even civil war, if the Party is toppled in Eastern European fashion. The rapid implosion of the Soviet Union is a sobering lesson here and the Chinese themselves do not have to look very far into their own recent national history to fear the break-up of the nation into inter-regional strife and warlordism.

The first stage 'transition to authoritarianism' is all the more significant as a real political option because that is the direction in which the Chinese reforms were evolving before Tiananmen. In practical terms, steps were being taken to limit the power of the Party by separating it from the state administration (by abolishing leading Party member groups in governmental bodies and reducing the incidence of 'interlocking directorates' whereby the same person held both Party and government posts), by reducing the power of Party secretaries and committees in relation to professional managers in state enterprises, and by allowing other political institutions to acquire additional powers to act as a partial check on the Party (notably the National People's Congress). As we have seen, this reform thrust was given impetus by the Thirteenth Party Congress in 1987 when the then General Secretary, Zhao Ziyang, spelled out these and other measures in his official report. Moreover, the overall economic power of the state had also been undermined to some degree by the economic reforms, partly by the impact of the Open Policy, partly by the rapid emergence of a dynamic non-state sector and partly by the increasing operational autonomy of state enterprises.

At the theoretical level, this gradual process of political liberalisation was accompanied by the emergence of the notion of 'new authoritarianism' (*xin quanweizhuyi*). This emerged among a group of relatively junior intellectuals in both government and academe in Beijing between 1986 and 1989 and had apparently made some progress in attracting the attention and support of senior Party reformers, most importantly Zhao Ziyang.[10] The theory draws heavily on the example of the 'four little tigers' of East Asia and from the work of United States political scientists, notably Samuel Huntington (1968). Theorists of 'new authoritarianism' argue that China's political arrangements must reflect its current cultural and economic constraints as an underdeveloped country. In such a context, a rapid transition to some form of fully-fledged democracy is neither political feasible nor economically desirable. Full democracy is an ultimately desirable state which must await the establishment of its social, economic and political preconditions, notably the separation of political and economic life, the spread of markets, the formation of a diversity of socio-economic groups and interests in civil society, and a concomitant growth in political awareness and skills. The role of the 'new authoritarian' regime which is to emerge from the matrix of Stalinist 'totalism' is to organise this transition, establishing the social and economic basis for a longer-term, second transition towards democracy, in particular by introducing a market economy, increasing the space available for the expression and organisation of socio-economic interests, and gradually expanding the sphere of democratic participation, representation and competition.

Although the 'new authoritarian' project attracted high-level political attention in late 1988 and early 1989, any possibility for developing it further as a theoretical matrix for political reform was dashed by the Beijing Massacre of 4 June 1989. As a reform proposal, it has serious deficiencies. First, there would still be serious obstacles to be faced in moving from a 'totalist' to a 'new authoritarian' polity, notably the institutions and vested interests of the *ancien régime*. Second, there is the question of who is to hold power in such a system: on the one hand, it is likely that previous political and bureaucratic élites would retain the whip-hand (indeed, 'new authoritarianism' provides a convenient theoretical cloak for their continuing dominance); on the other hand, there would probably be some form of compact between the reform sections of the latter and a politically interested section of the intelligentsia. Thus in social terms, the 'new authoritarian' system would be highly élitist, matching its élitist project of political tutelage. Third, while the political rationale for 'new authoritarianism' was based on an attempt at hard-headed Huntingtonian realism about the need for political stability and order to tackle the difficulties of development, it would have to be 'translated' into something which was politically and ideologically more palatable. In the aftermath of the Beijing Massacre, such a theory would be even harder to sustain. In practical terms, moreover, authoritarian systems, once established, themselves tend to calcify and prove hard to remove. Without some form of enforceable constitutional and institutional guarantees from the outset, the result might be a highly unpleasant new form of despotism (albeit preferable to its predecessor).

If a first stage 'transition to authoritarianism' is still considered advisable, for the reasons advanced above, how can this be crafted to avoid the defects and pitfalls of 'new authoritarianism' and how can this be linked to the second stage of transition to democracy? First, let us consider the prerequisites for political liberalisation. The first of these is a change in the leadership of the Party and state, since it seems very unlikely, at the time of writing (November 1991) that the current leadership, in spite of its undercurrents of disagreement, can be expected to make any decisive moves in the direction of political liberalisation. The nature of the CCP leadership is crucial in assessing the feasibility of political reform since it is still the central nucleus of political power in China. The balance between conservative and reformist elements in the leadership had been shifting gradually during the 1980s under the tutelage of Deng Xiaoping. The student mobilisation of late 1986 and the more widespread uprising of early 1989 took place at times when the balance had still not shifted decisively in the reformers' favour. However, every day that passes brings an imperceptible weakening in the power of the conservative old guard and a strengthening of younger, more reform-minded political generations. Particularly important in this shift in the leadership balance within the Party/ state is the role of the armed forces, an institution which cannot receive here the attention it requires. However, we can assert the general point that, to the extent that the People's Liberation Army is not wedded to the political *status quo* and does not have a political project of its own (being content with the status of a professional army outside or above politics), the dual transition is more feasible.[11]

A second prerequisite of political reform is some kind of accommodation and compromise between reformers within the CCP and activists in the Democratic Movement which retains a shadow identity within China and has taken on a multi-faceted (and factionalised) organisational form overseas. This accommodation would not be easy to achieve given continuing resistance to it from conservative elements in the Party and state and the diverse nature of the democratic forces. It would ideally require a single leader or a number of skilful and authoritative leaders able to command support across the political divide. It is at cardinal moments of political transition such as these that the quality of political leadership becomes crucial.

The purpose of the 'grand accommodation' would be to work out a programme of political reform, define the measures needed to achieve it and establish a coherent alliance of competing forces to provide the political basis to carry this out. The political reform would also be accompanied by a renewed commitment to continuing and deepening the economic reforms with the ultimate aim of achieving some form of market economy. The basic function of this political pact would be to design and engineer the dual transition: a short/medium-term transition from totalism to some form of circumscribed authoritarianism and a longer-term transition to ultimately fully-fledged democracy. I use the term circumscribed authoritarianism because the diverse character of the alliance of political forces underlying the pact would lead towards a degree of dispersion of political power and moves towards democratisation in the *short*, not merely the long term.

Steps towards democratisation could take place in at least three spheres – the constitutional, institutional and social. Constitutional changes would require legal changes to guarantee basic citizen and economic rights, to define the institutional mechanisms necessary to establish and enforce them (notably through the legal system), and to set the rules of the game for a new system of political institutions. Institutional changes would involve a redefinition of the position of the dominant Party, the CCP (even though in the short and medium term the Party might remain hegemonic) and its relationship with other political institutions; reforms in the internal structure and external behaviour of the Party (for example, permission for organised factions within the Party, or multi-candidacies and secret ballots for Party elections); and encouragement of more political 'pluralism' by ceding power to other institutions, such as the People's Representative Congresses, the non-communist 'democratic parties', the Chinese People's Political Consultative Conference, or local communities in both cities and countryside. The latter institutions already exist, having been set up in an earlier era of accommodation in the 1940s as the Revolution came to power. Their virtually lifeless bodies could have fresh political air breathed into them, though this would not mean that new kinds of political institutions would not be necessary in a new era which calls out for political innovation. Social democratisation would involve an expansion of social space to allow for the organisation of group interests in 'civil society', greater freedom of ideological and cultural expression and the establishment of more autonomous mass media.

It is probable also that such a 'grand accommodation' would attempt to set a timetable and define a process whereby these initial moves towards democratisation, which might still guarantee the Party's hegemonic position albeit in attenuated form, would be followed by successive further moves leading towards some ultimate end-state of 'mature' democracy, such as a fully-functioning multi-party system in which the Communist Party would no longer play a hegemonic role. Participants in the 'grand accommodation' would certainly wish to define the concrete policies necessary to achieve the first stage of reform: the separation of the Party from the state administration, the removal or weakening of Party organisations within enterprises, the radical reduction of direct official controls over economic activity, measures to bring about the internal restructuring of the Party itself, abolition or reform of existing 'mass organisations', and greater space for autonomous organisations in 'civil society'. These specifically political measures would be reinforced by politically significant changes in the economy, notably changes in the ownership system which, through privatisation or some alternative reform, would undermine the economic dominance of the state.

In the short and medium term, the resulting political system would be a hybrid form, like its counterparts in countries such as Singapore, Taiwan, South Korea or Mexico where elements of single-party dominance co-exist (or have co-existed) with elements of institutionalised democratic politics. Its political basis would be diverse, but at least this diversity would receive public acknowledgement and find more available channels of self-expression than the previous system of artificially imposed uniformity under the mendacious and suppressive banners of 'democratic centralism' and 'socialist democracy'. To be optimistic, this more pluralistic system would also be more flexible, allowing for a rolling process of continuing political accommodation which could not only provide the stability essential for coherent developmental policies and the transformation of the economic system, but also underpin successive stages of ever-deepening political reform leading towards higher levels of democratisation and an eventual consensus on the political rules of the democratic game. In the long term, the social and economic changes brought about by this transitional polity would ideally strengthen the basis for more developed forms of political organisation and participation in the framework of a competitive yet consensual political society.

A political accommodation of this kind could prove capable of breaking the deadlock in Chinese reform, the depressing cycle of élite conflict and policy oscillation which we witnessed during the 1980s. Though the Beijing massacre has made this kind of accommodation much more difficult and the possibility of an Eastern European style collapse more likely, it is worth remembering that, in political terms, there are substantial differences between the Chinese and Eastern European political situations. While most of the Eastern European parties were foreign transplants, representing the hegemonic interests of a hated imperial neighbour, the Chinese Communist Party has its own independent history and is much more deeply rooted in society, particularly in the countryside where the vast majority of the population still lives. China also lacks a tradition of a strong civil society and experience of democratic governance, which have facilitated both the removal and the replacement of the ruling parties of Eastern Europe. In spite of the fissiparous forces present in Chinese society, moreover, they cannot compare in intensity with the nationalist hostilities which have torn apart the Soviet Union. Moreover, the economic impact of the reforms in China has been far more impressive than in Eastern Europe and the Soviet Union where they came too little or too late.

The two-stage process of political transition faces powerful constraints, but there are some reasons for optimism. Ideological obstacles may prove less damaging than one might expect since the traditional ideology of Marxist–Leninist socialism has lost most of its intellectual and emotional appeal. Social tensions and conflict are a natural concomitant of the transition process, but they can be managed by a skilful and flexible leadership with a sufficiently wide and firm base of consensus and support, both inside and outside the Party. Indeed, the key constraints are political: the availability of skilled and progressive leadership, the coherence of any political alliance forged between reformist elements inside and outside the Party, and their ability to neutralise opposition from the older generation of Party leaders and their potential allies within the armed forces. A new regime would also have to face challenges from more radical reformist forces dissatisfied with the degree and pace of political change. Yet the latter are also necessary as 'gadflies' to keep any project of gradual democratisation on-track.

However, even if the 'political pact of transition' is able to overcome these obstacles, it will need to live by its results. If it cannot deliver what it promises in terms of political stability, transformation of the economic system and improvements in material welfare, it faces a fate similar to its predecessor and the prospect of a radical, possibly violent, political break becomes more likely.

Concluding Remarks

The only aspect of China's political future which is predictable is its unpredictability. In spite of the basic political forces and trends which I have tried to identify in this book, the range of possible political futures is still wide. There may be a form of Chinese 'Brezhnevism' to see out the millenium as the current leadership manages to stay in power. If this is indeed the case, then the political contradictions and trends which I have identified will intensify and make it more likely that the transition, when it comes, will be sudden, radical and possibly violent. By that time, the Chinese Communist Party will have finally forfeited its residual claim to political legitimacy and will end up on the dust-heap of history along with some of its Eastern European equivalents. On the other hand, a single event in the near or very near future (my own estimates begin from tomorrow, which is 2 December 1991!), such as the death of the paramount leader, may spark off a rapid train of events with unforeseeable consequences, ranging from the gradua-listic scenario I have portrayed above, or a radical swing to liberal democracy, or a military dictatorship. In any of these, cases, the nature of the transition – gradual or sudden, violent or 'velvet' – will crucially affect both the nature of the political system which emerges from it and the political fortunes of the Chinese Commu-nist Party. The more radical the break, the more likely that the Communist Party will disintegrate; the more gradual, the more likely that it can adapt and evolve (like its counterparts in Bulgaria, Hungary and Soviet Central Asia) in ways which retain its political credibility and usefulness for the nation.

Over the longer term, the basic social, economic and political trends I have identified in this study will come into play to carry forward a process of socio-economic pluralisation and political democratisation which will be reinforced by changes in the international political environment. These trends are bringing with them a crop of political funerals. Marxist–Leninist state socialism is on its deathbed, even though it may linger on for a while in certain countries such as China, North Korea and Vietnam. This means that the attempt to reform it through the 'market socialist' (or rather 'market Stalinist') project is also moribund. As in Eastern Europe and the Soviet Union, moreover, no credible alternative vision of a 'socialist' society has arisen to take its place. In politics as in economics, liberalism will most likely be the guiding force for change, though this will be grafted on to elements of the previous system (not only Chinese state socialism but also its 'traditional' imperial precursor). At the risk of stating a truism, whatever the result is, it will be distinctively Chinese. The most likely scenario is a form of state capitalism along East Asian lines (comparable to Japan and South Korea/ Taiwan since the mid-1980s) with a competitive political system and a capitalist economy with a high degree of state involvement. However, while such a combination promises to be economically dynamic, it may well be socially exploitative and politically unequal if politics and economics operate according to the intersecting logics of class structure and market dynamics. While some of the basic elements of Chinese state socialism – such as subsidies, basic welfare services, job security and relatively egalitarian distribution – might have reflected the actions of a quasi-patriarchal, totalist state and posed problems from the point of view of economic efficiency, they are also valued attributes of a humane society. While Russia and some of the post-socialist Eastern European nations seem prepared to throw out the social baby with the socialist bathwater, there are elements of the old which can be made complementary with the new in the form of some kind of social democracy along Western European lines. Indeed, it is the hope of some contemporary Chinese political theorists, such as Su Shaozhi, that China may evolve, in both economics and politics, towards a form of social democracy which steers a middle course between and away from the Scylla of authoritarian state socialism and the Charybdis of unfettered capitalism. While this is, of course, a long way away from their original goal of 'market socialism', this outcome may go some way towards meeting the aspirations of Chinese reformers who set out in the post-Mao era to build a society which combined the virtues of state and market, equity and growth, individual incentives and collective responsibility, socialism and capitalism.

Notes

Introduction

1. It is now the usual practice to use the official Chinese system of Romanising Chinese words (called *pinyin*), but Chinese names are often transcribed in terms of an earlier system. To avoid confusion, I shall use the *pinyin* form in the text with the earlier form in brackets after it.

1 The Failure of the Maoist Developmental State and the Rise of the Economic Reformers

1. For a similar analysis of these two strands of Maoism, see Young and Woodward 1978.
2. The intellectual quality of Mao's pronouncements in the 1960s lacked the clarity and order of his earlier thinking. His contribution to the elaboration of radical Maoism came in discursive speeches and brief Delphic 'highest directives'. Indeed, already in his seventies, Mao was no longer the dynamic traveller and intervener of the 1950s, and was losing touch with the increasingly kaleidoscopic realities of the early 1960s. To the extent that radical Maoism was fleshed out into a coherent body of thought, this was done by other ideologues, notably Zhang Chunqiao, Chen Boda, Lin Biao and small groups of radical intellectuals in various institutions. For two classic statements of radical Maoism in the 1970s, see Yao Wenyuan, 'On the social basis of the Lin Piao anti-Party clique', *Peking Review*, 10, 1973, pp. 5–10 and Zhang Chunqiao, 'On exercising all-round dictatorship over the bourgeoisie', *Peking Review*, 14, 1975, pp. 5–11.
3. Hua Guofeng, 'Speech at the Second National Conference on learning from Dazhai (Tachai) in agriculture', *Peking Review*, no. 1, 1 January 1977, p. 41.
4. For an outline of this strategy, see the State Planning Commission, 'Great guiding principle for socialist construction', *Peking Review*, no. 39, 23 September 1977; for Hua's analysis of the Plan, see his 'Unite and strive to build a modern powerful socialist country', 26 February 1978, in *Peking Review*, no. 10, 10 March 1978, pp. 7–40.
5. The noted economist Hu Qiaomu argued against those 'who take the will of society, the government and the authorities as economic laws which can be bent to political expediency... politics itself cannot create

other laws and impose them on the economy', in 'Observe economic laws, speed up the Four Modernisations', *Peking Review*, 45, 10 November 1978, p. 8.

6. For attacks on the economic thinking of the Gang of Four, see Chi Wei, 'How the "Gang of Four" opposed socialist modernisation', *Peking Review*, no. 11, 11 March 1977, p. 8 and Lin Kang, 'Is it necessary to develop the productive forces in continuing the revolution?', *Peking Review*, no. 14, 1 April 1978, pp. 6–10.

7. For authoritative statements of this principle, see 'Practice is the only criterion for verifying truth', *GMRB*, 11 May 1978 and 'One of the fundamental principles of Marxism', *RMRB*, 24 June 1978.

8. For the 'Resolution on Hua Guofeng's Errors' issued at the Sixth Plenum, see *NCNA* (English), 30 June 1981.

9. For an analysis of these imbalances, see Jin Ping, 'Make a success of comprehensive balancing; advance in the course of making adjustment', *GMRB*, 25 March 1979, in *FBIS*, 4 April 1979.

10. For example, see Zhong Renfu, 'Inquire into the reasonable rates of accumulation for our country from historical experience', *RMRB*, 15 May 1980, in *FBIS*, 20 May 1980.

11. Yu Youhai, 'US$1000 by the year 2000', *Peking Review*, 43, 27 October 1980, pp. 16–18.

12. For an authoritative exposition of such arguments, see Xue Muqiao, 'A study in the planned management of the socialist economy', *Peking Review*, 43, 26 October 1979.

13. Liu Guoguang *et al.*, 'The relationship between planning and market as seen by China in her socialist economy', *Atlantic Economic Journal*, no. 31, 1979, p. 15.

14. Yuan Wenqi *et al.*, 'International division of labour and China's economic relations with foreign countries', *Social Sciences in China*, no. 1, 1980, p. 30. For an opposing analysis, see Yao Xianhao, 'The international division of labour and the foreign economic relations of a socialist state', *Jingji Kexue* (*Economic Science*), Beijing, no. 4 1980.

2 Reform: An Overview

1. Deng Xiaoping, *Build Socialism with Chinese Characteristics*, Beijing, Foreign Languages Press, 1985, p. 49.

2. For an excellent discussion of this 'conservative' model, see Cyril Zhihren Lin 1989, pp. 117–18.

3. Zhao Ziyang, 'Advance along the Road of Socialism with Chinese Characteristics', 25 October 1987, in *Beijing Review*, 9-15 November 1987, pp. xi–xii.

4. The 'Four Basic Principles' are: Marxism-Leninism – Mao Zedong Thought; the socialist road; the dictatorship of the proletariat; and the leadership of the CCP. For a more detailed discussion, see Chapter 5.

5. Zhao, 'Advance along the Road of socialism', pp. xv–xxi.

6. 'Economist examines problems of "grim" economic situation', *NCNA*, 6 September 1989, in *SWB* 0561, 14 September 1989.
7. 'Resolution on the guiding principles for building a socialist society with an advanced culture and ideology', translated in *SWB* 8377.

3   The Politics of Agrarian Reform

1. By 'agriculture', I do not merely refer to farming the land, but also to forestry, animal husbandry, fishery and various kinds of 'sideline' production which the Chinese refer to collectively as 'big agriculture' (*da nongye*).
2. *NCNA* (English), 7 May 1982.
3. There is a series of interviews with the vice-governors in *Peasants' Daily* (Nongmin Ribao), 30 November, 1989, in *SWB* 0645.
4. Du Runsheng offered a rebuttal to these criticisms at a national conference on the rural situation in late 1983: reported in *NCNA* (Chinese), 28 December 1983, in *SWB* 7530.
5. For example, this position was laid down by the Party theoretical organ *Hongqi* (Red Flag), no. 13, 1 July 1982 in an article by Zhang Dajian, 'Implement the agricultural responsibility system and maintain the direction of collectivisation', pp. 32–5.
6. Zeng Jianwei and Feng Jian, 'Always keep in mind the 800m. peasants – a report from Zhongnanhai', *NCNA* (Chinese), 19 May 1981, in *SWB* 6730.
7. 'Some opinions on strengthening and improving ideological-political work in the rural areas', *NCNA* 6 November 1982.
8. 'Ten policies of the CCP Central Committee for the further invigoration of the rural economy', *NCNA* (Chinese), 24 March 1985, in *FBIS* 057.
9. The main elements of the new strategy can be found in Zhao Ziyang's speech to the National Rural Work Conference on 21 December 1984 (*NCNA* 30 December 1984) and in 'Shift rural production onto the path of a commodity economy', *People's Daily*, editorial, 31 December 1984.
10. For example, see the article by a Commentator, 'Augment the strength reserved for agricultural development' in *People's Daily*, 2 March 1987, in *FBIS* 047.
11. For an example, see 'The majority of peasants grow grain to feed themselves and build houses first when their income increases', *Nongmin Ribao* (*Peasants' Daily*), 9 September 1988, in *FBIS* 159.
12. For a fascinating account of the problematic state of relations between peasants and local cadres, see *Peasants' Daily*, 12 September 1988.
13. *Zhongguo Tongxunshe* (China Bulletin Agency), Hongkong, 1 January 1989, in *SWB* 0352.
14. Pan Xining, 'An analysis of the "instability" of rural policies', *Nongcun Jingji Wenti* (*Problems of Rural Economy*), Beijing, 23 October

1990, pp.14–18, cited in *Inside China Mainland*, 13: 2 February 1991, p. 20.
15. *NCNA* (English), 18 July 1989, in *SWB* 0513.
16. *NCNA* (domestic), 4 November 1988, in *SWB* 0305.
17. Liu Jintong and Yu Leiyan, 'Various aspects of the prices of the means of agricultural production', *Liaowang* (*Outlook*), no. 27, 4 July 1988, pp. 18–19, in *FBIS* 1988, p.142.
18. 'Strive for a bumper harvest next year', *People's Daily*, editorial, 16 November 1988, p. 1.
19. Xia Weiyi, 'An agricultural situation in which old and new problems are intertwined', *Wenhuibao*, Hongkong, 26 February 1990, in *FBIS* 040; and 'The pros and cons of grain trade', *Guoji Shangbao* (*International Trade News*), 24 August 1990, in *FBIS* 115.
20. For the relevant State Council decision, see *NCNA* (domestic), 13 October 1988.

4 The Politics of Industrial Reform

1. This meeting is reported in *People's Daily*, 11 February 1988, p. 1, in *SWB* 0080.
2. 'Persist in reform, open up a new path for progress and invigorate the enterprises', *NCNA* (domestic), 6 February 1985, in *SWB* 78874.
3. 'Strive to create the conditions for invigorating large and medium enterprises', *NCNA* (domestic), 6 September 1985, in *FBIS* 175.
4. 'Ma Hong writes to a leading comrade of the State Council offering proposals for accelerating the renewal and transformation of old enterprises', *People's Daily*, 30 November 1986, in *SWB* 8435.
5. *Guowuyuan Gongbao* (State Council Bulletin), no. 10 1983, pp. 475–8.
6. 'The officials of the Ministry of Finance again answer the questions concerning the changing of profit into tax for state enterprises', *People's Daily*, 28 April 1983, cited in Wang 1984, p. 65.
7. See the statement by Lu Dong, vice-minister of the State Economic Commission, in *NCNA* (English), 9 May 1984.
8. The introduction of the contract responsibility system was heralded and defended by three authoritative articles by a 'commentator' in the *People's Daily*, 22 April, 15 and 19 May 1987. Responsibility systems for industry were also mentioned by Zhao Ziyang in his report to the Fifth Session of the Sixth National People's Conference in March–April, 1987, the text of which was in *Beijing Review*, vol. 30, no. 16.
9. For example, see the reservations expressed by Dong Fureng, interviewed in *China Daily*, 30 December, 1987, p. 4.
10. For example, see Zhao's remarks when he visited Shanghai in April 1987, reported by *NCNA* (domestic) on 25 April 1987, in *SWB* 8553.
11. For example, see the article by Cao Siyuan in *Jingji Ribao* (*Economic Daily*), 16 Nov 1985, in *SWB* 8134; and Sun Yaming 'China's

enterprise bankruptcy law which is being formulated', *Liaowang* (outlook) (overseas edition) 27 January 1986, in *FBIS* 030.

12. For an overview of different opinions on this issue, see Liu Guoguang and Zhao Renwei, 'The share system, a new task in changing ownership relations', *Jingji Ribao* (*Economic Daily*), 2 November 1985, in *SWB* 8110.

13. Zuo Mu, 'On the contract management responsibility system', *People's Daily*, 15 June 1987.

14. Personal communication, 29 May 1991.

15. Akio Takahara, interview with the Guangdong Provincial Economic Commission, reported in a personal communication, 29 May 1991.

16. *Zhongguo Caizheng yu Jinrong* (*Chinese Fiscal and Financial Affairs*), Beijing, Beijing University Press, 1985, pp. 134–5.

17. For one example, see the case of Song Beifang, manager of a motor vehicle plant in Zhengzhou, Henan province, in *People's Daily*, 23 April 1986, in *SWB* 8253.

18. 'Some tentative remarks on reforming the industrial enterprise leadership system', *Jingji Guanli* (*Economic Management*), no. 12 (December 1980), p. 14, cited in Chamberlain 1987, p. 633.

19. As late as 1983, 96.8 per cent of the state workforce were 'fixed workers' with the effective right to stay in their initial enterprise for life. This privileged status gave them access to a range of welfare benefits provided by the enterprise itself, such as medical and labour insurance, housing, child-care facilities, pensions and even guaranteed jobs for their children. In fact, state enterprises had tended to become a sort of 'urban village', 'small societies' with their own mini 'welfare states'. In consequence, the workforces of state enterprises tended to be stable, with high rates of overstaffing (what Kornai [1980: p. 254] calls 'unemployment on the job') and low levels of mobility between enterprises, sectors and localities.

20. For examples of debates from the late 1980s, see the articles by Ni Dinghua of the Central Party School, by Tian Xiaobao of the Ministry of Labour's Labour Science Institute, and by Zhang Shishu, all in *Banyuetan* (*Fortnightly Talks*), no. 14, 25 July 1988, p. 34, in *FBIS* 156; and the opposing articles in the same journal (25 September 1988, in *SWB* 0292) by Li Yanrong and Wang Bensun.

21. For example, see the interview with a veteran army officer published in Hongkong's *Zhengming Daily*, 24 July 1981, who linked growing unemployment with prostitution and criminal violence (in *FBIS* 27 July 1981).

22. For example, see Li Peng's remarks at a meeting of managers at the China General Petrochemical Company, reported by *NCNA* (domestic), 21 December 1989, in *SWB* 0649.

23. *NCNA* (English), 16 June 1988.

24. *Liaowang* (Outlook), 15 February 1988, in *SWB* 0104.

25. Zhang Xuehu, 'A fatal knock at the door – exploration and analysis of unemployment in China', *Gongren Ribao* (*Workers' Daily*), 28 September 1988, pp. 1–2, in *FBIS* 197.

5 **Economic Reform and Ideological Decay: The Decline of Ideocracy**

1. Schurmann makes a distinction between 'pure' and 'practical' ideology, mirroring the Chinese distinction between *lilun* (theory) and *sixiang* (thought) (1968: ch. 1).
2. The 'two whatevers' was enshrined in a *People's Daily* editorial of 7 February 1977, allegedly published under the aegis of Hua Guofeng and Wang Dongxing, vice-chairman of the CCP Central Committee (Dittmer 1984: p. 350).
3. *Guangming Daily* (*Glorious Daily*), 11 May 1978.
4. See the article by Lin Honglin in *People's Daily*, 11 November 1980, in *SWB* 6576.
5. See the Commentator's article on 'enlightenment in ideological work' in *Banyuetan* (*Fortnightly Conversations*), 14, 25 November 1980, in *SWB* 6588.
6. For an early critique, see Chi Wei, 'How the Gang of Four opposed socialist modernisation', *Peking Review*, 11 March 1977.
7. For a detailed analysis of the Plenum and the Resolution, see Gardner 1982: pp. 189–96. For contemporary commentaries on the Resolution, see the article in *Liberation Army Daily*, 8 July 1981, in *SWB* 6787 and Lu Zhichao, 'Correctly understand and deal with Mao Zedong Thought', *Xin Shiqi* (*New Times*) no. 7, July 1981, in *FBIS* 177.
8. This speech, unpublished at the time, was translated in *Issues and Studies*, Taibei, March 1981, pp. 78–103. A Chinese text can be found in Deng 1983: pp. 280–302.
9. For example, see the article of this title by Jin Feng in *Liberation Daily*, 10 November 1980, in *SWB* 6592.
10. Hu Chen, 'Opening up a labour power market is not based on regarding labour power as a commodity', *GMRB*, 25 October 1986, in *SWB* 8412.
11. Zhuang Hongxiang, 'Recognising labour power as a commodity will not cause the negation of the socialist system', *GMRB* 7 September 1986, in *SWB* 8368.
12. Zhao Guoliang, 'A brief discussion on socialist labour as a commodity', *GMRB*, 23 August 1986, in *SWB* 8357 and Dong Fureng, 'A brief discourse on the labour system and labour power as a commodity', *GMRB* 4 October 1986 in *SWB* 8397.
13. Dong Fureng, *op. cit.*
14. The report, entitled 'Advance along the Road of Socialism with Chinese Characteristics', can be found in English in *SWB* 8709 or *Beijing Review*, vol. 30, no. 45, 1987.
15. For a retrospective survey of this political see-sawing over ideology by a leading conservative ideologist, see Wang Renzhi, Director of the CCP Propaganda Department, 'On opposing bourgeois liberalisation', Beijing Radio, 15 February 1990, in *SWB* 0697. For an excellent Western scholarly account of the period up to 1984, see Schram 1984.

16. For examples, see Li Lianke, 'Discussion on 'Marxism and Humanism' over recent years', *People's Daily*, 11 January 1983, in *FBIS* 010; Ruo Shui, 'In defence of humanism', Wen Hui Bao, Shanghai, 17 January 1983, in *SWB* 7244; Zhou Yang's statement at an academic symposium, reported in *NCNA*, 7 March 1983, in *SWB* 7280; and Ru Xin, 'New tasks facing Marxist philosophy', *People's Daily*, 20 July 1983, in *SWB* 7399.

17. *NCNA*, 30 August 1985.

18. 'Resolution of the Central Committee of the CCP on the guiding principles for building a socialist society with an advanced culture and ideology', *NCNA*, 28 September 1986, in *SWB* 8377.

19. There were attempts by political theorists to adapt Marxism to the new realities of capitalism and the international economy: for example, see Feng *et al.* 1984.

20. For example,a large survey was conducted in 1986–7 to ascertain the socio-political attitudes and the effectiveness of ideological-political education in the universities of Beijing. Some of the results have been translated in the magazine *Chinese Education*, vol. 22, no. 3 (Fall 1989) and vol. 23, no. 1 (Spring 1990).

6   The Party's Over? Economic Reform and Industrial Decay

1. Deng Xiaoping, 'On the reform of the system of Party and state leadership', in *Selected Works of Deng Xiaoping (1975–1982)*, Beijing, Foreign Languages Press, 1984, p. 316.

2. Xin Tongwan, 'Correctly carry out the Party's democratic centralism – on the Party's highest organ of power' (part 1), *People's Daily*, 24 July 1981, in *FBIS* 145.

3. Deng Xiaoping, *loc. cit*, p. 310.

4. Xin Tongwan, *op. cit.*, part 3, *People's Daily* 10 August 1981, in *FBIS* 159. Compare the CCPCC circular on 'Party Organisational Life' which attempted to lay down rules about the frequency and conduct of meetings, *NCNA* (Chinese), 6 October 1981, in *SWB* 6849.

5. For discussion of the regularised role of Party schools, see a report on the CCP Central Committee decision about them in *NCNA* (Chinese) 19 May 1983, in *SWB* 7341. For a report on the activity of Party schools at the provincial level, see Shaanxi Radio, 27 July 1983, in *FBIS* 147.

6. For the Twelfth Congress Party Constitution, see *NCNA* (Chinese), 8 September 1982, in *SWB* 7126 and for a commentary on it see 'The new Party Constitution's special features of the era', *People's Daily*, editorial, 22 November 1982, in *SWB* 7194. For revisions incorporated into the Thirteenth Congress Party Constitution, see *NCNA* (Chinese), 1 November 1987, in *FBIS* 211.

7. Deng Yingchao, a member of the CCP Politburo, referred to the regulations on the living arrangements of senior cadres in her speech

to the Central Discipline Inspection Commission, reported in *People's Daily*, 28 March 1981, in *FBIS* 060; for the use of deadlines (in replying to documents), see Zhang Lizhou, 'One must dare to give oneself problems to solve', *People's Daily*, 28 August 1981, in *SWB* 6823; for CCP Central Committee strictures on the 'reckless sending of delegations abroad', see *NCNA* (Chinese) 28 January 1986, in *SWB* 8176.

8. Wang Renzhong, 'Unify thinking, conscientiously rectify Party work-style', *Hongqi (Red Flag)*, no. 5, 1982, in *SWB* 6971.

9. *Guangming Ribao (Glorious Daily)*, 26 July 1982, in *SWB* 7096.

10. Deng Xiaoping, *op. cit.*, 1980, p. 311.

11. Deng Xiaoping, *op. cit.*, l980, p. 310.

12. This view is cited in *Hongqi (Red Flag)*, no. 2, 1981, in *SWB* 6633.

13. Huang Kecheng, 'On the problem of the Party's workstyle', *People's Daily*, 28 February 1981, in *FBIS* 046.

14. Ibid.

15. For example, see Ma Wenrui, 'Inherit and carry forward the Yan'an workstyle...', *Shaanxi Ribao (Shaanxi Daily)*, 30 June 1981, in *FBIS* 137.

16. Deng wrote the official report on the 1957 movement: *Report on the Rectification Campaign*, Beijing, Foreign Languages Press, 1957. For the classic analysis of rectification campaigns in the pre-reform era, see Teiwes 1979. For a detailed description of the 1983–7 Rectification, see Dickson 1990.

17. 'The Party's urgent tasks on the organisation and ideological fronts' (12 October 1983), in Deng 1987: pp. 24–40.

18. For example, see the report on the situation in Guangxi province in *Guangxi Ribao (Guangxi Daily)*, 28 September 1983, in *SWB* 7453.

19. Bo Yibo, 'A number of questions concerning Party rectification and building party organisations', *Hongqi (Red Flag)*, 16 October 1985, in *FBIS* 211.

20. Zhang Yun, 'Improving the quality of Party members...', *Hongqi*, No. 10, 16 May 1986, in *SWB* 8263.

21. Bo Yibo, 'A basic summary of party rectification and the further strengthening of Party building', *NCNA* (Chinese), 31 May 1987, in *FBIS* 87:105, 2 June 1987.

22. For an analysis of the Central Control Commission, see Franz Schurmann 1968, pp. 156–9. For a history of control organs up to 1978, see Sullivan 1984, pp. 600–5.

23. *NCNA* (Chinese), 27 January 1980.

24. For example,see the report by the then Permanent Secretary of the CDIC, Wang Heshou, in *NCNA* (Chinese), 8 February 1985, in *SWB* 7873.

25. See Chen Yun's speech at the 6th Plenum of the CDIC, 24 September 1985, in *NCNA* (Chinese), 26 September 1985, in *SWB* 8067.

26. 'Step up case handling, punish the corrupt and strictly enforce Party discipline', *Dang Jian (Party Building)*, no. 9, 1989, in *SWB* 0542.

27. *Shanxi Ribao (Shanxi Daily)*, 3 June 1983.

28. *NCNA* (Chinese), 15 September 1983, in *SWB* 7444.
29. *NCNA* (Chinese), 13 July 1985, in *SWB* 8004.
30. *NCNA* (Chinese), 28 July 1989, in *SWB* 0526.
31. Liao Gailong, 'Historical experiences and our road of development', a report to a forum of the National Party School, 25 October 1980, translated in *Issues and Studies*, Taibei, vol. xvii, nos 5, 10, 11 and 12 (Oct. to Dec. 1981) – the relevant section is in no. 12, pp. 95–8.
32. Deng Xiaoping (1980), pp. 303, 310–12.
33. Deng (1980), pp. 304–9.
34. Ibid., p. 303 and 'Reform the political structure and strengthen the people's sense of legality', 28 June 1986, in Deng 1987, pp. 145–8.
35. Ibid., pp. 315 and 322.
36. For a detailed discussion of these structural reforms, see Saich 1991.
37. Zhao Ziyang, 'Advance along the road of socialism with Chinese characteristics', *Beijing Review*, vol. 30: no. 45 (9–15 November 1987), section V.
38. Yi Li, 'It is necessary to strengthen building of intra-Party democracy and regulations . . .', *Liaowang (Outlook)*, no. 26, 27 June 1988, in *FBIS* 135.
39. Hu Yaobang, 'Create a new situation in all fields of socialist modernisation', (1 September 1982), *NCNA* (English) 7 September 1982.
40. 'Constitution of the CCP' (adopted on 6 September 1982), *NCNA* (English), 8 September 1982.
41. 'Revision of some articles of the CCP Constitution', no. 5, *NCNA* (Chinese), 1 November 1987, in *FBIS* 211.
42. See the report on a meeting of the CCP Organisation Department in *NCNA* (Chinese) 21 July 1983, in *SWB* 7394 and the report on the 'third echelon' in Beijing in *Beijing Daily*, 26 August 1983, in *SWB* 7435.
43. 'The policy of making the contingent of cadres younger will remain unchanged', *Liaowang (Outlook)*, overseas, no. 22, 1 June 1987, in *FBIS* 110.
44. For example, see Bao Xin, 'Something about the third echelon', in *Liaowang (Outlook)*, overseas, no. 46, 17 November 1986, in *FBIS* 226.
45. Chang Xing, 'Princes' Party?', *Ming Bao*, Hong Kong, 30 December 1985, in *FBIS* 251.
46. Liu Ming, 'CCP conservative forces dish up a leftist programme . . .', *Ching Pao*, Hong Kong, 16 June 1987, in *FBIS* 117.
47. 'Organisation Department of the CCPCC issues document . . .', *GMRB*, 17 January 1984; General Office of the CCPCC, 'Report on recruiting large numbers of outstanding intellectuals into the Party', *NCNA* (Chinese), 14 March 1985, in *SWB* 7905.
48. Beijing TV, 24 October 1987, in *FBIS* 206 (Supplement).
49. Rosen, 1989, Table 2.
50. *NCNA* (English), 28 October 1987.
51. *NCNA* (English), 6 September 1988.
52. Hunan Radio, 26 March 1985, in *SWB* 7913.

53. *People's Daily*, 6 April, 1984, in *SWB* 7617.
54. *NCNA* (English), 15 October 1989 and *Ming Bao*, Hong Kong, 23 October 1989.
55. *Qiushi*, no. 20, 1989, in *SWB* 0590.
56. *People's Daily*, 18 December 1980, in *FBIS* 246.
57. For a detailed and thoughtful report on one experiment in Hebei province, see 'Division of work between Party and governmment must go ahead . . .', *Hebei Ribao* (*Hebei Daily*), 21 October 1982, in *SWB* 7175. In March 1986, 16 cities were chosen as experimental sites for this political reform.
58. Zhao Ziyang, 'Advance along . . .', *loc. cit.*, p. xvii.
59. Zhao Ziyang, *op. cit.*, p. xvi.
60. *NCNA* (Chinese), 12 October 1989, in *SWB* 0589.
61. Li Ximing made this charge in a speech to a meeting of the Beijing Municipal Party Committee reported by *NCNA* (Chinese), 19 October 1989 in *SWB* 0595.

7   The Social Impact of Economic Reform: The Rise of Civil Society?

1. This picture of the 'official' social structure is complicated by the fact that the radical Maoists continued to use an obsolete set of 'class' categories which derived from the period of revolutionary change in the early and mid-1950s when people were classified in terms of their pre-revolutionary socio-economic status.
2. For a broad analysis of the social impact of the reforms by Chinese sociologists, see Li *et al.* n.d.; for a Western analysis, see Selden 1986. For a Chinese analysis of the changing constellation of interest groups in Chinese society, see Gu Jieshan and Zhang Xiang, 'On interest groups in the initial stage of socialism', *Guangming Ribao* (*Glorious Daily*), 29 February 1988, in *FBIS* 055.
3. This concern can be discerned from opinion polls conducted in the late 1980s; for some results, see *ZGSHTJZL*: pp. 312–13.
4. The source of these statistics is *Gongren Ribao* (*Workers' Daily*) 9 August 1988, cited in Saich 1990: fn.80.
5. For several reports on this accelerating labour migration, see *SWB* 0402, 7 March 1989.
6. *Guangming Ribao* (*Glorious Daily*), Beijing, 15 January 1990, excerpted in *Inside China Mainland*, 12:4 (no. 136), pp. 7–9.
7. For some information on the political impact of the Polish events in China, see Benton 1982: 82–7).
8. In 1981, the breakdown of trade union membership was 85 per cent in state and 15 per cent in collective enterprises, with 370 000 branches and 243 000 full-time cadres: *NCNA* (Chinese), Beijing, 28 April 1981, in *FBIS* 082. At the same time, trade unions ran 3669 workers' schools with an enrolment of 1.3 million and 130 rest and recreation homes with 27 000 beds.

9. For a discussion of the continuing relevance of Lenin's theory in the reform era, see Chen Ziyun, 'Study Lenin's thesis on the role of trade unions in providing "two kinds of protection"', *Gongren Ribao (Workers' Daily)*, 30 September 1981, in *SWB* 6855.

10. For example, see the speech by Ni Zhifu (head of the national federation of trade unions) in *Gongren Ribao (Workers' Daily)*, 13 October 1981, in *SWB* 6870; for a statement of the official Party position; cf. his speech at the Trade Union Congress in October 1983, in *People's Daily*, 27 October 1983, in *SWB* 7489.

11. This account describes Party manipulation of trade union elections in a Tianjin shipyard: *Gongren Ribao (Workers' Daily)*, 4 August 1980, in *FBIS* 164.

12. Take the example of the trade union chairman of a textile mill in Liaoning province who supported workers in demands to improve working conditions and health services for women and was dismissed in May 1983 on the grounds that he was 'buying popular support' in a bid to 'assume leadership of the mill' – he was later reinstated: *NCNA* (Chinese), 9 August 1983, in SWB 7411. For a case of union weakness in 'contracted-out enterprises', see *NCNA* 7 April 1988, in *SWB* 0135.

13. For example, see *NCNA* (Chinese), 15 April 1981, in *SWB* 6703, where a 'small number of trade union cadres' were criticised for thinking that 'trade unions should only defend the interests of staff and workers'; cf. Tong Chengmin, 'A discussion on questions concerning urban trade unions participating in and discussing government administration', *Gongren Ribao (Workers' Daily)*, 27 February 1986, in *FBIS* 062.

14. For example, see the ideas reflected in Han Xiya, 'Perfect the socialist democratic system ... exploring the trade union issue in socialist society', *People's Daily*, 3 July 1986, in *SWB* 8318.

15. *Zhongguo Xinwenshe* (China News Agency), 14 October 1986, in *SWB* 8393.

16. For a good example, see the interview with Luo Gan, ACFTU vice-president, reported in *Liaowang (Outlook)* 10 August 1987, in *SWB* 8655.

17. *China News Agency*, 18 December 1987, in *SWB* 0038. It is interesting to compare this with the results of a survey of 900 enterprises in 1985 which discovered that 80 per cent of employees believed that the manager represents the interests of the factory or its workers and only 8 per cent that the manager represented the interests of the state (reported in Yang Guansan *et al.*, 'Enterprise cadres and reform' in Reynolds 1987, p. 83, and in Walder 1989a, p. 251.

18. For a report on this law by the Minister of Civil Affairs, Cui Naifu, see *NCNA* (Chinese), 29 August 1989, in *SWB* 0550; for reports of discussion of the law at the National People's Congress, see *SWB* 0551.

19. *NCNA* (Chinese), 18 April 1990, in *SWB* 0745.

20. *NCNA* 6 January 1988, in *SWB* 0192.

21. For the latter, see *People's Daily*, 27 October 1986, in *SWB* 8411 for a report on Cangzhou Prefecture in Hebei province; compare Hunan

Radio, 30 December 1987, in *SWB* 0041 for a comparable trend in Hunan province.
22. *NCNA* (Chinese), 21 January 1987, in *SWB* W1426.
23. *NCNA* 18 March 1988, in *FBIS* 88 and *NCNA* 1 March 1989, in *SWB* 0400.
24. 'Laws essential for mass organisations', *China Daily*, 2 September 1989. I am grateful to Peter Geithner for drawing this to my attention.
25. Beijing Radio , 15 February 1990, in *SWB* 0697.
26. See Gong Zuozhou and Jin Can, 'Let's see what Chen Yizi really is', *People's Daily*, 21 April 1990, in *SWB* 0752.
27. Beijing Radio, 15 February 1990, in *SWB* 0697.

8 From Market Socialism to Social Market?

1. *The Observer*, London, 10 November 1991.
2. Huntington (1991: p. 7) gives a 'procedural' definition of democracy as follows: a nation's political system is democratic 'to the extent that its most powerful collective decision makers are selected through fair, honest, and periodic elections in which candidates freely compete for votes and in which virtually all the adult population is eligible to vote'.
3. For an analysis of East Asian experience, see White (ed.) 1988. The more successful NICs (Newly Industrialised Countries) of Latin America also embody a similar pattern, notably Brazil under a military regime and Mexico with its effectively one-party system.
4. For discussions of the notion of the 'autonomous' developmental state, see the 'Introduction', by myself and Robert Wade, in White (ed.) 1988 and White 1984.
5. Huntington (1991: p. 105) appears to make a similar argument in relation to China when he states that 'China {in 1989} was far from the political transition zone'.
6. This was the central focus of the public debate on political reform which took place in late 1986. For an important example of reformist arguments at the time, see Liu Beixian, 'Political system reform is inevitable – interview with Yan Jiaqi, Head of the Political Research Institute, Chinese Academy of Social Sciences', *Zhongguo Xinwenshe* (China News Agency), Hong Kong, 17 June 1986, in *FBIS* 117.
7. For an analysis of this system, see Tang Tsou 1986: ch. 5. Tang Tsou uses the term 'totalitarianism' in his analysis.
8. Robert Wade, 'State intervention in "outward-looking" development: neoclassical theory and Taiwanese practice', in White (ed.) 1988; see also Hung-mao Tien 1989 and Winckler 1984.
9. Lee Kuan Yew has himself gone on record recommending economic reform before democratisation, as the following excerpt from an interview in *Time* shows:

> *Question*: Are you saying these societies {including China} must choose between democracy and economic development?

Answer: In most cases. The more dissension, the more contention and the less consensus, the less you get on with the job. In the early stages you need to achieve clear-cut goals like universal education, high savings, high productivity, low consumption...And you can't have contention over these simple truths indefinitely.

This is a rather crude version of the developmental case against democratisation and it ignores the important political reasons why some form of democratisation is necessary in the Chinese case in the short not merely the longer term.

10. For an excellent analysis of the origins and content of 'new authoritarianism', see Hao Wang, 'Which way to go: strategies for democratisation in Chinese intellectual circles', Department of Political Science and Public Administration, Beijing University, mimeo, n.d. Also see Du Ruji, 'Reflections on new authoritarianism', *Zhengzhixue Yanjiu* (Political Studies Research), Beijing, 3: 1989, pp. 21–5 and Rong Jian, 'Is new authoritarianism feasible in China?', *Shijie Jingji Daobao* (*World Economic Herald*), Shanghai, 6 January 1989 and Hao Wang, 'A theory of transitional democratic authoritarianism', *Political Studies Research*, 3: 1989, pp. 16–20. Particularly useful also is the collection of articles on the subject in Liu and Li (eds) 1989; also compare Petracca and Mong 1990).

11. For useful analyses of the political role of the Chinese military, see Cheung 1990 and Shambaugh 1991.

Bibliography

Andors, Stephen (1977) *China's Industrial Revolution: Politics Planning and Management, 1949 to the Present* (New York, Pantheon Books).

Ash, Robert F. (1988) 'The evolution of agricultural policy', *China Quarterly*, 116 (December), pp. 529–55.

Aziz, Sartaj (1978) *Rural Development: Learning from China* (London, Macmillan).

Bachman, David (1987) 'Implementing Chinese tax policy', in D. M. Lampton (ed.), pp. 119–53.

Barnett, A. Doak (1967) *Cadres, Bureaucracy, and Political Power in Communist China* (New York, Columbia University Press).

Benton, Gregor (ed.), (1982) *Wild Lilies, Poisonous Weeds* (London, Pluto Press).

Bernstein, Thomas P. (1977) *Up to the Mountains and Down to the Countryside: the Transfer of Youth from Urban to Rural China* (New Haven, Yale University Press).

Bernstein, Thomas P. (1984) 'Reforming Chinese agriculture', paper prepared for the conference on 'To Reform the Chinese Political Order', Harwichport, Mass. (June).

Blecher, Marc J. (1978) *Leader–Mass Relations in Rural Chinese Communities: Local Politics in a Revolutionary Society*, Ph.D. thesis (University of Chicago).

Blecher, Marc J. (1991) 'Developmental state, entrepreneurial state: the political economy of socialist reform in Xinji municipality and Guanghan county', in White (ed.), pp. 265–94.

Bowles, Paul and White, Gordon (1989) 'Contradictions in China's financial reforms:the relationship between banks and enterprises', *Cambridge Journal of Economics*, 13:4, pp. 481–95.

Brugger, Bill (ed.) (1985) *Chinese Marxism in Flux 1978–84, Essays on Epistemology, Ideology and Political Economy* (London, Croom Helm).

Brus, Wlodzimierz (1972) *The Market in a Socialist Economy* (London, Routledge and Kegan Paul).

Burns, John P. (1987) 'Civil service reform in contemporary China', *The Australian Journal of Chinese Affairs*, 18 (July), pp. 47–83.

Byrd, William (1983) *China's Financial System: the Changing Role of the Banks* (Boulder, Westview Press).

Chamberlain, Heath B. (1987) 'Party management relations in Chinese industries: some political dimensions of economic reform', *China Quarterly*, 112 (December), pp. 631–61.

Chang, Gordon H. (1988), 'A symposium on Marxism in China today: an interview with Su Shaozhi, with comments by American scholars and a response by Su Shaozhi', *Bulletin of Concerned Asian Scholars*, vol. 20 no.1 (January–March), pp. 11–35.

Cheng Tizhong (1986) 'An inquiry into certain problems concerning a comprehensive implementation of the contract system', *Zhongguo Laodong Kexue* (Chinese Labour Science), no. 5 (May) pp. 10–12.

Cheung, Tai Ming (1990) 'The PLA and its role between April–June 1989', mimeo, paper presented at the Third Annual Workshop on PLA Affairs (National Sun Yat-sen University, Kaohsiung, Taiwan).

Chevrier, Yves (1990) 'Micropolitics and the factory director responsibility system, 1984–87', in D. Davis and E. F. Vogel (eds), *Chinese Society on the Eve of Tiananmen: the Impact of Reform* (London, Harvard University Press) pp. 109–34.

Conroy, Richard (1985) 'Laissez-faire socialism? prosperous peasants and China's current rural development strategy', *Australian Journal of Chinese Affairs*, no. 12.

Croll, Elisabeth (1983) *Chinese Women Since Mao* (London, Zed Press).

Croll, E., Davin D. and Kane P. (1985) *China's One-Child Policy* (London, Macmillan).

Deng Xiaoping (1983) *Deng Xiaoping Wenxuan* (Deng Xiaoping's Selected Works 1975–1982) (Beijing, People's Publishing House).

Deng Xiaoping (1987) *Fundamental Issues in Present-Day China* (Beijing, Foreign Languages Press).

Dickson, Bruce J. (1990) 'Conflict and non-compliance in Chinese politics: Party rectification, 1983–87', *Pacific Affairs*, vol. 63, no.2 (Summer), pp. 170–90.

Dirlik, Arif and Meisner Maurice (eds) (1989) *Marxism and the Chinese Experience* (London, Sharpe).

Dittmer, Lowell (1982) 'China in 1981: Reform, readjustment, rectification', *Asian Survey*, vol. XXII, no.1 (January), pp. 41–2.

Dittmer, Lowell (1984) 'Ideology and organization in post-Mao China', *Asian Survey* vol. XXIV, no. 3 (March), pp. 349–69.

Dreze J. and Sen A. (1989) *Hunger and Public Action* (Oxford, Clarendon Press).

Fathers, Michael and Higgins, Andrew (1989) *Tiananmen: the Rape of Peking* (London, the *Independent*).

Feng Lanrui, Sun Kaifei and Liu Shiding (1984) 'The worldwide new industrial revolution and China's socialist modernisation', *Selected Writings on Studies of Marxism*, Chinese Academy of Social Sciences, no. 3.

Field, R. M. (1983) 'Slow growth of labour productivity in Chinese industry, 1952–81', *China Quarterly*, 96 (Dec.), pp. 641–64.

Friedman, Edward (1989), 'The crushing of the Democracy Movement in China and the struggle to reform the Leninist dictatorship' mimeo, Department of Political Science, University of Wisconsin.

Gardner, John (1982) *Chinese Politics and the Succession to Mao* (London, Macmillan).

Gerth, H. H. and Mills, C. W. (1958) *From Max Weber: Essays in Sociology* (Oxford University Press).

Gold, Thomas B. (1985), 'After comradeship: personal relations in China since the Cultural Revolution', *China Quarterly*, no. 104, pp. 657–75.

Gold, Thomas B. (1988) 'The social implications of private business', paper at a conference on 'Social Consequences of the Chinese Economic Reforms' (May) (Harvard University).

Gold, Thomas B. (1990) 'The resurgence of civil society in China', *Journal of Democracy*, 1:1 (Winter), pp. 18–31.

Goodman, David S. G. (1981) *Beijing Street Voices: the Poetry and Politics of China's Democracy Movement* (London, Marion Boyars).

Gray, Jack (1973) 'The two roads: alternative strategies of social change and economic growth in China', in S. R. Schram (ed.), *Authority Participation and Cultural Change in China* (Cambridge University Press) pp. 109–57.

Gray, Jack (1988) 'The state and the rural economy in the Chinese People's Republic', in White (ed.), 1988, pp. 193–234.

Habermas, J. (1976) *Legitimation Crisis* (London, Heinemann).

Harding, Harry (1987) *China's Second Revolution: Reform after Mao* (Washington D.C., The Brookings Institution).

Hartford, Kathleen (1985) 'Socialist agriculture is dead: long live socialist agriculture! Organizational transformations in rural China', in Perry and Wong (eds), op. cit., pp. 31–62.

Howell, Jude (1989) *The Political Dynamics of China's Open Policy*, D.Phil. Thesis (University of Sussex, Brighton).

Huang Yasheng (1990) 'Web of interests and patterns of behaviour of Chinese local economic bureaucracies and enterprises during reforms', *China Quarterly*, 123 (September), pp. 431–58.

Huntington, Samuel P. (1968) *Political Order in Changing Societies* (London, Yale University Press).

Huntington, Samuel P. (1991) *The Third Wave: Democratization in the Late Twentieth Century* (London, University of Oklahoma Press).

Ishikawa, Shigeru (1983) 'China's economic growth since 1949 – an assessment', *China Quarterly*, 94 (June), pp. 242–81.

Jefferson, G. H., Rawski, J. G. and Zheng Yuxin (1992) 'Growth, efficiency, and convergence in China's state and collective industry', *Economic Development and Cultural Change* vol. 40, no. 2 (January), pp. 239–66.

Jiang Yiwei, 1985 'If all workers are on the contract system, it will not be conducive to the socialist character of the enterprise', *Jingji Tizhi Gaige* (Economic Structural Reform), no.1, pp. 11–13.

Keane, John (ed.), (1988) *Civil Society and the State: New European Perspectives* (London, Verso).

Kelliher, Daniel (1991) 'Privatisation and politics in rural China', in Gordon White (ed.), pp. 318–41.

Kitching, Gavin (1983) *Rethinking Socialism: A Theory for a Better Practice* (London, Methuen).

Kornai, Janos, 1980 *Economics of Shortage*, Vol. A (Amsterdam, North Holland).

Kornai, Janos (1985) 'Comments on papers prepared in the World Bank about socialist countries', *CPD Discussion Paper*, no. 1985–10 (March).

Lampton, David M. (1987a) 'Chinese politics: the bargaining treadmill', *Issues and Studies*, Vol. 23: No. 3, Taibei (March), pp. 11–41.

Lampton, David M. (1987b) 'The implementation problem in post-Mao China', in Lampton (ed.), 1987c, pp. 3–24.

Lampton, David M. (1987c) (ed.), *Policy Implementation in Post-Mao China* (London, University of California Press).

Latham, Richard J. (1985) 'The implications of rural reforms for grass-roots cadres', in Perry and Wong (eds), op. cit., pp. 157–74.

Lee Hong Yung (1991) *From Revolutionary Cadres to Party Technocrats in Socialist China*, Oxford, University of California Press.

Lee, Peter N-S. (1986) 'Enterprise autonomy policy in post-Mao China: a case study of policy making, 1978–83', *China Quarterly*, 105 (March), pp. 45–71.

Lewis, John Wilson (1963) *Leadership in Communist China* (Ithaca, New York, Cornell University Press).

Li Hanlin *et al.* (n.d.) *Xunqiu Xinde Xietiao* (Seek a New Co-ordination) (Survey Publishing House).

Lieberthal, K. and Oksenberg, M. (1988) *Policy Making in China: Leaders, Structures and Processes* (Princeton, Princeton University Press).

Lin, Cyril Zhiren (1989) 'Open-ended economic reform in China', in Nee and Stark (eds), pp. 95–136.

Lipton, Michael (1977) *Why Poor People Stay Poor:A Study of Urban Bias in World Development* (London, Temple Smith).

Liu Lansheng (1985) 'A discussion about strengthening the construction of residents' committees', *Difang Zhengquan yu Renmin Daibiao* (Local Government and People's Representatives) (Shenyang, Masses Publishing House).

Liu Jun and Li Lin (eds) (1989) *Xin Quanweizhuyi: Dui Gaige Lilun Ganglingde Lunzheng* (Neo-Authoritarianism: A Debate on the Theoretical Reform Programme) (Beijing, Beijing Economics Institute Publishing House).

Manion, Melanie (1984) 'Cadre recruitment and management in the PRC', *Chinese Law and Government*, vol. XVII, no. 3 (Fall).

Manion, Melanie (1985) 'The cadre management system post-Mao: the appointment, promotion, transfer and removal of Party and state leaders', *China Quarterly*, 102 (June), pp. 203–33.

Mann, Michael (1986) *The Sources of Social Power*, vol. I (Cambridge: Cambridge University Press).

Meisner, Maurice (1989) 'Marx, Mao and Deng on the division of labour in history', in Dirlik and Meisner (eds), op. cit., pp. 79–116.

Meyer, Alfred G. (1966) 'The functions of ideology in the Soviet political system', *Soviet Studies* vol. 17 no.3 (January).

Moore, Mick (1988) 'Economic growth and the rise of civil society', in White (ed.) pp. 113–52.

Naughton, Barry (1988), 'The Third Front: defence industrialisation in the Chinese interior', *China Quarterly*, 115 (September), pp. 351–86.

Naughton, Barry (1991) 'Macro-economic management and system reform in China', in White (ed.), pp. 50–82.

Nee, Victor and Stark, David (eds) (1989) *Remaking the Economic Institutions of Socialism: China and Eastern Europe* (Stanford University Press).

Nelson, Joan M. *et al.* (1989) *Fragile Coalitions: The Politics of Economic Adjustment* (Oxford, Transaction Books).

Nelson, Joan M. (ed.) (1990) *Economic Crisis: Policy Choice* (Oxford, Princeton University Press).

Nolan, Peter (1988) *The Political Economy of Collective Farms* (Oxford, Polity Press).

Nolan, Peter (1990) 'Introduction', in Nolan and Dong (eds), pp. 1–38.

Nolan, Peter (1991) 'Prospects for the Chinese economy', *Cambridge Journal of Economics*, 15, pp. 113–24.

Nolan, Peter and Dong Fureng (eds) (1990) *The Chinese Economy and its Future* (Cambridge, Polity Press).

Nolan, Peter and White, Gordon (1984) 'Urban bias, rural bias or state bias? Urban–rural relations in post-Revolutionary China', *Journal of Development Studies*, vol. 20: no. 3.

Nove, Alec (1977) *The Soviet Economic System* (London, Allen and Unwin).

Nove, Alec (1983) *The Economics of Feasible Socialism* (London, Allen and Unwin).

Oi, Jean C. (1989) *State and Peasant in Contemporary China: the Political Economy of Village Government* (Oxford, University of California Press).

Oksenberg, Michel (1982) 'Economic policy-making in China: summer 1981', *China Quarterly*, 90 (June), pp. 165–94.

Oksenberg, Michel and Tong, James (1991) 'The evolution of central-local fiscal relations in China, 1971–1984: the formal system', *China Quarterly*, 125 (March), pp. 1–32.

Ostergaard, C. S. (1989) 'Citizens, groups and a nascent civil society: towards an understanding of the 1989 student demonstrations', mimeo, University of Arhus.

Parish, W. L. and Whyte, Martin K. (1978) *Village and Family in Contemporary China* (Chicago: Chicago University Press).

Perry, Elizabeth J. and Wong, Christine (1985) *The Political Economy of Reform in Post-Mao China* (London, Harvard University Press).

Perry, Elizabeth J. (1985) 'Rural collective violence:the fruits of recent reforms',in Perry and Wong (eds), op. cit., pp. 175–92.

Petracca, Mark P. and Mong Xiong (1990) 'The concept of Chinese neo-authoritarianism: an exploration and democratic critique', *Asian Survey*, XXX:11, (November), pp. 1099–117.

Reynolds, Bruce L. (ed.) (1987) *Reform in China: Challenges and Choices* (New York, M. E. Sharpe).

Riskin, Carl (1987) *China's Political Economy: the Quest for Development since 1949* (Oxford University Press).

Riskin, Carl (1990) 'Where is China going?', in Nolan and Dong (eds), pp. 41–62.

Rosen, Stanley (1988) 'China in 1987', *Asian Survey* vol. XXVIII no. 1 (January).

Rosen, Stanley (1989) 'The CCP and Chinese society: popular attitudes towards Party membership and the Party's image', mimeo, Department of Political Science, USC, Los Angeles.

Saich, Tony (ed.) (1990) *The Chinese People's Movement: Perspective on Spring 1989* (London, M. E. Sharpe).

Saich, Tony (1990) 'Urban society in China', mimeo, prepared for the International Colloquium on China at Saarbrucken (July).

Saich, Tony (1991) 'Much ado about nothing: Party reform in the 1980s', in Gordon White (ed.) (1991), pp. 149–74.

Schram, Stuart R. (1984) *Ideology and Policy in China since the Third Plenum, 1978–84*, London, SOAS Contemporary China Institute, Research Notes and Studies no. 6.

Schurmann, Franz (1968) *Ideology and Organization in Communist China* (London, Cambridge University Press).

Selden, Mark (1986) 'Class, state and the political economy of reform in China', mimeo, SUNY Binghamton.

Sen, Amartya (1981) *Poverty and Famines* (Oxford, Clarendon Press).

Shambaugh, David (1991) 'The soldier and the State in China: the political work system in the People's Liberation Army', *China Quarterly*, 127 (September), pp. 527–68.

Shen Liren and Dai Yuanchen (1990) 'Woguo "Zhuhou jingji" de xingcheng ji qi biduan he genyuan' (The form of our country's "ducal economy" and its abuse and origin'), *Jingji Yanjiu* (Economic Research), Beijing, no. 3.

Shirk, Susan (1985) 'The politics of industrial reform', in Perry and Wong, op. cit., pp. 195–222.

Shirk, Susan (1989) 'The political economy of Chinese industrial reform', in Nee and Stark (eds), pp. 328–62.

Shue, Vivienne (1984) 'The new course in Chinese agriculture', *Annals, AAPSS*, 476 (November).

Shue, Vivienne (1989) 'Emerging state–society relations in rural China', mimeo, European Conference on Agricultural and Rural Development in China, Sandbjerg Castle, Denmark.

Sicular, Terry (1988) 'Agricultural planning and pricing in the post-Mao period', *China Quarterly* 116 (December), pp. 671–705.

Simmie, Scott and Nixon, Bob (1989) *Tiananmen Square* (Seattle, University of Washington Press).

Solinger, Dory J. (1987) 'The 1980 inflation and the politics of price control in the PRC', in Lampton, ed., 1987, pp. 81–118.

Solinger, Dory J. (1989), 'Capitalist measures with Chinese characteristics', *Problems of Communism*, vol. 38, no. 1 (January/February), pp. 19–33.

State Statistical Bureau of the PRC, *China: Statistical Yearbook 1990*, Beijing.

Su Shaozhi (1983) 'Tentative views on the reform of the economic mechanism in Hungary', *Selected Writings on Studies of Marxism*, no. 3 (Beijing, Chinese Academy of Social Sciences).

Sullivan, Lawrence R. (1984) 'The role of control organs in the CCP, 1977–83', *Asian Survey*, vol. XXIV, no. 6 (June).

Sullivan, Lawrence R. (1988) 'Assault on the reforms: conservative criticisms of political and economic liberalisation in China, 1985–86', *China Quarterly*, 114 (June), pp. 198–222.

Sullivan, Lawrence R. (1989–90) 'The emergence of civil society in China', in Saich (ed.), pp. 125–43.

Tang Tsou (1986) *The Cultural Revolution and Post-Mao Reforms: A Historical Perspective* (London, University of Chicago Press).

Teiwes, F. C. (1979) *Politics and Purges in China: Rectification and the Decline of Party Norms* (White Plains, New York, Sharpe).

Tien Hung-Mao (1989) *The Great Transition: Political and Social Change in the Republic of China* (Stanford University, Hoover Institution).

Travers, S. Lee (1985) 'Getting rich through diligence: peasant income after the reforms', in Perry and Wong (eds), op. cit., pp. 111–30.

Unger, Jonathan (1985–6) 'The decollectivization of the Chinese countryside: a survey of twenty-eight villages', *Pacific Affairs*, 58:4 (Winter), pp. 585–606.

Unger, Jonathan (1987) 'The struggle to dictate China's administration: the conflict of branches vs. areas vs. reform', mimeo, Contemporary China Centre, Australian National University, Canberra.

Vogel, Ezra F. (1989) *One Step Ahead in China: Guangdong under Reform* (Cambridge, Mass.: Harvard University Press).

Wade, Robert, *Governing the Market: Economic Theory and the Role of Government in East Asian Industrialization* (Princeton University Press).

Walder, Andrew G. (1986), *Communist Neo-Traditionalism: Work and Authority in Chinese Industry* (Berkeley, University of California Press).

Walder, Andrew G. (1987) 'Actually existing Maoism', *The Australian Journal of Chinese Affairs*, no. 18 (July), pp. 155–66.

Walder, Andrew G. (1989a), 'Factory and manager in an era of reform', *China Quarterly*, 118 (June), 242–64.

Walder, Andrew G. (1989b) 'The political sociology of the Beijing upheaval of 1989', *Problems of Communism*, 38:5, pp. 30–40.

Walker, Kenneth R. (1984) 'Chinese agriculture during the period of the readjustment, 1978–83', *China Quarterly* 100 (December), pp. 783–812.

Wang Guichen, Zhou Qiren *et al.* (1985), *Smashing the Communal Pot – Formulation and Development of China's Rural Responsibility System* (Beijing, New World Press).

Wang, Chuanlun (1984) 'Some notes on tax reforms in China', *China Quarterly*, 97 (March), pp. 53–67.

Warner, M. (1985) 'Training China's managers' *Journal of General Management*, vol. 11, no. 2 (Winter) pp. 12–26.

Wei Lin and Chao, Arnold (eds) (1982) *China's Economic Reforms* (Philadelphia, University of Pennsylvania Press).

White, Gordon (1983) 'The post-revolutionary Chinese state', in Victor Nee and David Mozingo (eds), *State and Society in Contemporary China* (Ithaca, New York, Cornell University Press).

White, Gordon (1984) 'Developmental states and socialist industrialisation in the Third World', *Journal of Development Studies*, vol. 21, no. 1, pp. 97–120.

White, Gordon (1985) *Labour Allocation and Employment Policy in Contemporary China* Brighton, IDS China Research Report No. 2.
White, Gordon (1988) (ed.) *Developmental States in East Asia* (London, Macmillan).
White, Gordon (1988a) 'State and market in China's socialist industrialisation', in White, G. (ed.) *Developmental States in East Asia* (London, Macmillan) pp. 153–92.
White, Gordon (1988b) 'State and market in China's labour reforms', in E. V. K. Fitzgerald and M. Wuyts (eds), *Markets Within Planning: Socialist Economic Management in the Third World* (London, Frank Cass, pp. 180–202).
White, Gordon (1990) 'Chinese economic reform and the rise of civil society' (Geneva, UNRISD).
White, Gordon (ed.) (1991) *The Chinese State in the Era of Economic Reform: the Road to Crisis* (London, Macmillan).
White, Gordon (1991a) 'Basic-level government and economic reform in urban China', in White (ed.) (1991), pp. 215–42.
White, Gordon and Benewick, Robert (1986) *Local Government and Basic-Level Democracy in China: Towards Reform?*, China Research Report, IDS (University of Sussex, Brighton).
White, Gordon and Bowles, Paul (1987) *Towards a Capital Market? Reforms in the Chinese Banking System*, China Research Report, IDS (University of Sussex, Brighton).
Whiting, Susan (July 1989) *The Non-Governmental Sector in China: a Preliminary Report* (Beijing, The Ford Foundation).
Whyte, Martin K. and Parish, William L. (1984) *Urban Life in Contemporary China* (Chicago: Chicago University Press).
Winckler, Edwin A. (1984) 'Institutionalization and participation on Taiwan: from hard to soft authoritarianism?', *China Quarterly*, 99 (September), pp. 481–99.
Wong, Christine (1987) 'Between plan and market: the role of the local sector in post-Mao China', *Journal of Comparative Economics*, 11, pp. 385–98.
Wood, Adrian (1991) *China's Economic System: a Brief Description, with some Suggestions for Further Reform* (April), CP no.12, The Development Economics Research Programme (London School of Economics).
World Bank (1986) *China: Long-term Development Issues and Options* (Washington DC).
Xue Muqiao (1988) 'Establish and develop non-governmental self-management organisations in various trades', *People's Daily*, 10 October, in *FBIS* 201.
Yahuda, Michael (1979) 'Political generations in China', *China Quarterly*, 80 (December), pp. 793–805.
Yang Baikui (1987) 'Some questions on China's political reform', *Guangzhou Yanjiu* (Guangzhou Research), no. 2, pp. 30–33.
Yang, Dali (1990) 'Patterns of China's regional development strategy', *China Quarterly*, 122 (June), pp. 230–57.

Yi Duming (1986) 'In defence of the "iron rice-bowl" system', *Yangcheng Wanbao*, (Guangzhou Evening News), 23 February, in CREA, no. 347.

Young, Graham and Woodward, Dennis (1978) 'From contradictions among the people to class struggle: the theories of "uninterrupted" and "continuous revolution"', *Asian Survey*, vol. XVIII, no.9 (September), pp. 912–33.

Zhang Shaojie and Zhang Aurei (1987) 'The present management environment in China's industrial enterprises' in Bruce L. Reynolds (ed.) *Reform in China: Challenges and Choices* (London, Sharpe) pp. 47–58.

Zhang Yonggang (1990) 'A summing up of all kinds of thinking about the deepening of enterprise reform', in *Zhongguo Qiye Gaige Shinian* (Ten Years of Enterprise Reform in China) (Beijing, Reform Publishing House) pp. 316–23.

Zhang Yulin (1982) 'Readjustment and reform in agriculture', in Wei and Chao, op. cit., pp. 123–46.

Zhongguo Shehui Tongji Ziliao 1990 (ZGSHTJZL) (Statistical Materials on Chinese Society 1990), edited by the Social Statistics Office of the State Statistical Bureau, Beijing, Chinese Statistics Publishing House.

Zhu Xigang and Tian Weiming (1989) 'The system of decision-making for agriculture in China', *Australian Journal of Chinese Affairs*, no. 21 (January), pp. 161–70.

Zweig, David (1983) 'Opposition to change in rural China', *Asian Survey*, vol. XXIII: 7 (July), pp. 879–900).

Zweig, David (1987) 'Context and content in policy-implementation: household contracts and decollectivisation, 1977–1983', in Lampton (ed.), 255–83.

Index

Dictatorship Development
Reform in the '80s